T0285262

TRUE IDENTITY

Cracking the Oldest Kidnapping Cold Case and Finding My Missing Twin

PAUL JOSEPH FRONCZAK

and Alex Tresniowski

A POST HILL PRESS BOOK

True Identity:
Cracking the Oldest Kidnapping Cold Case and Finding My Missing Twin

ISBN: 978-1-64293-667-4
ISBN (eBook): 978-1-64293-668-1

Cover photo by Greg Preston and Sharon Sampsel, Sampsel Preston Photography
Cover design by Paul Fronczak and Alex Tresniowski
Interior design and composition by Greg Johnson, Textbook Perfect

This book is a work of nonfiction. All people, locations, events, and situations are portrayed to the best of the author's memory. While all of the events described are true, some names and identifying details have been changed and one event slightly fictionalized to protect the privacy of the people involved.

Post Hill Press
New York • Nashville
posthillpress.com

Published in the United States of America
1 2 3 4 5 6 7 8 9 10

"We all have to decide for ourselves
how much sin we can live with."

—ENOCH "NUCKY" THOMPSON
Atlantic City Boss, *"Boardwalk Empire"*

For my mom, Dora Fronczak,
thanks for always being there,
for your unconditional love,
and for being my best friend.

And for my dad, Chester Fronczak,
I miss you every single day,
and will love you always.

And for all the other searchers, lone wolves,
and lost sons and daughters out there.
You are not alone; we are each other's family.

PROLOGUE

Far Northern Wisconsin
Fall, 2020

We sat across from each other on folding chairs in his backyard, a hilly half-acre with scrub grass and scattered gravel and a sawed-off, rusted steel barrel on blocks for a smoker. We were bundled up against the cold lake winds, me more than him, and we talked about the past.

"Look, you can wish and dream all day, but that ain't reality," the old man said, frustrated that I hadn't already caught on. "Reality is two things. It's what you can remember having, and it's what you have in front of you now, and that's it."

"The rest is history," he said.

He was in his early eighties, with wispy white hair and a thin white beard, and every wrinkle on his face and bend to his body spoke of some lesson learned along the way. He had been around, he told me, seen a lot, mixed it up. Played in country bands, hustled pool, rode the trains for a while. Lived in a ditch for a few days. He took pride in how much he understood about life—not life the way some people pretend it is, but life as it happens in the hard places, like the one-bar town where he lived up north, by the big lakes, frozen half the year, forsaken the rest.

"I don't go looking for trouble, never have, but if it finds me, I don't back away," he said. "Come bleed or blister, what are you gonna do to me, whip my ass? It's been whipped before, you ain't gonna get a cherry for it."

I had to keep pushing him to tell me again, to explain it further, to connect the dots that I obviously wasn't connecting. He didn't seem to mind talking about it—though he said he had never spoken about it with anyone before, and never would again once I was gone—but he was running out of ways to make me understand the futility of what I was doing.

I began to feel like Fox "Spooky" Mulder on *The X Files,* meeting the Well-Manicured Man for the first time and prodding him for information.

"I know your head and your heart is hurting and all you got for it is a bunch of lies and unanswered questions," the old man said. "But life is about *whats,* not *whys.* You ain't ever gonna get to the real rock-bottom truth. That's 'cause there ain't no bottom. The bottom's gone. The sooner you accept that, the better."

I told him I couldn't accept it. A boy had been kidnapped out of his mother's arms. I was raised believing I was that boy, but I wasn't. I had everything taken from me—my name, my identity, my history. I needed answers. I needed the truth. And he *knew* the truth. He just wouldn't tell me what it was.

"Why?" I pushed him. "Why is the truth so unknowable?"

"You can't ever open that door 'cause if you do, it's already too late and you'll be dead," he said.

"But what about the FBI? What if they find you?"

"The FBI?" he said. "The FBI ain't a pimple on a truly bad man's ass. And I'm talking about some truly bad men."

"Okay, then," I begged, "so just tell me. Just give me the name. Who took him from his mother? Who kidnapped that boy?"

The man turned his weathered face to mine and looked at me like I was the dumbest person he'd ever met.

"Kidnapped?" he said. "Son, haven't you figured it out already? There *was* no kidnapping. *The boy wasn't kidnapped.*"

CHAPTER 1

Atlantic City, New Jersey
March 6, 2020

It was early March on the East Coast—wet, windy, and cold. I'd taken a red-eye from Las Vegas and landed in Newark, New Jersey at 7:00 a.m. with only a couple of hours of sleep. The whole Covid thing was just beginning to be talked about. I felt tired and weary, and I wondered if I'd caught it on the plane.

I rented a red Jeep Wrangler and drove two hours south to Atlantic City. It was my sixth or seventh time crisscrossing the country to get to the gambling mecca since I started my investigation in 2013. The Jeep's GPS guided me to the Clayton G. Graham Public Safety Building, the four-story, stone-and-brick police headquarters on Atlantic Avenue, across from the towering Tropicana casino.

I found a parking spot around the corner. This was a visit I'd resisted making ever since I discovered a shocking truth about my identity in 2013. But now, the time had come. Embedded in the sidewalk in front of the building were several large bronze plaques commemorating fallen police officers, the plaques half-puddled with rain now. I walked past them, up three stairs, and went inside. I cleared the metal detector, and an officer pointed me to a door, past which I found two marked windows. I said hello to a middle-aged woman sitting behind Window 1 and told her why I was there.

"It's a missing persons case," I said.

"How long has the person been missing?" she asked.

"Fifty-five years."

The woman looked at me like I was joking. I told her a little more about the person I was searching for, and about our relationship, and the strange circumstances of her disappearance. I explained how I'd spent the last eight years of my life trying to track her down, turning over every rock, asking every question, sparing no expense or sacrifice, trying *everything*.

"Have you tried Google?" she asked.

Now I thought *she* was joking. But she wasn't. I told her that, yes, I'd tried it, but even so, she spent the next fifteen minutes plugging away at Google, hoping to stumble across some information that somehow I had overlooked. I let her go ahead and try. Who was I to turn down help of any kind?

Finally, the woman pushed a sheet of paper through the slot beneath the bulletproof glass. She told me to fill it out and come back. I took out a pen and, in twenty-seven blank lines headlined *Please Describe What Happened*, I wrote down a story I'd told hundreds of times before.

> *In 1965, I was found abandoned outside a department store in Newark, New Jersey. The Newark PD and FBI mistook me for Paul Fronczak, a baby kidnapped from a Chicago Hospital in 1964. I grew up as Paul Fronczak, but in 2012 I took a DNA test and discovered my true identity—Jack Thomas Rosenthal. I was born to Gilbert and Marie Rosenthal and I have a twin sister, Jill Rosenthal. Through investigations I learned that at the time I was abandoned in Newark, my twin sister Jill disappeared without a trace. More investigations showed that something bad might have happened to Jill—though there is no evidence or clues to suggest where she is or if she's still alive. She simply vanished, and family members were told never to mention the twins. I have Jill's birth certificate, but my biological relatives who might know what happened—including Jill's*

sister Linda and brother Fred—refuse to talk to me. I need to find my twin sister, because I believe she is still out there.

Signed,
Paul Fronczak
March 6, 2020

What I didn't include on the form, or tell the woman behind the window, was that Jill Rosenthal, my twin sister, wasn't even the *first* missing person I'd devoted hundreds of hours to finding—and that the other person had *also* been missing for more than fifty years.

Two colossal mysteries, each a half century in the making, and there, smack in the middle of both, was me.

The search for my twin sister was relatively new to me, but in a way, I'd spent my whole life looking for the other missing soul. Many times, I was certain I'd found him, only to realize I hadn't found anything at all. A farmer in Arkansas. A lawyer in Florida. A teacher in North Carolina. A salesman who looked *exactly* like the age progression photo. For a while, they were all the man I was looking for, until they weren't. Every dashed hope was another cruel reminder that I might not ever find him, no matter how desperately I wanted to, or how hard I tried.

This is not some pulp crime novel that wraps up neatly in the end, I kept reminding myself. *This is life. Sometimes it doesn't add up.*

Even so, I never stopped looking. Why?

Because the truth mattered. Finding the missing man *mattered.*

We tell ourselves stories about who we are, what we're made of, what legacies our parents left us, as a way to shape the events of our past into what we call an identity. If we can't find a way to tell these stories, the stories begin to tell us. Maybe we dream them. Maybe we act them out. Maybe we start behaving in ways we can't understand. Or maybe, if the story is too painful, too unspeakable to tell, we allow ourselves to be defined by stories other people tell us.

When I was young, I was told my name was Paul Fronczak. That was a lie.

I was told I was kidnapped as an infant, and returned to my grieving parents two years later. That wasn't true either.

I was told the date of my birth, my family history, the ways in which I was or wasn't like my parents and brother. None of these things were true.

Everything about my life was a story invented by other people, not out of malice, but out of fear of confronting a lie.

Finally, eight years ago, I did face down that lie, and I started hunting the truth.

The circumstances of the lie connected me to another person I had never met—the real Paul Fronczak. I'd been bound to him for half a century, and him to me, in deep and complicated ways, though for most of that time, neither of us knew the other existed. We were flip sides of the same coin—him, the boy who was stolen; me, the boy who was thrown away. Neither of us knew our real names or birthdays, and both of us had been deprived of the same vital thing—our true stories.

I've spent quite some time searching for this man, this shadow me, and I've paid a high price for my resolve—my marriage fell apart, my parents and brother stopped speaking to me for two years, jobs came and went. So many people told me I would never find him, and even if I did, it would be too late. Leave it alone, they said. Let it go.

But I couldn't. So I didn't.

In 2017, I wrote *The Foundling*, a book about my life and the search for my true identity. The book began with two unsolved mysteries and ended with two unsolved mysteries, even though, in between, against all odds, I actually *did* solve the mystery that was most personal to me—the puzzle of who I really was. With heroic help from a team of genealogists, led by the brilliant CeCe Moore but staffed mostly by amateur sleuths, I learned my real given name—Jack Thomas Rosenthal—as well as the identities of my biological parents and relatives.

The very instant this riddle was solved, however, it was replaced by another astonishing mystery.

Because in the same phone call in which CeCe changed my life by revealing my real name, she absolutely floored me with another discovery:

I'd been born a twin, and my twin sister, Jill, had been missing for more than fifty years.

Imagine learning you weren't born alone, as you'd assumed all your life. Imagine learning the person closest to you—the person most *like* you, and most likely to *know* you—was a twin sister who hadn't been heard from in more than fifty years.

Imagine twins named Jack and Jill, except Jack never knew about Jill, and Jill was God knows where.

The Foundling ended on two cliffhangers:

Where was Jill?

And where was the real Paul Fronczak?

This book picks up the story of those two searches, and of the incredible clues, leads, and disguised truths that led me to the very edge of what was, for me, the promised land.

And then, incredibly, at the very end of this book, you will read about yet another bizarre twist in my story—and the beginning of yet *another* family mystery, this one going back sixty-three years. This new mystery, as it unravels, could change everything I thought I knew about my biological family so far.

The story that follows is about many things.

It's about how the past calls out to us in the present, just as the present sometimes bleeds back into the past. It's about how we don't move on from history so much as replay it through our decisions and actions, wittingly or not.

It's about how the vagaries of human nature act as spoilers in our quest to nail down our true identities, revealing at once the necessity of the quest, and its utter folly.

And it's about how a mission of self-discovery changes you, so that you're inevitably a different person from who you were when you began the quest—yet one more thing that makes neat conclusions all but impossible.

Mostly, though, this book is about our instinctual need to belong.

Look at wolves. Wolves may haunt the dark corners of our dreams, but in truth they aren't that different from us. Like humans, they travel in packs, form borders, fight each other over domestic disputes, and protect each other from outside threats. They are defined by the blood that runs through the family line, and if they disperse, instinct reunites them. They can recognize a prodigal wolf after many years apart.

Then there is the lone wolf.

Sometimes, a wolf separates from its pack and strikes out on its own. Different things cause the break—a desire to mate, dissatisfaction with the hierarchy, or even the simple mistake of wandering away and getting lost. The lone wolf roams the forest without a family structure, left to forge paths and fight aggressors alone. In the mythology of the American Male, the term *lone wolf* suggests a strong, uncompromising individualist, happy to go his own way rather than run with the pack.

But this metaphor for rugged masculinity is a lie.

A lone wolf does *not* want to be alone. No creature on earth seeks a life of long-term isolation, least of all wolves, who favor groups, make friends, choose mates. Every fiber of a wolf's being, every twist and wrinkle of its nature, draws it to other wolves. The lone wolf is an outlier, a freak, doomed to struggle, and deprived of the comforts of pack life.

The lone wolf yearns, and what it yearns for is home.

This is the story of lone wolves, yearning to be home.

CHAPTER 2

Las Vegas, Nevada
Early 2019

It came in like hundreds of other tips, leads, and dead ends—a whistle on my cell, meaning a message on my website. The subject line got straight to it:

This is the baby you're looking for.

No other description—just, *the baby*. Not that any description was needed. I knew exactly who they meant.

They meant the man whose life I'd been living.

At that point, it was just a crumb of information, neither true nor false. I would need to break it down, tear it apart, race it around. The process would involve mistakes, setbacks, undercover work, and the help of an expert genealogist. It would require more than a little bit of luck.

But as I dug deeper into the anonymous tip, I began to feel as if it could be *the* big break I'd been so desperate for. As if, against absurdly long odds, I might be on the brink of cracking the oldest kidnapping cold case in the history of U.S. law enforcement. As if all the years of pain and dejection and loss and expense had all been worth it, and I might be able to deliver on a sacred promise I made to my mother back when it all began—*Mom, I'm going to find the son they took away from you.*

But first, I had to answer two fundamental questions.

Was this baby—now a fifty-five-year-old man and father of three living in a small town in northern Michigan—the very same baby who was kidnapped out of his mother's arms in a Chicago hospital in 1964?

And if he was, could I somehow go back in time—more than fifty years back, through decades of dust and cobwebs and secrets and lies and shadows—and finally make things right?

My hope, my prayer, was that maybe, just maybe, I could.

So I went back to the past—a past that began in Chicago.

Chicago, Illinois
April 27, 1964

Chicago PD Detective Ed Kearns, badge number 11705, got the call from Central Command at 2:45 p.m. on a foggy Monday—*proceed directly to the Michael Reese Hospital,* at 29th and Groveland Streets, in Chicago's Bronzeville neighborhood, on the city's rough South Side.

The crime—a possible kidnapping.

Det. Kearns revved up his blue-and-white Chevy Biscayne cruiser and raced to the hospital, a few hundred paces from the western shore of Lake Michigan. Fifteen minutes later, he parked near the entrance to the six-story, dark-brick, Prairie-style building. Several squad cars were already there. An unmarked sedan pulled up at the same time, carrying FBI Special Agent Girard Annino, an Air Force veteran charged with starting the FBI's own investigation that day. Kearns made his way to the fourth floor, where the first officers at the scene, Lt. Reingold and Sgt. Kelly, filled him in.

"An infant was supposedly kidnapped by a female dressed in a nurse's white uniform," Reingold explained.

Kearns got straight to work interviewing witnesses. The story that emerged was both simple and maddening—a low-tech crime with the very highest stakes.

At its center was a woman named Dora Vuckson, the daughter of Croatian-born parents who, seven years earlier, moved to Chicago from Escanaba, Michigan, a small town bordering Little Bay de Noc on the state's Upper Peninsula. Dora found work as a bank teller, and one day handled a deposit for Chester Fronczak, a Chicago factory worker whose parents came from Poland. It took Chester five years of asking, but eventually he persuaded the pretty young teller to go on a date with him. They got married in a Catholic church, and two years later, Dora Fronczak checked into Michael Reese Hospital to give birth to their first child.

Paul Joseph Fronczak was born at 1:20 a.m. on April 26, 1964, in Room 418 of Meyer House, the maternity wing of Michael Reese Hospital. Paul weighed seven pounds, two ounces, and he had a healthy head of black hair and slightly olive skin. He was as perfect as could be.

Dora, darkly pretty with a shy smile, and Chester, who had a machinist's thick forearms to go with doleful eyes, briefly met and held their son that first day, though the infant spent most of his time in the hospital's nursery unit. The next day, Monday, April 27, Chester went to work at the Hewitt-Robins factory with a box of cigars to hand out to co-workers, while Dora was allowed to hold her baby for longer spells while feeding him. At 9:00 a.m. that morning, a nurse brought the swaddled boy from the nursery and gave him to Dora, who fed him peacefully for thirty minutes, until another nurse entered Room 418.

Without a word, this other nurse walked over to Dora's bed, lifted the blue cotton blanket that was covering baby Paul, studied the infant's face for a moment, then lowered the blanket and walked out.

In retrospect, this might have seemed like odd behavior to some, but at the time it didn't strike Dora as alarming.

Later that day, at 1:40 p.m., that same nurse walked back into Room 418.

"One of the pediatricians wants to examine your son," she calmly explained to Dora, who was holding her child for another feeding. "I need to take him now."

Dora handed the boy to the nurse. The nurse left and walked briskly down the fourth-floor hallway, clutching Baby Fronczak in a white blanket. A young nurse's aide at the hospital, Alice Pemberton, spotted her in the hallway, while another nurse, Lillian London, watched her exit the floor through a south end door, which led to the stairwell. At 1:50 p.m., ten minutes after the mysterious nurse took Dora's baby, Martha Vinson, the nurse assigned to the hospital's newborn nursery, walked into Room 418 and saw that Dora was empty-handed.

"Where's your baby?" Vinson asked. "I need to take him back to the nursery."

Dora explained how a different nurse had already come and taken the infant. Betraying nothing, Nurse Vinson left to sort out the confusion.

In fact, she knew by then that there was a problem. A very big problem. She immediately notified the hospital's chief of security, Lindberg Dell, who quickly contacted every nurse and supervisor in the maternity ward to ask about the mysterious nurse. Several people had seen her. Oscar Moore, a laboratory assistant in the hospital's pathology department, even watched her leave the building and walk away onto 29th Street.

Not a soul knew where Baby Fronczak was.

Now there was no question in Lindberg Dell's mind—the newborn had been stolen.

At 2:45 p.m., a little over an hour after the kidnapping, Dell notified the Chicago Police Department.

Central Command pulled nearly every beat cop and officer from Chicago's 21st District onto the case. They issued an All-Points Bulletin and began a door-to-door search of the ten-block area around Michael Reese Hospital. Two lieutenants, six sergeants, and several patrolmen, as well as four detectives from the homicide division—plus nine FBI Special Agents—were all at work on the case within two hours of the kidnapping. The Chicago PD Crime Lab was notified at 3:00 p.m., and two technicians from the mobile unit were sent to fingerprint and photograph Room 418.

Around that time, police called the foreman at the Hewitt-Robins machine parts factory and asked to speak with Chester Fronczak, the proud father who earlier distributed the fine cigars he had bought to celebrate his first child's birth. The message they gave him was blunt and brutal.

"Your son is missing," they said.

Chester Fronczak hurried to the hospital and up to Room 418. The staff had not informed his wife Dora that their child was taken, so it fell to Chester to break the unthinkable news. As he knelt by his wife's bed and took her hand, Chester knew the next words he spoke would profoundly change her forever, because those same words had profoundly changed him. He understood this would be their before-and-after moment, the dividing line between when they knew happiness, and when happiness became something they could never truly know again.

This was how Dora finally learned her baby was gone.

Det. Kearns interviewed Lisa Cohen and Hope Rudnick, two expectant mothers in the room next door to Dora. They, too, had been visited by the mysterious nurse that morning. When they asked her what she wanted, the nurse said she was from the eye, ear, nose and throat department, but then quickly left without further explanation. The two women agreed on a detailed description—the nurse was white, approximately forty years old, five feet, five inches tall, about 145 pounds, with dark, possibly graying hair, a ruddy complexion and noticeably red cheeks, and a build they referred to as "plump." She wore a white frock like "the type worn by beauty operators and possibly made of nylon," they told Kearns, as well as white shoes and stockings. Police sketch artist Otis Rathel later used their descriptions to create a composite drawing of the suspect.

Mrs. Richard Shure from Room 425 told Det. Kearns the mysterious nurse had checked out her baby too.

Finally, Kearns spoke to Joyce Doane, Dora's roommate in 418. Joyce confirmed Dora's account of what happened earlier that day. Were there any other details about the nurse she could provide? Kearns asked. "I didn't get the impression she was a motherly, kindly sort of woman," Joyce said. "From looking at her, I think she must have hated the world."

The Chicago PD contacted local taxi companies and had their dispatchers broadcast an alert about the kidnapping. Lee A. Kelsey, a thirty-four-year-old driver for the Yellow Cab Company, heard the alert and called the police. He explained that, earlier that day, he'd been parked outside Michael Reese Hospital, waiting for a fare, when the phone at the cabstand rang. A woman told him she was in the Butler Building and would be right down.

"There is no Butler Building," Kelsey told her.

The woman corrected herself and said she was just south of the main building, on her way down.

"Look for a nurse," she said.

Kelsey drove around the corner of 29th Street, and three minutes later, the woman with the baby appeared.

She fit the suspect's description, Kelsey said, right down to the baby she was carrying in a white blanket.

"Take me to 35th and Halsted," the woman said.

Kelsey drove south, then west on 35th Street, until the woman changed her destination—35th and Union, four blocks short of Halsted. Kelsey dropped her off at the corner and went on his way. He later told cops he was sure he had driven the woman before. "I once picked her up in the area of 35th and Wallace and took her to a restaurant, and then returned her to 35th and Wallace," Kelsey recalled.

Chicago's Area 1 Homicide Task Force dispatched several officers to search the area around 35th Street, but found "no further information and no other leads."

By the end of April 27—Day One of Records Division Case No. C-128014—some two hundred policemen and FBI Special Agents had worked the streets of South Side Chicago, searching six hundred homes and talking to more than one thousand people. After that, the pace of the investigation only intensified. More than 2,600 Chicago area hospital employees were interviewed, while the files of hundreds of registered nurses were examined. Police combed through the medical records of any women with recent stillborn babies, along with the case histories of thousands of babies whose births were suspicious or complicated. Both the Chicago PD and the FBI set up offices to field the hundreds of calls and tips that poured in every day.

Eventually, investigators on the case questioned nearly forty thousand people across the country.

It was the largest police manhunt in Chicago history—more aggressive, even, than the citywide search for public enemy number one, John Dillinger, in the 1930s.

There were dozens and dozens of promising tips. An anonymous caller identified a woman who, he said, had worked as a nurse in several maternity wards, and who, when her ex-husband gained custody of their child, tried to burn down his house. A woman who strongly resembled the police sketch of the kidnapper was approached and interviewed at the Lincoln Park Children's Zoo. A passenger in a taxi told police he'd overheard the driver say he'd killed the Fronczak baby. A Miss V. Fox, the chief operator for the Stewart Exchange of the Illinois Bell Telephone Company, listened in on a patched call and heard the party say, "We took that baby from the hospital."

Not a single lead panned out. Every woman who looked like the police sketch had an alibi. Interesting tips turned out to be prank calls. Most of the hundreds and hundreds of supplementary police field reports led nowhere. Mothers on trains who appeared to be trying to conceal their infants were merely bundling them against the cold. Both Dora and Chester Fronczak appeared on TV, their haunted, exhausted faces pale in the camera lights, and appealed directly to the kidnapper.

"Take good care of him and see that he gets enough to eat," Dora, too weak to stand and speaking in a whisper, pleaded several days after her son was taken. "He is everything we built our hopes for the future on. Please return the baby to us."

Nothing came of their pleas either.

Many years later, Bernard Carey—one of the two FBI Special Agents assigned to live in the Fronczaks' Chicago home and monitor incoming telephone calls for two weeks—recalled what it was like to work on such a heartbreaking case.

"It was a very sad detail," Carey said. "There was such a sadness in that house. We were waiting every day for anything that seemed like a ransom call, but it never came. We didn't get even one slightly suspicious call. That was the hardest part. Having to go up and talk to the parents every night and say, 'I'm sorry, but there was nothing. No calls, no leads, nothing.' It's very sad to say, but when I finally left the house detail, I remember thinking that this case would never be solved."

Decades later—a lifetime, really—my mother Dora finally talked to me about what happened to her that awful day in Room 418-B.

"I felt so terrible for handing the baby over," she told me. "More terrible than you can know. People say, 'Well, she was dressed like a nurse, how could you have known?' But I should have known. I *should* have known. I shouldn't have just handed him over. A mother should know."

Weeks passed, then months. What would have been Baby Fronczak's first birthday, and then his second, came and went without any news of where he might be. At the one-year mark, Lt. John T. Cartan of the Chicago PD told reporters that one hundred volumes of testimony had been pored over, with no breakthrough—partly because, as Cartan put it, the stolen boy was "a 99% perfect baby with no blemishes or birth marks," and thus nearly impossible to compare to other infants.

Still, he said, "We haven't given up yet. Two detectives are working on it. We average a couple of leads a week."

At the two-year mark, the task force actively working the case was down to a single detective.

The story faded from the headlines, then from newspapers altogether. Officially, Case No. C-128014 stayed open, though the reality was that the investigation had been all but shelved. There was no list of suspects to monitor, no leads to pursue, nothing of any substance to hold on to. Whoever it was that took Baby Fronczak from his mother Dora's arms had, in effect, committed the perfect crime.

Short of a miracle, it was an unsolvable case.

This is when I entered the story, and became forever entwined with it—the miracle that wasn't a miracle at all.

CHAPTER 3

The first thing I should say is that I don't remember the day I was abandoned. Lord knows I wish I did. I've sat down and thought hard and really focused on peeling back layers of trivial memories to get closer to the details of that day, to this fundamental imprint on my brain, but I just can't get there. I cannot get myself back to July 2, 1965—432 days after the Baby Fronczak kidnapping.

The place was Newark, New Jersey, three states and eight hundred miles due east of Chicago. It was around 3:00 in the afternoon, and it was eighty degrees and partly cloudy. I was a little boy, not even two years old, wearing a clean blue suit and a blue boy's cap, sitting in a stroller on the sidewalk outside McCrory's, an enormous, four-story, eleven-bay, brick department store on the corner of Broad and Cedar Streets.

The stroller—and I—were unattended.

Back then, Broad Street was one of the busiest streets in all of New Jersey. It was part of what had once been called Ladies Mile—a strip of high-end department stores that catered to Newark's wealthiest women. On that day in 1965, the sidewalk outside McCrory's was undoubtedly bustling, both with shoppers and passersby. The entrance to McCrory's, where I was, was especially narrow, creating a funnel of people going in and out. Buses and trains discharged even more people right on or near Broad Street. The area was Newark's Times Square.

Even so, I sat in that stroller for close to two hours without a parent or guardian or any adult stopping to see if I was okay. I may have cried during those two hours in the stroller; I have no way of knowing. But I imagine I did.

Finally, at 5:00 p.m., someone called the Newark Police Department to report an abandoned child outside McCrory's. The caller declined to give his or her name.

"Child in distress," the dispatcher radioed to all patrol cars.

I was taken directly to Newark Hospital for a health check. I weighed twenty pounds and stood thirty inches tall—both below average for a twenty-one-month-old boy—and I had a cold and a runny nose, but otherwise I was in decent shape. I spent the night in the hospital, nameless, unidentified. The next morning, the police notified the Newark Bureau of Children's Services, and a case file was opened. I was given an official designation that has stuck with me all my life.

I was labeled a "foundling"—an infant abandoned by its parents and left for others to care.

The job of finding out who I was fell to a random Newark detective named Joseph P. Farrell. It turned out Farrell had a particular sensitivity to cases involving missing children, and that sensitivity played a big part in shaping my future.

Farrell's father, Joseph Farrell Sr., was a New York City police lieutenant who was known as a national expert in pickpocketing. Farrell Jr. followed his father into law enforcement, and was twenty-six years old when he started training to become a New Jersey state trooper. The agency, created eleven years earlier, was led by the legendary Norman Schwarzkopf Sr., a West Point graduate who personally trained the earliest troopers. Their mandate was to go after Mafia drug dealers, rumrunners, moonshiners, and gambling rings. Joe Farrell was still in training when, on March 1, 1932, he was summoned to East Amwell Township, in New Jersey's Hunterdon County. He couldn't have known he was being pulled into one of the most infamous kidnapping cases in U.S. history.

Soon enough, he learned that Charles Lindbergh Jr., the twenty-month-old son of aviation hero Charles A. Lindbergh, had been abducted from his family's home in the dead of night.

Along with other trainees and troopers, Farrell spent hours searching the thick woods around the Lindbergh home, desperate to find any sign of the missing boy. They turned up evidence—a ladder, footprints—but not the child. The search for Charles Jr. lasted ten weeks. On May 12, 1932, a delivery truck driver named William Allen stopped on the side of Princeton-Hopewell Road, near the small town of Mount Rose and 4.5 miles from the Lindbergh home. He stepped into a grove of trees to relieve himself and saw something peculiar on the ground. When he looked closer, he could tell it was a partial skeleton, the skull caved in, much of the body torn away by animals.

"My God," he yelled to his co-worker Orville Wilson, "there's a child, a dead child, over there!"

A genetic defect—overlapping toes on the small right foot—helped Charles Lindbergh identify the remains of his son. The best guess was that the body had been in its shallow dirt-and-leaf grave for seventy-two days, which meant the child was likely killed on the very night of the kidnapping. Joseph Farrell's intensive search of the woods, and every subsequent search, had all been for a body, not a child.

They'd all been chasing a ghost.

The Lindbergh case stayed with Farrell as he moved on from the troopers and became a Newark police officer. He took great pride in being part of New Jersey's largest police force. "He loved the uniform," Farrell's daughter Elizabeth Stewart told me when I visited her in 2019 to talk about the case. "Back then they wore these long overcoats that buttoned all the way down in front, and you had to unbutton your coat to get your gun out, but he loved all that. He liked pressing his uniform shirts."

Newark was not as dangerous as it would become in later decades, but it was still a rough place in the 1950s and '60s, rife with vice and gambling. But Joe Farrell was a big man, six foot two and stocky, and he could more than handle himself. "I remember being at a party with him, and a fight broke out in a crowd," Elizabeth remembered. "I turned around to say, 'Hey, Dad,' but he was already in the middle of it, breaking it up. He was powerful, but he never used his power until he absolutely had to."

On July 3, 1965, Det. Farrell was assigned to my case—the foundling case. He quickly covered the bases, running ads in local newspapers with my description, questioning contacts, taking my picture to send out to other departments. He came to assume—rightly so, it turned out—"that someone living outside the Newark area must have abandoned the child," he told a reporter. Farrell also surmised that the choice to leave me at McCrory's meant that "someone wanted me to be found and cared for."

Still, Farrell could not produce a single good lead. No one had seen who pushed my stroller up to McCrory's, or at least no witness had come forward. Nor was it possible back then to do any testing that would reveal a connection to any relatives. Farrell's only hope was that someone would reach out with information about me, but no one did.

The only inference to draw was that whoever my parents had been, they had no interest in being my parents any longer.

Instead, I became a ward of the state, in the custody not of a human being but of an agency. After spending weeks at Newark Hospital with an unshakeable cold, I was officially handed over to the New Jersey Bureau of Children's Services, which placed me in an adoption home—a sort of holding place for orphans—in the central New Jersey town of Watchung. In late July 1965, on an evening when I was running a temperature and still showing signs of a cold, a Children's Services official covered my head with a blue blanket and brought me to the door of Claire and Fred Eckert, who ran the adoption agency out of their Tudor-style home and became my new guardians. I was wearing a half-sleeve shirt and a diaper. Claire and Fred were waiting for me at the door, along with their daughter Janet. Claire took me in her arms and looked at my face.

"You smiled," Janet Ingrassia would tell me many, many years later, when we finally met again. "Your eyes were so big."

The Eckerts gave me a name, just as they did with every nameless child they took in. I became Scott McKinley. Claire chose it because she felt it was a strong, American name. She also picked a birthday for me, April 15, which roughly aligned with the age I appeared to be. And she gave me a religion—Roman Catholic. She did these things so she could baptize me at St. Joseph's Church in Watchung, in a brand-new white outfit she bought for me with her own money. Again, this was something the Eckerts did for all the children in their care, so that in the eyes of God, at least, we would no longer be strays or outcasts or wastrels. We wouldn't just be case numbers and police files. Claire gave me an identity—a claim to my own humanity—just as she did for the hundreds of other foundlings she embraced.

I wound up spending nearly a year with the Eckerts, though I don't remember any of it. But I came to learn that Fred and Claire had a very special relationship with me. "He is one of the most perfect boys I have ever known," Claire wrote in a letter in 1966. "He has charmed us all with his dearness and kind little ways. He has such a great love of life, and he has made us aware of so many things. He was my special boy."

The children in the Eckerts' care were all wards of the state, and they stayed with the couple only until the state found them permanent homes with adoptive parents. But Claire's daughter Janet later told me that if no one came forward to claim me, the Eckerts—who have since passed on—planned to keep me and raise me as their own.

"My parents did not want to let you go," said Janet, who was barely out of her teenage years when I was there. "They took such a shining to you, and they really just gravitated to you. We all did. I have so many memories, vivid memories, of the days and afternoons we spent with you. You playing your toy guitar, swimming in the pool, running down the driveway to meet my father when he came home from work. Even what you liked to eat"—soup with saltines, milk and cookies, soft-boiled eggs with butter. Some mornings, Janet recalled, Claire would give me a little dash of her morning coffee in my glass of milk.

"You became part of our family," Janet said.

Perhaps I had the same feelings as the Eckerts did—that they had become my new family. As I said, I can't remember anything from back then. But even if I did embrace the Eckerts as my new parents, it was not my destiny to be their son. Even though I'd settled into a wonderful and apparently joyous routine with the Eckerts, I was soon separated from my second family, and sent off to a third—all before I turned three years old.

Newark Det. Joseph Farrell was three weeks into my case when he had an idea. "He would tell us it was just a hunch," his daughter Elizabeth explained to me. "He was sensitive to the crime of kidnapping and sensitive to the sadness of a child being taken from his family. So he played a hunch."

My case was not a kidnapping case—it was an abandonment case. But Farrell remembered another recent case that did involve a kidnapping—the Baby Fronczak case, still unsolved after more than a year. It had been a national story, and the one existing photograph of Dora and Chester's son—the official hospital photo—had been circulated across the country. In his office in Newark, Det. Farrell dug up that picture, and held it up against the photo he'd taken of me at the start of the case. He did not see a striking resemblance.

Then he tracked down photos of Dora and Chester Fronczak, to see if any of their facial features matched mine. Again, there was nothing to persuade him there was a match.

But neither was there anything to make him give up on his hunch.

Farrell wrote a letter to the Chicago PD chief of detectives, Otto Kreuzer, and asked him to forward the Baby Fronczak file. Kreuzer obliged. He also alerted the FBI, which pounced on the fresh lead. The Special Agent in Charge of the Chicago office, Marlin Johnson, ordered medical tests to be performed on me—blood, bone, skin, and hair tests, plus an examination of my ear configurations. One of our unique human characteristics is the specific shape and contour of the rims of our ears, and police sometimes used this ear test to identify people. Because the staff at Michael Reese Hospital did not make a set of foot or fingerprints for me—the practice wasn't yet customary—and in a time when DNA analysis was still two decades away, the ridges of my ears were pretty much the best identifiers authorities had to work with.

Two FBI agents showed up at the Eckerts' home and made clay molds of my left ear—the only ear visible in Baby Fronczak's hospital photo. The FBI also had Claire Eckert take me to a local hospital to have blood samples drawn, and to the Trenton office of the Bureau of Children's Services, so staffers there could take current photos of me. The FBI agents assigned to the case pored over all this new evidence for eight months, conducting what the FBI called "extensive investigations and exhaustive medical studies." They scrutinized the ear ridges of ten thousand children, to compare against those of the stolen boy.

All ten thousand children were eliminated, except for one.

Me.

The eight-month investigation into Farrell's hunch could not "absolutely establish that Mr. and Mrs. Chester Fronczak" were my biological parents, an official report declared.

"But," it concluded, "neither has this fact been excluded."

In other words, it was worth it for the FBI to take the next, potentially painful, and surely fateful step—have the Fronczaks look me over in person, to decide if I was theirs.

CHAPTER 4

I can't say that what happened next was a crime. It was well intentioned, and not particularly reckless. In fact, it was an act of benevolence, and on some level, it made sense. A child without a family, and a family without a child—wasn't the instinct to bring them together a profoundly human one?

It started with Dora and Chester Fronczak receiving a letter from the FBI in April 1966, just about two years after the kidnapping. "An unknown male child was found abandoned in Newark, New Jersey," the letter read. "Extensive investigation was conducted by the Newark Police Department in an effort to determine who abandoned this child; however, no positive information in this regard was developed."

Even so, the letter went on, the child was roughly twenty-two or twenty-three months old, which put him in the age range to possibly be the Fronczaks' missing son. With that in mind, the FBI explained, they sent the boy's blood sample to Michael Reese Hospital for analysis, and now they wanted the Fronczaks to do the same.

Technicians from three different hospitals wound up examining the blood samples, all in search of some rare blood trait that would have linked the boy to the Fronczaks. It took more than a month to run all the samples, but in the end the results were "inconclusive," according to one FBI report.

After that, the science pretty much ran out. Ears and blood, the best bets, hadn't established any connection. All that remained was guesswork, which was fitting for a lead that began as a hunch. The FBI asked officials at the New Jersey Bureau of Children's Services, my legal guardians at the time, for their professional opinion on whether or not I was Baby Fronczak.

In truth, Bureau staffers hadn't seen very much of me at all, apart from several days after I was abandoned. The people to ask were probably the Eckerts, who by then had spent months with me and knew me pretty well. Yet no one asked Fred or Claire or Janet for their opinions.

Meanwhile, the Children's Services Bureau, working from photos of the Fronczaks and I, stepped into the science gap and offered a surprisingly conclusive opinion. Their assessment was that I looked "like Mrs. Fronczak from the front and like Mr. Fronczak from the side view," the FBI relayed in a report. That wasn't exactly a detailed analysis, but it was enough for a Bureau to declare, "It is our impression that Paul Joseph, who was abducted soon after birth, is in fact the child Scott McKinley."

Not *might* be Scott, or *likely* is Scott, or even *almost definitively* is Scott. No—they concluded that I was *in fact* the kidnapped boy. And so the FBI asked the Fronczaks to drive from Chicago to New Jersey so they could meet me in the district office of the New Jersey State Adoption Bureau, in the borough of Somerville, about thirty miles from where I was abandoned.

The meeting was set for June 9, 1966. Ralph Baur, an Illinois Children's Services director, sent the Fronczaks a letter explaining how the meeting would go. "The plan is for you to talk things over with the casework supervisor and then be introduced to Scott in the office of the Agency," Baur wrote. "The caseworker in New Jersey will show you a picture of Scott before you see him face to face."

The letter implied that the purpose of the meeting was to see if I triggered something in Dora to make her believe I was the same, one-day-old infant she had handed over two years earlier. What that something would be, I can't imagine—a physical resemblance, a feeling, a mother's intuition? Had Dora been given enough time to bond with her newborn son in any real way before he was taken? Were two or three brief feedings over the thirty-seven hours I spent in the hospital enough to establish a connection, an intimacy? Or were the authorities that set up the June 9 meeting—the Chicago PD, the FBI, the Children's Services directors in both Chicago and New Jersey—banking on Dora claiming me as her son no matter what?

Were they thinking, *How could she not take the boy?*

There is evidence to suggest they were. Before the Fronczaks had even been shown a photograph of me, they'd already been thrust into the long bureaucratic process of being approved as adoptive parents, should they decide I was theirs (since there was no scientific method that could prove I was their son, they would be legally required to adopt me). And since that process could end up lasting beyond the June 9 meeting in Somerville, Chicago authorities also granted the Fronczaks temporary licenses as childcare providers, which meant they could take me home even before they'd been approved as adoptive parents. "They are fine, decent people who are interested in the welfare of children," the New Jersey commissioner of agencies and institutions, Lloyd McCorkle, explained to a reporter. "They met all the tests."

And all of that was *before* the Fronczaks were even shown a photo of me.

My connection to the Baby Fronczak kidnapping dated back to Det. Farrell's hunch three weeks after I was abandoned. Every legal and bureaucratic authority involved in the case was aware that I was the FBI's best and possibly only lead—and perhaps the last significant chance anyone would have to reunite Dora and Chester with their son. In fact, the reason a state official put a blanket over my head as they walked me to the Eckerts' front door months earlier was to hide my identity should any reporters who somehow learned of the connection be lurking nearby. I was never just a missing child—I was always the world's best hope of finding Baby Fronczak and cracking an infamous case.

Did all of that add a palpable urgency to the June 9 meeting? Did it make that meeting a mere formality? Again, were authorities depending on a childless and traumatized Dora Fronczak being emotionally incapable of walking away from a healthy boy who was hers for the taking?

Either way, the pressure on Dora Fronczak must have been unfathomably immense. Whatever decision she made would be fraught with consequences. But as June 9 approached, she had no choice but to make a decision one way or the other. The burden of recognizing her own son, after spending less than one total hour with him two years earlier, fell to her and her alone. Science couldn't help. Law enforcement couldn't help. Even Chester Fronczak would not bear the same load as his wife, the infant's mother. Dora was trapped in an almost impossible situation. There was nothing she could do except show up.

The same was true of Claire and Fred Eckert, who had grown to love me yet had no choice but to give me up. As June 9 approached, Claire scraped up some of her savings—a full month's salary worth—and bought me several new outfits, including the white, striped jumper suit I would wear to the meeting. Claire also pulled together several photos she'd taken of me over the months, which she put in an envelope for Dora Fronczak, along with a lock of my hair taken from the haircut Claire's son-in-law gave me the day before the meeting.

Finally, Claire prepared a letter for the Fronczaks, and included a daily schedule that she called, "A Complete Diet of Hugs and Kisses." In it, she included all the foods I liked, my clothing sizes (3 in pants, 4 in pajamas, 6 in socks, 7D in shoes), and a brief report on my latest injury.

"Scott skinned his toe when he fell the other day, and he tells me about this, so maybe you could take his shoes off while he is riding in the car," Claire wrote. "Also, he does not like the floor if it is cold on his feet, so I use little slipper socks."

Then Claire added the sweetest thing anyone would ever say about me, as far as I can remember.

"For all the sadness you have both known, you are in for so much joy," she assured the Fronczaks, "for you will now see things through Scott's eyes, and he can make them lovely."

On the morning of June 9, Claire Eckert wrote her name, address, and phone number on a small piece of paper, and pinned the note to one of the undershirts she packed in my little suitcase. She did that so the Fronczaks could reach out to her, should they ever want to. The Eckerts and their daughter Janet drove me the seventeen miles from Watchung to Somerville and, at the New Jersey State Adoption Bureau office, a staffer took me and hustled me away. Claire, Fred, and Janet were allowed to stay in the room next door to where the Fronczaks would meet me, but that was as close as they could get.

Dora and Chester Fronczak were already in the district office, waiting, when a caseworker holding my hand walked me in. I stood in front of these two strangers as they looked me over. Within seconds, a decision had been made.

"My God!" Dora exclaimed. "That is my baby!"

In the next room, the Eckerts heard Dora's near-scream, and confronted their mixed emotions. "What a wonderful sound that was for us," Janet told me many years later. "We loved you very much, but in our hearts we were happy to see a family that had been apart for so long reunite again."

Janet told me about something else that happened at the Adoption Bureau office that day.

She said that just before the meeting took place, she overhead two police officers talking in the hallway.

One of them leaned in and whispered something in the other's ear, just loud enough for Janet to hear.

The officer whispered, "That ain't the same kid."

CHAPTER 5

There was a secret pact.

It involved the two most important law enforcement officials working the case—Marlin Johnson, the Special Agent in Charge of the FBI's Chicago Bureau, and the highly esteemed Lt. John T. Cartan of the Chicago Police Department, who was heading the Baby Fronczak investigation.

Johnson, an Iowa native, was only twenty when he joined the FBI as a fingerprint clerk. He stepped away from the job to serve in the Navy, but returned and rose through the ranks until he was given what was then the FBI's most high-profile assignment—heading up the Chicago force. He had a solid, stalwart appearance, topped off with thick, black-rimmed glasses.

Lt. Cartan had a reputation as a great policeman with a squeaky-clean nose. He worked long hours, brought his work home with him, seized on certain cases, and never let up. Johnson and Cartan recognized something pure and noble in each other and became quick friends during the Baby Fronczak investigation. That friendship would last both their lifetimes.

After I was abandoned in New Jersey, and drew attention as a possible Baby Paul, the decision of what to do with me fell to both Johnson and Cartan. Their job would have been easy if the blood analysis had shown some link between the Fronczaks and I, but when it didn't, they found themselves in a tricky spot. They could either pass the decision off to the Fronczaks and hope the couple accepted me as their son, or they could funnel me back into the child services system.

Only one of those options allowed the FBI and the Chicago PD to claim they had righted a terrible wrong.

The truth was that both Marlin Johnson and John Cartan had a strong suspicion, if not a near certainty, that I was *not* Paul Fronczak.

"My father would come home and say to my mother and me, 'The Fronczaks are such fine, good people, and my heart is heavy for them, but that is not their baby,'" John Cartan's daughter Mary Hendry told me many years later when we spoke about the case. "He believed they would make great parents, and he would never discourage them from taking you, but he was certain that you were not theirs. I can still see him standing in the kitchen shaking his head and saying, 'They are good people, they will do a really good job of raising him.'"

Lt. Cartan wasn't the only one convinced I wasn't Paul. Marlin Johnson felt the same way. "They agreed that neither one of them believed you were the kidnapped baby, but they also agreed to go along with it," says Mary Hendry. "They were sure the Fronczaks would be good parents, so they let it all unfold."

So it was that Dora and Chester Fronczak were forced into making an unimaginably pressurized decision—a decision I would later learn gave them no real choice at all.

For decades, Dora Fronczak refused to discuss the day she claimed me as her own, or allow that she had any doubts that I was her son. Eventually, though, I got the chance to ask her about the fateful moment when she called me her baby in that office in Somerville. Did she truly believe that I was Paul? Was she nearly convinced but not sure? Did she know I *wasn't* him?

When I asked about that moment nearly five decades later, Dora wiped away tears and let out a big sigh.

"I had to ask myself, 'Is this really him?'" she finally admitted. "I had to worry if you were really him. Could we have just said, 'That's not him,' and then be judged for not taking you? Or could we just take you and save a child?"

That sounded to me like she felt she couldn't say no. Which meant that when she claimed me as hers, she was voluntarily accepting a lifetime of questioning herself.

"In my heart," she told me, "I was hoping you were him."

Back in Somerville, Johnson and Cartan gave the Fronczaks two days to think about it before officially agreeing to take me. I don't know if they wavered in that time, but on the third day, they said they wanted to bring me home. A few days later, when the paperwork was finished, the Fronczaks took me to Chicago. Reporters clustered outside the Fronczaks' home, hoping for a glimpse of me, or a quote from one of the happy parents. A local paper reported a family friend saying, "Dora is really happy."

Not much later, the Fronczaks put me in a little white suit and brought me to Saint Joseph and Anne Catholic Church, where the Rev. James V. Shannon baptized me in the Catholic faith. In short order, the Fronczaks were awarded official legal custody of me before, in December 1966, the adoption process was finalized. "Chester and Dora Fronczak are husband and wife, of lawful age and under no legal disability," the adoption decree read. They are "reputable persons of good moral character with sufficient ability and financial means to rear, nurture and educate the said child in a suitable and proper manner." Thus, the decree went on, "Scott McKinley, a minor, shall be to all legal intents and purposes, the child of the petitioners. The name of said child shall be changed to Paul Joseph Fronczak."

Ironically, and for clarity's sake, the decree concluded that, "The petitioners are *not* related to said child." After all, how can you legally adopt a child who is your biological son?

Everyone involved in the decision regarding my placement with the Fronczaks faced the same, stark reality—there was simply no way to be certain of my identity. "There is presently no known method of positively establishing the descendancy of a two-year-old child," Edward Weaver, regional director of the Chicago Department of Children and Family Services, unambiguously declared in a newspaper interview. In other words, the best anyone could do was guess.

But if that was the simple truth that everyone understood, why was the situation not handled that way?

Why wasn't it honestly portrayed as a family that lost a son taking in a son who lost his family? Why did Dora have to definitively claim that I was her kidnapped boy?

"Is the missing baby your son?" one reporter demanded when he cornered her outside her home.

"Yes, it is," Dora said without hesitation.

Her insistence that I was the kidnapped child—whether she believed it or not—created an enormous disconnect between my new parents and I, as, over the years, I failed constantly to live up to the imposed truth that I was Paul. The handoff in Somerville created a situation that invited resentment—resentment of me because I was not Dora and Chester's true son, resentment of the Fronczaks for not being my real parents. What began as Det. Joseph Farrell's well-meaning "hunch," and ended with Johnson and Cartan's secret pact, wound up trapping us all in a situation that was far more emotionally and psychologically complex than anyone could have dreamed.

CHAPTER 6

For the first eight years I was with the Fronczaks, I had no idea how I came to be their son. Any early memories I had of meeting them in New Jersey and driving back with them to Chicago, if I even had any, would not have been helpful since I'd have been too young to understand what was happening. As far as I knew, I was just an ordinary kid in an ordinary family.

That all changed when I was ten.

I was snooping around for Christmas presents in the basement of my parents' Chicago home when I found a hatbox and three shoe boxes in a small crawl space. In the boxes were hundreds of old newspaper clippings about a crime—the kidnapping of a one-day-old infant from the arms of his mother, Dora Fronczak, in Chicago's Michael Reese Hospital in 1964. I recognized my parents in the photos that ran with the articles.

Then I found clips about a different event—a boy abandoned in New Jersey who was identified as the kidnapped child. The articles included photos of that boy.

I could tell right away the boy was me.

The discovery of the clippings, as dramatic as they were, was not so much a revelation to me as it was a confirmation of a vague but persistent feeling I had that I wasn't the Fronczaks' real son. It wasn't anything we ever talked about—in our family, we almost never sat down and discussed our feelings about anything—but it was there even before I found the clippings in the hatbox.

Here's what I mean. Shortly after the Fronczaks brought me home with them, they had a baby of their own—a boy named David. We grew up as brothers, unaware of the fact that we weren't related. But as the years went by, I noticed little differences in the way we were treated, and in the way we interacted with our parents. Dave seemed to have an easy camaraderie with our father, Chester, while my relationship with him wasn't nearly as free and relaxed. At the dinner table, I often had the feeling that our family was divided into three and one (the odd one out being me). Later on, my parents gave Dave a big bedroom of his own near their bedroom, while I—the older brother—was given the smaller bedroom further on down the hallway. No one ever explained to me this decision, even though it seemed too blatantly unfair to go undiscussed.

There was also the matter of my appearance. I simply didn't look like Dave or my parents. Dave, like my father, had a soft, roundish face. Mine was angular. Dave and my father had dark hair, while mine was a light reddish color. Even as a child, I had an adventurous, curious nature, while Dave was more cautious and reserved. Now, plenty of siblings and parents are different from each other, some in startling ways. But for me, it wasn't just the inequitable treatment or my appearance or our behavior or any one single thing—it was the combination of all the differences that often made me feel like an outsider.

So, when I found the newspaper clippings in the crawl space, it was a stunning moment of affirmation—there *was* something different about me. I put most of the clippings back in their boxes, but I kept a few with me, and that evening I went up to my mother in the kitchen and asked her about them.

"What are these?" I asked, holding out the clippings.

My mother's face reddened deeply, and for a moment she couldn't even speak. It was clear I wasn't supposed to know about those old articles, or at least not yet, and possibly ever.

"How dare you snoop around this house?" she demanded. "Those are none of your business."

"These are about me," I persisted. "Paul Joseph Fronczak. That's me, isn't it?"

My mother could tell that her initial approach—scolding me into dropping the whole thing—wasn't going to work. If I'd been younger when I found the boxes, it might have worked. But at ten, I wasn't going to be easily dissuaded from having my question answered. There was an urgency to my questions that surprised even me.

"Yes, those are about you," my mother finally conceded in a soft voice. "You were kidnapped, we found you, we love you, and that's all there is to know."

My mother's stunningly concise summation of the event—"You were kidnapped, we found you, we love you, and that's all there is to know"—would indeed be the very last words spoken between us about the kidnapping, not just for a few years, but for the next four decades of our lives.

Something so monumental, so impactful, so defining of our family, simply ceased to be an issue that required mention or discussion or even recollection. My parents wrote it out of their history, and mine, by refusing to confront its consequences in any way, and instead letting its memory gather dust, along with the boxes that held the old clippings of a now forgotten story.

What happened to me in those forty years of silence is, one could argue, the story of my life. But to me, it is only the story of my *first* life.

My second life began in October 2012, when I made a discovery about myself that changed just about everything. That is the date I wish to jump to now. I told the story of the previous forty years in my first book, *The Foundling*, and I don't think there's any need to do anything but summarize it now.

Basically, I was a wanderer, restless in my own skin, always chasing the next adventure, never sure of who I was or who I was supposed to be. I've often felt like Dr. Sam Beckett in *Quantum Leap,* jumping in and out of different characters trying to find my way home. The Fronczaks raised me with all the love and care they could give, which was substantial, and a blessing in every way. They were very, very good people and very good parents, caught, like me, in an impossibly awkward situation. My father worked long hours at a machine factory to feed and clothe and school his two sons, and my mother ran our home just as any loving mother would, with attention to detail and concern for our health and happiness. We were, in all apparent ways, a typical nuclear family—a new car every few years, annual two-week vacations, PTA nights, first dates, high school dances, fights and arguments, birthdays and Christmases, all the things that constitute family life.

But just below the surface, there was always tension and strife. My parents, understandably, were extremely strict with and protective of me. They'd lost a son to a kidnapper, and they weren't about to let me wander out of their sight. But as I got older, I rebelled against their shielding ways and constantly pushed for more freedom. I snuck out to see girls when forbidden to date, skipped college to join a band, and otherwise defied my parents' wishes at every turn. I alienated my brother David by failing to conceal my distaste for his conformity and allegiance to our parents. I let my hair grow long and shaggy, a stark contrast to my father's and brother's neat, trim cuts. I dreamed of being someone else—who, I didn't know.

As a kid, I dressed up as different characters and play-acted my way through childhood—a cop, a soldier, a reporter. As an adult, I did pretty much the same thing. I spent a year in the U.S. Army, toured with my own Rush-tribute band, repaired trunk amplifiers for a cable company, ran a premium cigar store in New York City, served as George Clooney's stand-in on *Ocean's Eleven,* played several different characters in a live Las Vegas *Star Trek* show, made infomercials that still run in Nevada's McCarran Airport, went broke, got married, got divorced, and held probably a hundred different jobs in all—without ever once feeling rooted to any one place or person. I left companies and relationships with equal ease, floating through the world rather than living in it. I didn't spend time wondering how much of this had to do with the trauma I might have endured as an infant, but in hindsight, it was clearly my identity issues—not feeling that I was the real Paul—that created this disorientation and lack of direction in my life.

Searching for something—anything, really—I placed an ad on Match.com (my unfortunate pitch—"A Cool Guy for a Cool Girl") and went on a date with a beautiful teacher named Michelle. I liked her because her profile photo showed her smiling and holding a martini glass. We got along well, and after I broke my sternum and collarbone in a car crash, Michelle nursed me through a two-week stay at her apartment. *She is good for me,* I kept thinking. *She grounds me.* I proposed in the snow on a bridge over the Chicago River, and we were married on a sunny day in Las Vegas. Not much later, Michelle was pregnant, and we had a child—an impossibly angelic girl we named Emma Faith.

Suddenly, I had something I never thought I'd have—a family of my own. A family that was unquestionably mine. And when I held Emma for the first time in the hospital, I was overwhelmed by how connected I felt to her. My blood ran through her, which bound us in a way I'd never experienced before. *This is what it feels like,* I thought. *This is what it means to belong to someone and someplace.*

This was an astonishing time in my life, but it was interrupted by a routine question put to me by Michelle's doctor.

"What is your family history?"

It was a question he'd probably asked of thousands of people, and yet I had no answer. The abstract worry in my brain that I wasn't the real Paul Fronczak suddenly wasn't abstract anymore. I could have recited the Fronczaks' family history to him, but that wasn't really my history, was it? Right there in the doctor's office, it struck me that the question of my identity was no longer just of concern to me. Now, it belonged to Emma too. What kind of father would I be if I couldn't even promise her the foundation of knowing who I was? What kind of incomplete legacy was that to hand off to your own flesh and blood?

It was instantly clear that I had to resolve the nagging questions about my real identity once and for all. It took some convincing, but I finally got my parents to submit saliva samples for DNA tests, and I took one myself. The long-neglected mystery of my true relationship to the Fronczaks was, I could hardly believe, on the verge of being solved.

I was in my office at the Art Institute of Las Vegas, where I worked as the assistant director of admissions, when, in October 2012, I got a phone call from a representative at the DNA analysis company Identigene. I told him my secret code, and he asked a few questions to confirm who I was. Then there was a long pause, and I heard my heart beating through my chest.

"We have the test results," the representative finally said. "There is no remote possibility that you are the son of Dora and Chester Fronczak."

There it was. *No remote possibility.* Not an opinion, not a hunch—hard science. Decades of doubt and questions and uncertainty tumbled away in a torrent of emotion—I felt relief, sadness, and fear all at once. What did it mean that I wasn't the real Paul Fronczak? Besides the fact that I no longer knew my own name, my birth date, my medical history, or anything about my true identity, what did it mean to me and my family that I wasn't who everyone thought I was? I called my wife Michelle and told her what the DNA tests showed, and she assured me that nothing had really changed; I was still her husband and Emma's father. *That* was my identity. It felt good to hear that, but the bottom line was that something *had* changed.

And in that moment, it felt like *everything* had.

That one five-minute phone call from the Identigene rep created a monumental mystery that would quickly consume my life—if I wasn't the real Paul Fronczak, who was I?

But in the same instant, it created a second mystery that would prove every bit as consuming as the first.

If I wasn't the real Paul, then who was, and where was he?

This may be hard to believe, but from the start I felt like I was more invested in the second mystery than the first. The gut instinct I felt that day was the desire to find the real Paul Fronczak—my parents' real son. That, I believed, was the true injustice—the wrong that needed to be righted. I felt like I owed it to Dora and Chester to figure out what had become of the real Paul, and then, if possible, to bring him back to them. Of course, learning my own identity was important, too, but from the start, my primary mission was figuring out what happened to my mother's kidnapped son.

That mission proved a lot harder than I ever imagined. One of my first decisions was to go public with my story, in the hopes that someone out there would have information about the real Paul. I contacted a well-known local reporter named George Knapp, news anchor for the Las Vegas station KLAS-TV, and told him my story. He was immediately interested in helping me. Both Michelle and I were interviewed for a TV report, but before it aired, I had to reach out to my parents and let them know about the test results. I didn't want them to hear it from George Knapp. I didn't call them right after I got the results because, frankly, I was scared to. I didn't know how to break it to them that I wasn't their real son. Maybe they already knew that, deep down, and maybe they didn't. Either way, it was bound to bring up terrible memories they had tried to bury.

I decided to write my mother an email, rather than break the news to her on the phone. That way, she and my father would at least have a little time to digest the news before we spoke. "First, I am your son, and I always will be," I wrote. But "the DNA test results came back, and it turns out I am not your biological son. I am not the kidnapped boy that you had stolen from your arms on April 27, 1964. This means the real Paul Joseph Fronczak may still be out there, not knowing who he is."

I told her about George's upcoming TV report on me, and I assured them my only goal was to finally learn the truth. "I hope you and Dad will be with me on this, and be part of the process," I wrote.

"Having you and Dad with me every step of the way would be the greatest thing I could ever hope for."

I didn't know how my parents would react. I expected them to be upset that I was going public with the story. After all, they had warned me repeatedly when I was young not to mention the story to anyone, ever. They had a fear that I might be kidnapped again, given how many people knew about us and even knew where we lived. Any kind of publicity at all was, to them, opening the door to possible catastrophe. Beyond this fear, my parents wanted nothing more than to be ordinary again. They didn't want to be known as "that family with the kidnapped boy." They just wanted to be the Fronczaks. Notoriety was, to them, deeply embarrassing and deeply hurtful. This was why they chose to bury the story—and why I knew they would be upset that I was now digging it back up.

Still, I hoped they would understand why I was going public, and understand how important it was for me to discover my own identity.

Sadly, they didn't.

After I sent the email to my mother, I didn't hear from her or my father for four days. Finally, the phone rang, and I recognized my parents' Chicago number.

"Hi, Mom," I said as calmly as I could, as if nothing at all had changed.

"How could you do this to us?" my mother said, with the same rising anger in her voice I heard the day I found the newspaper clippings four decades earlier.

"Do what?" I said.

"I can't believe you did this. We told you not to do it. I'm sorry we weren't good enough parents for you. I'm sorry you felt you had to do this."

"Mom, I just want to find Paul," I pleaded. "I want to do this for you."

"*You have ruined our lives!*" my mother yelled. "*Now we have to relive the nightmare again! Why would you do this to us?*"

I heard the phone drop on the kitchen counter, and I heard someone pick it up.

"Dad?"

"You're an asshole," my father said. "You should have left this buried."

After that, the phone went dead.

I would soon learn my brother Dave sided with my parents and refused to help my search in any way. I called my parents a few times after that, but they never picked up.

I would not speak another word to my mother, father, or brother about anything *for the next two years.* Complete radio silence. I'd been effectively cut out of the Fronczak family, just after learning I wasn't biologically a part of it.

Was it my own doing? Yes, I guess it was. I set it all in motion, against what I knew to be my parents' wishes. I could have done nothing—I could have left the past in the past—if only to spare my parents the pain of reliving the tragedy. In the months that followed, I would hear from many people who believed I did the wrong thing. "The Fronczaks *are* your parents," went a typical comment. "That's all you need to know."

The truth, however, was that I felt I didn't have a choice. To do nothing would be to accept living a lie. I'd spent most of my life unsure of my identity, so how could I pass up the chance to finally learn who I was? That uncertainty about my past had very real consequences in my life, and I didn't want to pass those consequences down to my daughter Emma. I owed her a father who was confident and complete—a man in full—not some rootless, restless imitation of a man. Once I sent in the DNA tests, it never occurred to me to not act on the results, should they prove what I suspected. Of *course* I had to act on this new information. Of *course* I had to dig up a long-buried secret, in order to search for a long-obscured truth.

Ask yourself—if you were in my place, what would *you* have done? Nothing? Or something?

Would you have been okay living a lie?

CHAPTER 7

The FBI investigation into the kidnapping of Paul Fronczak was never officially closed. Yet by 1966, two years after the abduction, it was essentially over. Once I was given to the Fronczaks, the investigation slowed to a crawl and then stopped altogether, and eventually the FBI's files were stacked in ten boxes and put in storage. As the years turned into decades, those boxes of case files were marked for destruction, to free up space for more pressing, and more recent, crimes.

By all rights, those files should have been fed through shredders or torched in burn bags long ago, thousands of pages of tips and leads reduced to ashes or pulp, an unsolved case fated to stay unsolved.

But that didn't happen. The ten boxes were not destroyed. When FBI agents went looking for them in 2013, they discovered that, due to a bureaucratic error, the files were still in storage, safe in their sealed boxes.

That cleared the way for the FBI's announcement on August 8, 2013.

Though it had never been closed, the FBI was officially reviving the Fronczak case.

"It was deemed appropriate to take a fresh look at the evidence we have," read the FBI press release, "and possibly re-interview sources that are still around."

The abduction of Baby Fronczak became the oldest kidnapping cold case to ever be reopened in U.S. history.

It was my DNA test that reopened it.

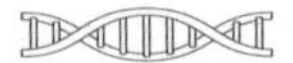

I went public with my story on April 25, 2013, in an I-Team report on an 8NewsNow broadcast on Las Vegas's KLAS-TV station. "I don't know how old I am, or who I am, or what nationality, all those things you just take for granted," I told the highly esteemed investigative reporter George Knapp, a hard-boiled, silver-haired, pound-the-pavement-style journalist. "But it's not just about me. It's about, is my parents' son still alive? Is he out there? Hopefully this story can help us find out."

The local scoop made international news. I received a call and then a visit from two FBI agents, who administered their own DNA test and asked me a series of questions. I also received phone calls and letters from nearly every major news organization—ABC, NBC, CBS, CNN—interested in telling my story nationally. After a lot of deliberation with my wife, Michelle, I went with Barbara Walters and the ABC News show *20/20*. My hope was that Barbara's popularity would help my story spread and prompt someone who knew something to come forward.

The two *20/20* segments I did with Barbara Walters were the show's most highly rated broadcasts in more than two years.

Sure enough, the tips began to arrive. ABC created an age progression image of what the real Paul Fronczak might look like today, and several men thought there was enough of a resemblance to reach out to us. They all had suspicious adoption histories and questions about their identities. We ran DNA tests, but none of them came up as a match to a DNA sample submitted by a Fronczak cousin (my parents and brother Dave refused to allow their DNA to be used in any efforts to identify the real Paul).

At the same time, a genetic genealogist named CeCe Moore contacted me with an offer to help me discover my identity. In the end, I had both CeCe and genealogists from the DNA website Ancestry.com working separately on my case.

It took me a while to figure out exactly what they were doing. I learned that they would start with a DNA sample from me and *reverse* build my family tree, until they could identify my parents, and then me.

Basically, when most people submit their DNA to a site like Ancestry, they are building a family tree that starts with them at the bottom of the tree. In other words, they are building upwards, to identify more and more ancestors and add more and more branches to the tree. It's a journey from the present to the past.

But with me, the genealogists had to do something different. They were starting with the many hundreds of relatives who are matched with any one sample of DNA—the vast majority of them very distant relatives—and then picking the closest matches and building *downward* from them, until they could find recent ancestors common to more than one tree. When they found these Most Recent Common Ancestors, they could unite their trees, and keep doing this until they narrowed it down to a single tree that contained my two biological parents—and me.

They were starting in the past, and ending at me.

Building down a tree is a lot more challenging and time-consuming than building up. You start with many dozens of possible family lines to pursue, but don't have any idea which line is the right one, or even if a line is worth spending time on. There are a lot of dead ends, blind curves, and hopeful guesses.

In my case, I knew absolutely nothing about who my family was or where I came from, other than that I was abandoned in Newark, New Jersey, suggesting I might have been raised somewhere in the Northeast. But even that kernel of information didn't mean we could rule out family lines rooted in other parts of the country. Essentially, we would need to build down several different family trees, persuade many, many people to take DNA tests, pore through many thousands of pages of family records, census data, birth certificates, and obituaries, and on top of all that, hope for a whole bunch of lucky breaks.

CeCe Moore assembled a team to help her. They were three remarkable, amateur sleuths—Allison Demski, Carol Rolnick, and

Michelle Trostler—who, like CeCe, were mothers of young kids working on the case for free, mainly out of their homes and in between other jobs and chores. Usually they worked late into the nights, or while on vacation, when the rest of their families were out enjoying themselves. I learned genealogists are a special breed, capable of absorbing and processing vast amounts of information, blessed with uncommon focus and drive, and absolutely relentless until they finally identify the previously unknown relative they have targeted.

I was really so lucky to have so many gifted, giving people working on my case. They wanted to find my true identity every bit as much as I did.

Even so, the process took thousands and thousands of hours over the course of many long months. The first surprise I received was when the team of Matt Deighton and Crista Cowen at Ancestry.com sent me the preliminary results of my DNA test. The test revealed that 94 percent of my DNA traced back to Europe, 5 percent to West Asia, and 1 percent to Africa.

It also revealed that I am Jewish.

Actually, as someone who grew up the son of Catholic parents, and who went to schools that steeped me in Catholicism, learning that 37 percent of my genetic ethnicity was European Jewish was more than just a surprise. It was the loss of one of my cornerstone beliefs about myself. I can't say that I was rocked by the discovery; I guess I took it in stride. But in retrospect, it's pretty amazing how such a huge building block in my identity—the religion I believed in—could have come tumbling down straight out of the gate. It showed how very little I actually knew about myself.

The DNA test produced a slew of possible relatives, as most tests do, but very distant relatives are not what you're looking for. Someone who shares just a bit of DNA with you, enough to make you fifth or sixth cousins, does not much help lead you to a closer relation. Your sixth cousin and you share the same set of great, great, great, great, great-grandparents (that's five "greats"), which is many,

many generations back in your family tree—too many to have to build down from. Tracing such a distant connection would involve an unimaginable amount of work, if it were even possible, given the difficulty of finding records that date that far back.

What you're hoping for is a much closer relation—say, a second or third cousin, or even closer. You and your second cousin share a set of great-grandparents, which is only three generations back in your tree—a much more reasonable place to start from if you're looking for even closer relations.

Among my many distant matches, the closest relation was a woman who was anywhere from a fourth to a sixth cousin.

Her name was Frances Kirby, and she was the first person on the planet who I knew for sure was a blood relation.

I wound up traveling to New York City in 2013 to meet Fran Kirby and her husband Larry. They were a lovely and friendly couple, and I really enjoyed the time we spent together, but all along I was aware that we were fairly distant relatives. I knew I had to keep pushing deeper into my family tree to find much closer relatives and, ultimately, my biological parents.

The team at Ancestry.com, led by Matt Deighton, did the pushing for me. They set out to identify sixteen key people—Fran Kirby's eight sets of great-great-grandparents—and began by testing two of Fran's first cousins, who were nice enough to agree to submit DNA samples for us. If either of them matched with me, we'd be able to drastically shrink our pool of family lines to research. Unfortunately, neither was a match, so Matt and his team had to cast a much wider net and do a lot more research.

Just about then, I got a wonderful Hanukkah gift.

In a town called Beacon, on the Hudson River about an hour north of New York City, the children of a man named Alan Fisch gave him an Ancestry DNA kit as a Hanukkah present. Alan was a rugged outdoorsman in his fifties. He owned a kayak company, volunteered as an EMT for the Beacon Ambulance Corps, and also worked as a ski patroller for the Thunder Ridge Ski Area in Patterson, NY. Alan submitted his DNA and, a few weeks later, got his results in the mail.

He had a match for a second cousin—me.

When he contacted me with the news ("I just received my DNA results and they matched us as second cousins," he wrote. "I would like to talk to you to see how we may be related."), I was extremely encouraged. A second cousin? Not only could Alan's family tree help lead us to my biological parents, but he also gave me a fairly close blood relation—someone I could meet and look at and talk to and relish being part of the same family with. I was so excited to meet him that one of the first things we agreed on was a date to connect in person in New York City.

But here's the thing about my journey of self-discovery—it came to be defined by unexpected and often shocking last-second twists and turns. Every lucky break or bit of good news was usually followed by a setback that knocked me to my knees. That's what happened with Alan.

First, Alan told me that he was adopted, and that he didn't know anything about his biological family. I was hoping he'd have a lot of knowledge about and insight into our shared relatives, and maybe even my own parents, but he had exactly zero information to share with us. That was a setback, but okay—we could still use his DNA to find and build the family tree that connected us. Plus, we could get his adoption records, and maybe the names of his biological parents would be in them.

Then, the second twist—New York State had sealed Alan's adoption records, and it was next to impossible to access them.

That left researching his DNA matches as our only option, but even that was okay, because I still had Alan himself, and I was still going to get to meet someone who shared blood with me.

Then, just two days before our scheduled meeting in New York City, Alan's wife called to tell me that Alan was dead.

It happened quickly. He woke up one morning and struggled to catch his breath. He had no major health issues that he knew of and resisted going to the hospital. Finally, his wife, Randi, convinced him to go. Tests revealed he had a blocked blood vessel in his lungs. Doctors gave him clot-busting medicine, and he seemed okay. The nurses said all he could talk about was going to New York City to meet his new cousin. Alan had a peaceful night at the hospital, but the next morning, he had a heart attack.

Just like that, Alan was gone.

At first, I simply couldn't believe it was true. I mean, just two days before our meeting? It seemed ridiculous, implausible. Then, I felt horrible for Alan's family—his wife, Randi, and his children, Jason, Jenna, and Julie. I didn't even know Alan, and his passing devastated me. But these people who had known and loved him for so long—what must they be going through? I couldn't even conceive of such loss.

To my surprise, Alan's children decided they didn't want their father's dream to die with him, and they asked if I would go through with the meeting in New York City. I said of course, and I flew to New York and met with Randi and her son Jason in a hotel. We all cried together, and we tried to make some sense of the strange confluence of events. Jason, a strapping young man, said he wanted to stay involved in finding Alan's biological parents. I hugged him and thanked him, and only then, when I took a good look at him, did I realize that he and I were related too. The same blood ran through him, his father, and me.

Jason was my family.

Just a few days later, we did manage to get Alan's adoption records unsealed, but then we hit another series of roadblocks. His birth certificate listed no father, and his biological mother refused to help us. Not much later, we learned from 23andMe that Alan's DNA sample was unusable—he'd probably put too much saliva in his vial. This would have been a minor hiccup if Alan was still alive, but of course when we lost Alan, we lost his DNA too. Now we wouldn't be able to take advantage of the larger pool of possible relatives 23andMe would have given us.

To me, it all seemed like a tragic and total loss.

I was wrong. When Alan Fisch received his results from Ancestry.com, he didn't just match with me—he matched with a young woman named Aimee Gourley, who was listed as a possible third cousin. It turned out that Aimee had a passionate interest in her family history—thanks to long walks and talks she and her grandfather, Alan Rinaldi, took through cemeteries filled with lost ancestors. Aimee volunteered to help us build out Alan's family tree, so that we could get closer and closer to identifying my nearest relatives and, ultimately, me.

At the same time, we got perhaps our biggest break when a woman named CeCe Moore joined our team. CeCe started out as an amateur family-tree builder but soon became one of the nation's most resourceful genetic genealogists. CeCe heard about my case and contacted me with an offer to help. She assembled her squad of amateur genealogists—Allison Demski, Carol Rolnick, and Michelle Trostler—and got to work building out my family tree. CeCe worked independently of Matt and Crista at Ancestry.com, and sometimes it felt like they were in a race to see who would crack the case first. I was just happy to have these supremely skilled people guiding me through the complex and labyrinthine world of DNA analysis.

I devote a large part of my first book, *The Foundling*, to telling the story of how CeCe and her crack squad heroically plowed their way through thousands and thousands of matches to continually narrow down the field of prospective close relatives, overcoming obstacles at nearly every turn with guile and smarts and pure determination. They left a trail of text messages to each other that could fill their own book, and they pushed through several apparent dead ends that would have flummoxed lesser talents. It was not a quick process—it took many months. But I know that they never stopped working, squeezing in a few hours pecking away at their laptops in between the already impossible demands of their jobs and their lives.

In a word, they were relentless.

I wish I could retell the whole story of their remarkable mission in this book, but I can't. There is so much more about my search that I need to share with you. So, I hope you'll forgive me for jumping ahead to a warm, sunny afternoon in Las Vegas, when I was at work and received a text message from CeCe Moore.

"Can you call me?"

I went down to the parking lot and sat in my car for privacy. I dialed CeCe and asked her what was up.

"What do you think of the name Jack?" she asked.

I didn't understand why she was asking, but I told her I thought that Jack was a fine name.

"Well," CeCe said, "that is your name."

It took a couple of seconds for the gears in my brain to engage and begin whirling through the news. CeCe was telling me my name—my real name. I was Jack. Not Paul, not Scott—Jack.

But before I could say a single word or fully process the significance of what CeCe was telling me, she went on.

"There's something else," she said.

Something else?

"You have a twin sister," CeCe said, "and her name is Jill."

CHAPTER 8

It felt like a miracle. Like an impossible thing made possible. How could someone with no known relatives and next to no information about his past be identified straight down to the very human being he was born with? How could a past that was nothing more than a dark and featureless abyss now exist in the shape of a busy, blooming family tree? I tried very hard to remain optimistic during the many months that CeCe and her team fleshed out my roots, but if I am being honest, there were times when I felt my hopeful outlook begin to crumble. I never lost all hope, but I sure did brush up against hopelessness.

And yet—here it was. My family tree. A miracle, all right, but not a celestial one. A technological one. The result of years and years of advancements in DNA testing and analysis—the inevitable progress of science. Starting with only a small sample of my deoxyribonucleic acid molecules, each made up of two polynucleotide chains forming a coiled double helix, CeCe was able to extract enough of the genetic information carried by those helixes to find the *exact* place where I fit into the world around me. Imagine that!.

I learned a lot about DNA and DNA analysis during that time, but I'm not sure that I ever truly understood it. It still strikes me as, at times, almost impossibly complex.

But one thing I did learn is that DNA doesn't lie.

And I understood that what CeCe was telling me was the truth about who I am. Not an interpretation of it, or a cover story, or a guess—the indisputable biological truth about my identity.

And the truth was this—my name is Jack, and I was born with a twin sister, Jill.

It all started with Alan Fisch. His death was a terrible setback, both for the search and for me personally. But the team kept going, and we eventually identified Alan's biological mother as well as a man who could have been Alan's biological father. His name was Lenny Rocco, and he was a semi-famous former doo-wop singer who grew up in south Philadelphia and went to the same high school as Alan's biological mother. When we called him and asked him if he remembered Alan's mother, or knew that he might have a son, Lenny was incredulous. "It was a long time ago," he said. "Maybe it's true."

Still, Lenny agreed to take a DNA test, and the result confirmed he was not only Alan's biological father, but also my first cousin. Lenny was the first truly close match for me. From there, the team identified Lenny's grandfather, John Rocco, and his four children—Bertha, Jean, Thomas, and David. Further analysis showed that Thomas Rocco was Lenny's biological father.

So where did that leave me? We couldn't be sure yet. We ruled out Thomas as my biological father since, if he were, Lenny and I would be brothers or half-brothers, not cousins. Did that mean David had to be my father? Not necessarily, put possibly.

Then Lenny told us a story. He said he remembered that David had fathered twins. "I was little when it happened, so I don't remember much," he said. "There was something wrong with the twins, and David gave them up. He got rid of them. And we weren't supposed to talk about it, so no one ever brought it up."

The team kept going. We found an obituary for David's sister Bertha Rosenthal that said she was survived by two sons, Gilbert and Leonard. Another obituary for Gilbert Rosenthal revealed that he had a wife, Marie, and three children, Linda, Karen, and Fred, who all lived not far from Bertha in Atlantic City in New Jersey. We were able to find records and information about all three of Gilbert's children, which suggested I didn't fit into his particular family tree. If I did, surely there would have been some record of Gilbert's fourth child—me. But there wasn't.

We were running out of slots in the Rosenthal family where I could fit. It was still possible I was one of David's mysterious twins, but we couldn't find a single record that showed they even existed. Around this time, we located a relative who recalled seeing Bertha Rosenthal's brag book—the photo album she kept to record the births of her children and grandchildren. There was no mention of twins anywhere in the book.

But the relative remembered noticing that several pages in the middle of the book had been inexplicably ripped out.

What did that mean? Were the Rosenthals hiding something? Were they hiding the existence of the twins? Before we could formulate any workable theory, we needed to find at least some proof that the twins had existed at all.

Then, two things happened. First, we identified and contacted Leonard Rosenthal's ex-wife, who lived in Florida. She explained that her time with Leonard had been traumatic, that he had been horribly abusive and controlling, and that, after finally divorcing him, it took her ten years to feel like a functional human being again. She was hesitant to do anything that involved Leonard in any way, as if merely invoking his name would somehow bring him back into her life. But when we mentioned David's missing twins to her, she told us we were wrong.

"The twins didn't belong to David," she explained. "They were Gilbert's. It was Gilbert and Marie who had the twins."

That put us straight back on Gilbert's trail, despite documents that said he had only three children and no twins. Allison Demski, the only member of CeCe's team who lived on the East Coast, drove three hours north from her Maryland home to the Atlantic City Free Public Library, and dug up a reel of microfilm labeled *The Atlantic City Press.* She sat down and scrolled through every edition of the newspaper that came out in October 1963, which was when we deduced the twins, if they existed, had to have been born. She was looking for a birth announcement—a long shot, but not impossible. She went through hundreds and hundreds of pages, all the way to October 30, the second to last day of the month, before she found it.

It was a column headlined *By The Seashore*, listing several events of note along the Jersey shore: a doctor's lecture, a campaigners' reunion, other significant dates. One of the listings, in tiny, nearly illegible type, gave Allison goose bumps. It read:

> *The 27th day of the month holds significance for the increasing family of Mr. and Mrs. Gilbert Rosenthal of 201 Seagull Drive, Cardiff. The Rosenthals became parents of twins, a boy and a girl, Sunday, October 27, in Atlantic City Hospital. They were born on the birthday of the Rosenthals' oldest child."*

There it was! The twins *did* exist, and they *did* belong to Gilbert and Marie. Were it not for the statistical improbability of three of the Rosenthals' five children being born on the same date, the births would almost surely not have been featured in the local paper. But they had been, and now, fifty long years later, that tiny listing gave us the confirmation we sorely needed. The likely reason CeCe and the team had not been able to find a slot for me in the Rosenthal family was because that slot had been erased. The twins, apparently, had been written out of the family history.

But now, suddenly, there were two new slots to fill—and it was possible that I belonged in one of them.

CeCe did some further analysis and tree building just to be sure, and eventually connected two different family branches through the migration of one woman from Tennessee to New Jersey. That woman was Marie, future wife of Gilbert Rosenthal. When CeCe made that connection, she felt 99 percent sure that I had to be one of Marie's children—and one of the missing Rosenthal twins. That's when she called me and told me my name was Jack.

And in that instant, I became ensnared in yet another complicated fifty-year-old mystery: Whatever happened to Jill?

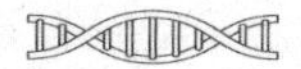

A friend who lives in New York City agreed to drive two hours to Trenton, New Jersey to try and dig up my official birth certificate, and Jill's, if they still existed. While there, he could also search for the birth certificates of the other Rosenthal children: Fred, Linda, and Karen. This would help us fill in the facts of my family—and, not incidentally, provide me with an actual record of my birth for the first time in my life.

My friend filled out some paperwork at New Jersey's Office of Vital Statistics and Registry, and then waited anxiously in a drab seating area while a staffer dug around for the documents. Ten minutes later, the staffer emerged with a manila envelope. Inside were copies of birth certificates. There was one for my brother Fred, another for Linda, and a third for Karen.

That left two more birth certificates. One was for my twin sister, Jill Lynne Rosenthal, born at 10:32 a.m. on October 27, 1963, in Atlantic City Hospital.

The other one was mine.

I was Jack Thomas Rosenthal, born fourteen minutes after my twin, Jill.

When my friend texted me a photo of my birth certificate, I was floored. Here it was, at long last—proof of my real identity. A single piece of paper that, out of the many, many billions of documents the world has known, secured my particular place in the vast history of existence, like a push pin on a giant map. Stamped by a New Jersey registrar on November 1, 1963, the certificate was the buried treasure beneath the *X* drawn on barren land—the prize that rewarded my tenacity and justified my decision to put aside my regular life and unearth the past.

Except—I didn't feel like I'd won anything at all. Yes, I was dazzled by the certificate itself: the names and dates and times manually penned into tiny squares on the form; the registrar's wobbly signature; the astounding square marked *This Birth,* and below it, the second of three options—Single, Twin, or Triplet—selected with a bold check. Yes, I felt a sense of satisfaction in being able to see and read this document that answered so many questions I'd feared were unanswerable only months earlier.

But a reward? Not really. To be honest, I did not feel elated, or even all that happy. In fact, I felt a little empty. The certificate, I realized, wasn't any kind of reward, it was only another step that led to—what, exactly? I wasn't sure. The only thing I was sure of was that my business was unfinished. My search was far from over. Every new answer, I came to understand, only created more questions. The goalposts kept getting moved, until the finish point became blurry. What was it that I was searching for? Closure? Family? Information about who I am?

Or did I even know?

In the end, I decided, it didn't matter what my original goal had been. Things had changed. Discoveries had created new mysteries. I had a twin sister who was missing, and how could I even consider quitting without finding out what happened to her? Maybe there never *would* be a reward waiting for me at some distant finish line. Maybe I just had to keep slogging through this quest until, hopefully, my heart and my head told me I was done.

Once we knew who my parents were, we were able to start finding other relatives—aunts, uncles, cousins, grandkids—and figuring out who was still around and who would agree to talk to me, so that I could put all the pieces together and solve the riddle of my abandonment, and Jill's disappearance.

My parents, sadly, had died many years earlier. But my mother Marie's brother, Frank Duncan, and my father's brother, Leonard Rosenthal, were both still alive. So were Leonard's ex-wife and daughter, and several other fairly close relatives.

The two most important surviving relatives, of course, were my three newly discovered siblings.

One of them—my sister, Karen—had passed away from a heart illness years earlier, at the age of forty-seven. But both my biological sister, Linda, and my biological brother, Fred, were alive and well. We figured out that Fred had been born just a few months before the twins disappeared, and surely would not remember them. But my sister Linda was four years old at the time, and conceivably could remember the twins, or at least might have heard something about what happened to them.

My immediate goal was to contact Linda and Fred, and introduce myself as their long-missing brother. I had no idea how they would react, or if they would even talk to me. I didn't know anything about them, except for the fact that the same blood ran through us all. We were all part of the same family; that was a fact. But what, exactly, did that mean?

I found my brother Fred's phone number on a database and sat down to call him one afternoon. I was nervous. He had spoken to someone on CeCe's team about my search, so he was at least vaguely aware of it, even though he'd wanted nothing to do with it. Still, I was making the kind of call you usually only see in movies—"Hi, I'm your long lost brother, back from the dead. What's new with you?" The best I could hope for was that his shock would be mild, and he would give me time to tell my story. The worst, I guess, was him thinking I was some kind of scammer and hanging up on me.

Most likely, he wouldn't even pick up the call and never return my message. I thought, "How would Chili Palmer in *Get Shorty* handle this? Fred, look at me!"

To my surprise, Fred *did* pick up after three rings, and I introduced myself first as Paul Fronczak. Then I told him who I really was.

"I'm Jack Rosenthal," I said. "I'm one of the twins."

Fred said he had no idea what I was talking about. He didn't know what twins I was referring to. He'd been born five months before Jill and I disappeared from the family, yet he had no clue that he had an additional brother and sister. Not only had we been erased from the family, but we'd been *thoroughly* erased, to the point where, apparently, our existence was never discussed. I told Fred the harsh truth about Gilbert and Marie Rosenthal: our parents gave birth to twins who inexplicably ceased to be part of the family nearly fifty years earlier. Put simply, he'd been lied to.

"How could a family keep something like this secret forever?" he asked me, in a way that suggested it was simply not possible to hide such an event for so long.

"I don't know," I said. "But they did."

That first call with Fred was short, but we began exchanging friendly emails. It took a lot of convincing—through newspaper articles, birth certificates, testimony from other relatives—but Fred eventually overcame his disbelief and, at least temporarily, accepted that I was his missing biological brother.

"I feel sick inside," he told me. "If you are Jack, I am so sorry that this happened to you."

What he said next filled me with hope that we might be able to work together to solve the puzzle of our strange family.

"Paul," he said, "I want to know what happened to Jill."

Still, I could tell the news was hitting him pretty hard. In one email, Fred asked me how I'd reacted when I first learned who I was, and how I had handled the pain of confronting the truth. I told him it was a struggle, but that the closer I got to knowing the truth of what happened, the better I felt.

"They say the truth hurts," Fred answered, "but this is beyond hurt."

Fred agreed to talk to his sister Linda about me, so that she would be ready for my call. He even gave me her phone number. But when I called it, no one answered, and there was no way to leave a message. I tried several times, but no one ever picked up. Finally, I dug up Linda's address and decided to just show up at her door. She lived clear across the country from me—I was in Las Vegas, and she was in a trailer park on the outskirts of Atlantic City, the city where my parents had lived and where the twins were born in 1963. It was a long trip, but I thought it was worth the effort. Linda was four years old when the twins disappeared, which, possibly, was old enough to remember something about them. And I just didn't want to wait any longer to find out.

I booked an overnight flight and landed in New Jersey early one spring morning, and I rented a car and drove down Interstate-95 to meet my sister. On the way, I stopped in a variety store and bought a small gift—a fake but realistic white orchid in a small brown pot. It was the only thing in the store that struck me as a semi-appropriate gift for the occasion, which was not exactly the kind of occasion Hallmark writes sentiments for.

Linda lived in a brown and tan double-wide trailer with an aluminum roof, on a small piece of land dominated by a tall, shady oak tree. I walked the four steps up to a wood deck outside the trailer and took a deep breath before knocking on the door. It felt like I was on the threshold of some great realization about who I was and what had happened, and I was nervous. I took another deep breath as I waited for someone to come to the door.

No one did.

Fifteen minutes passed with no sign that anyone was inside the trailer. I knocked again, and then again, louder each time, but still, nothing. I felt the familiar wave of disappointment begin to wash over me. Before I left, I decided to try one last time. I knocked really hard on the front screen door and announced myself for the first time.

"Is anyone there? This is Paul. Paul Fronczak."

I turned around to leave when, out of the corner of my eye, I thought I saw something move through the dark, mostly curtained window of the trailer. Then I thought I heard feet shuffling. I froze in place and waited, and in a few seconds, I heard the sound of a lock turning, and then the screen door began to open.

"Hi," I said to the woman suddenly standing in the doorway. "I'm Paul. I'm your brother."

"I know who you are," Linda said softly. "Come inside."

My very first impression was that she didn't look anything like me. Our faces were different shapes, and our features didn't match. But what did I expect? Some siblings look a lot alike for all their lives, but many don't. And faces change. The circumstances of your life have a lot to do with what you look like. And anyway, that was only a first impression. Once we sat down inside her dark trailer, me on a sofa, her on a chair across from me, I began to notice that Linda *did* look like me. Our chins were similar. So were the ways we smiled and laughed. It's hard to explain, but within just a few minutes of our time together, I *felt* like we were brother and sister. There was something about her that was familiar to me, in a way I couldn't quite grasp.

But it felt good. It felt good to find my biological sister, my flesh and blood. It felt *real.* I did my best to process all these emotions while at the same time focusing on the moment. I wanted Linda and I to make an authentic connection. And, of course, I wanted to find out if she knew anything about Jill.

I asked her what it was like growing up with my parents, Gilbert and Marie. Linda said it was difficult, without elaborating, other than to say that Gilbert, in particular, could be a hard person to be around. She told me that when Gilbert died, no one attended his funeral. I realized the story she had to tell was grim, which should not have come as a surprise. After all, I knew that Gilbert and Marie had committed one of the very worst sins a parent can commit—abandoning their child. How likely would it have been if—other than that grievous offense—the Rosenthals had all lived normal, happy lives?

Finally, I asked Linda about the twins. Her answer was short and definitive.

"I don't remember them at all."

Nothing? Not a single scrap of memory or bit of history about the twins? No, she said, just a void, absent of anything. Sitting there across from Linda, I didn't believe it was possible she neither remembered nor had heard anything about the twins, and was instead oblivious to their existence. How in the world could that be true? How could someone as near to them as a sister and brother be so cleanly wiped from their memories, even if they only knew us when they were three or four years old? Perhaps that was *exactly* how the brain worked—softening the edges of childhood trauma until the memory itself vanishes. I just didn't know. Even so, I doubted it could be true.

Still, I didn't press Linda any further. That was my one and only question to her about the twins. My plan had been to stay only a short while, and not force anything. Just say hello, let her see I wasn't a threat, maybe make a friend. After fifteen minutes of talking, I asked Linda if we could meet for lunch the next day.

"We'll go anywhere you want," I said, probably too excitedly. "We can pick a really nice place."

"I'd like that," Linda replied with a little smile I recognized as my own.

We made plans for me to pick her up at noon the following day, and I left with a final hug. Even though she hadn't said anything about the twins, I was elated that our first meeting had gone as well as it did. I felt we made the authentic connection I was hoping for. I could hardly wait for the next day to come.

That evening in my hotel room, I checked my emails and saw I had a message from my brother Fred. It was only a few lines, but when I read them, my body seized up.

> *Hi Paul, I have to be honest with you. I am not interested in meeting you nor establishing a relationship with you. I'm not convinced that we're related, but even if we were, I would feel the same way. So please don't try to make contact with me, I wish to be left alone. Thank you.*

The next day, no one answered when I knocked on Linda's front door at noon. I waited again, and knocked a few more times, just like I had the day before. Linda never appeared.

I stood on her front porch and stared out at the clear spring sky and watched an acorn drop out of the big oak tree. The blood family I'd just found after fifty years was, in an instant, lost again.

CHAPTER 9

I never learned why Fred suddenly shut me out, or why Linda disappeared after our one and only meeting. My best guess was that Linda and Fred spoke after my visit with her, and she told him I was asking questions about the twins, and somehow that spooked them, so they decided to stop communications. I chose to think they didn't consider the emotional impact of their rejection, as opposed to knowing how hurtful it would be and simply not caring. But that was only a guess too.

The big question was—why? Why, if neither of them knew anything about the twins, as they claimed, would they feel threatened by me asking about them? Did they know more than they were saying? Were they trying to protect their memories of our parents? Or did they simply not wish to dig up the past for fear of what they might learn? Did they think it would be easier to pretend that the twins—and I—never even existed?

What I couldn't grasp back then, no matter how much I thought about it, was how someone could so easily turn their back on a blood relation. I assumed that finding a long-lost brother would be a positive thing for Fred and Linda—I thought it was human nature to gravitate *towards* family.

But now, as I look back on that time in my journey, I realize I was being naïve. Our relationships with our families can be enormously complex, and can also change wildly over time. The same tides that keep some families together can wrench others apart. There was so much I didn't know about the Rosenthals—and, indeed, about Fred and Linda—that it would be impossible for me to predict how they would react to my sudden presence in their lives, with all its implications, good and bad. I should not have been that surprised that they reacted by telling me to get lost.

I would learn this lesson the hard way—by encountering many more such rejections as I located more and more members of my biological family.

To be fair, many of the relatives I met or spoke with were friendly and lovely and inviting, and with their help I was able to piece together a patchwork history of the Rosenthals.

The portrait that emerged was of a cursed family.

Cursed—but also tough as hard wood. My great-grandfather on my father's side, John Rocco, was a prizefighter who fought under the name Thomas Murphy. In the one photograph I have of him, he is posing with his family for a formal portrait, and he's sitting on a chair as the rest of his family stands around him—the patriarch, stalwart, immovable. His face is square and his black hair slicked back, and of course he's not smiling. His hands rest on his knees, balled up tightly into fists.

John Rocco's son was the hard-boiled boss of a Mack truck union, and he once defecated on a neighbor's front lawn to settle a dispute. As I wrote in my first book about him, "He had a maniacal laugh and a lightning-quick temper. I heard different versions of the story, but apparently David went to jail for killing a man in a fight—then may have killed another man in prison." Even David's wife Shirley once punched a woman for suggesting her baby was cuter than Shirley's own.

John Rocco's daughter, Bertha—my grandmother—was another character. My cousin Joy Rocco told me she remembered Bertha as a compact ball of endless energy. "We used to say she was four by four—four feet tall by four feet wide," Joy said. "She was tiny, but she was also big, this big body balanced on two tiny feet. We heard her shoes were only size four." One afternoon, Joy and some other children watched Bertha make an enormous sandwich in the kitchen, believing she was making it for them.

Instead, "she just raised it to her mouth and took a giant bite and went on to eat the whole thing. Right in front of us!"

Bertha had a very sad story to tell. Back in 1932, when she was only twenty-one years old, she was sent to the Burlington County Hospital in Philadelphia after trying to kill herself by swallowing poison. The reason for her rash act: a fight with her estranged husband, Harry Rosenthal, who she was suing for non-payment of child support. Eight years later, Harry finally left the family over a gambling debt, most likely owed to the Philadelphia mob.

"Family Faces Starvation Unless Husband Returns," a 1940 Philadelphia *Inquirer* newspaper story began. "'Come back home, Harry Rosenthal: come back and save your wife and two children from starvation and from eviction from the home that was once yours!' That was the message Bertha Rosenthal, of 124 South 5th Street, last night asked to be sent to her husband, wherever he is."

Wherever he was, he didn't get the message. Bertha was forced to sell her furniture and pawn her jewelry just to buy groceries, while both the eighty-seven dollars she owed in back rent—and Harry's gambling debt of some $1500—went unpaid. A kindly stranger left the Rosenthals a bag of groceries on their stoop overnight, but soon the electricity was cut off. Finally, a constable served the inevitable eviction papers at the doorstep of the apartment Bertha Rosenthal already lost.

"I've thought of everything since my husband disappeared," she told the reporter who had been documenting her miseries. "Sometimes I thought of jumping in the river, but I couldn't do that because of the boys."

When the day came, Bertha and one of her sons—Gilbert, six, or Leonard, ten, we don't know which—went to Mt. Sinai Hospital to have doctors check them out. A doctor treated the skinny boy for sores on his head and hands, the result of bad nutrition. Bertha, they said, "was on the verge of nervous collapse."

We don't know where they went to next, or what happened to them in the next few years. Eventually, Bertha married a cheerful taffy maker name Auggie, and settled her family in a quiet, white-board, two-story house on North Georgia Street, in the Ducktown section of Atlantic City. The Rosenthals lived less than two blocks from where Nicodemo Domenico Scarfo Sr.—"Little Nicky"—grew up and became the boss of the merciless Philadelphia crime family. Scarfo became the capo di tutti capi after Phil Testa, a temporary boss known as Chicken Man, was killed by a huge nail bomb that exploded beneath the front porch of his twin house on Porter Street in South Philadelphia.

"Well, they blew up the Chicken Man in Philly last night," Bruce Springsteen sings in *Atlantic City*, his somber ode to the troubled town. *They*, of course, were mobsters—hard, violent men like Nicky Scarfo. I've often wondered what kinds of things Bertha Rosenthal's two sons, the elder, Leonard, and the younger, Gilbert—my father—witnessed while growing up in the backyard of the ruthless Philly mob. How much of that life did they get to see? How many stories about Little Nicky and the Chicken Man did they hear? How many vile acts did they have to imagine after hearing whispers about some hit job?

Perhaps what I was really wondering was, "Did something evil make its way into my father's heart, and make him capable of abandoning his baby boy on the street?"

I met new relatives and heard more stories about my father, Gilbert Rosenthal, and the very pretty Ohio woman he would marry, Marie Duncan. Marie's father, Cecil Duncan, was born in Overton County, Tennessee, and eventually moved to Ohio and married Jeannie Noga. Cecil and Jeannie were my maternal grandparents. Cecil was a barber by profession, until he had his arm ripped off in a terrible accident. Doctors reattached the arm, but it never functioned again. After that, Cecil became a tire salesman. Marie, his only daughter with Jeannie, was the one who moved to New Jersey—I'm not sure why—where she married Gilbert Rosenthal and had five children.

When Jill and I were born, in 1963, Gilbert was twenty-nine and Marie was twenty-eight, and we were their third and fourth children. The fifth, my brother Fred, arrived about a year later. Our older sisters, Karen and Linda, were two and four. To me, that seemed like a lot of kids to have in the span of just five years.

I asked a lot of questions about what the Rosenthals were like as a family in those early days, and from what I gathered, they were not the happiest people on the block.

"We were a very dysfunctional family," my brother Fred told me in an email before cutting off all contact. His only memories, he said, were from after the twins had mysteriously disappeared, and in his words, the Rosenthals "were a family of five people living separate lives. We never sat around the table laughing and talking and having fun."

This was a theme that kept repeating—the Rosenthals were plagued by some mysterious darkness, some inherent turmoil, that seemed to deprive them of the capacity for joy. Relatives on both my paternal and maternal sides confirmed this.

"This family—if something good happened, they had to make it wrong," one relative told me, in an attempt to persuade me to stop digging deeper into the Rosenthal clan. "They were strange people and they turned good things into bad." There were harbored grudges, family secrets, festering hostilities, and "all these people who were really angry with each other, and it just wasn't pleasant." This relative drifted away from the Rosenthals, she said, because "after a while, I didn't want to be a part of a family where nobody liked each other."

Lenny Rocco, a former doo-wop singer who we identified as Alan Fisch's father—and who, as my second cousin, became a good friend—explained it in even starker terms.

"There's a streak," Lenny said to me after we had dinner in Philadelphia one night. "It runs through the family. It's a mean streak, an edge. Maybe it's destructive. Maybe it's self-destructive. But it's there. It runs through all of us. I have it too."

Lenny explained how his own stubbornness and negativity derailed what could have been a bigger, more rewarding career as a singer. "My bass player told me, 'If I had your talent, I'd be rich, but you're a defeatist, Len,'" he said. "That's the streak. The streak that runs through our family. We bring defeat on ourselves."

Then Lenny put his arm around me, as if to emphasize the point that I, too, was susceptible to the streak. "There's an emptiness in you, Paul, I can sense it," he said. "You're searching for something, and I'd like to help you find it if I can."

Lenny remembered my father, Gilbert, as "a nice guy," and not nearly as mean and sadistic as his brother Leonard. But then Gilbert served in the war, I was told, and when he came back, he had changed. Physically, he walked with his upper body bent forward, the result of either a war injury or a severe back condition. Emotionally, he became darker and more distant. "He just sort of dropped out of view," another relative said. My sister Linda, with whom I spoke only briefly in her trailer near Atlantic City, said simply, "Our father was not a nice man."

I wondered if my mother, Marie, was also caught up in this notion of an inescapable family curse. She married into the Rosenthals; might she have been immune to their genetic defeatism? Sadly, I learned, my mother brought her own problems into the family. CeCe Moore and her team were able to locate Marie's younger brother, Frank Duncan, who shared with me that Marie was a loner. "She was the eldest, and she always kept to herself," Frank explained. "Like when it was time for supper, she would come out and take a plateful of food and take it back to her room to eat it with the door closed. She stayed in her room all the time, and I never saw her. A very, very private person."

Part of the problem, apparently, was her father, Cecil. "He was an alcoholic, and he mistreated everyone," Frank told me. "He was verbally abusive, and he hit my mother and all the kids. That's why I left when I was young. I grabbed my girlfriend and took off."

Frank also told me that Marie became a drinker herself.

It was clear that Gilbert and Marie had several problems, but did any of them explain the disappearance of the twins when we were roughly two years old? I had no idea what happened to Jill, but I did know they left me on a busy Newark street, where I sat unclaimed for two hours before the police found me. What compelled the Rosenthals to take such a drastic action? I kept asking questions, trying to understand the pressures they faced in the fateful months before Jill and I disappeared.

Frank Duncan told me one of those pressures was financial. Not long before the twins went missing, Gilbert and Marie lost a home they owned and were forced to move.

"They lost it because Marie wasn't making the house payments," Frank said. "She didn't pay the mortgage or the utilities or anything. I don't know where the money went instead. But like I said, my sister drank—quite a bit. She was under a lot of pressure because of the children, and she drank a lot of wine."

It was right around that time, when the Rosenthals were forced out of their home, that Gilbert walked out on his family.

He was gone for six months, Frank explained. That's all he knew for sure; for instance, he could only presume that Gilbert left because his family situation was so dire. Was there a fight? Was he angry with Marie for not making the payments? Did it have something to do with the twins? No one knew—or at least no one I could find and ask.

What became clear was that Marie was deeply unhappy with having five young children to care for.

"Whenever I talked to Marie, all she did was complain," Frank said. "She'd say, 'Every year I get pregnant and have another baby, and I really don't like it.' That's why she drank."

Knowing that my parents, and particularly my mother, were under that much pressure did explain their unhappiness, but to me it still didn't explain the fate of the twins. I may have been wrong—the whole thing might have been as simple and straightforward as my mother or father or both abandoning the twins on the street in order to lessen their burden, and, in a twisted way, save their family. But I had a hard time accepting that. My mother wasn't a sixteen-year-old runaway on the streets leaving her baby at the church doorstep. She was a grown woman with five children and grandparents living nearby. Surely, friends and neighbors and relatives *knew* about the twins, or had seen them, or otherwise could vouch for their existence. That alone would likely deter most people from abandoning two children and having to somehow explain them away. There had to be something more.

There had to be a precipitating event.

Something that happened. Something jarring, unexpected, final. Something that left the Rosenthals no choice.

No choice but to leave me on the street.

So I asked more questions. A lot more questions. I asked, "What happened? What happened that made my parents abandon me?" Most relatives told me they had no idea. But others shared little scraps of information they remembered hearing four or five decades earlier. By putting them together, an event did emerge.

A possible precipitating event.

"We heard that Jill was dropped," Lenny Rocco's sister Sandy told me, recalling something she heard as a child. "One day my mother sat me and my sister down and told us, 'The twins are dead. Jill was dropped.' That's all she told us. But when she told us, she sort of trailed off, like there was more to the story that she couldn't tell us. Like an insinuation of something."

Another relative remembered that Jill had been sent to an institution, possibly because our parents believed she was mentally challenged. Most family members I spoke with could only remember asking about the twins when they were young, and being told never to ask about the twins again. If a friend or neighbor pried too deeply, one relative explained, the Rosenthals would say the twins were away with their grandparents. If a paternal relative asked about them, they'd be told the twins were under the care of Marie's parents in Ohio; a maternal relative, meanwhile, would hear that Bertha and Auggie had them.

Apparently, after a while, people simply stopped asking about the twins. Life moved on, and the sudden disappearance of two neighborhood children no longer needed explaining.

As for me, I still felt there was more I needed to uncover. What did it mean that Jill was "dropped"? Did she fall in an accident and suffer fatal injuries? Was she deliberately dropped or otherwise harmed on purpose? I felt like I had only a few scattered pieces of a much larger mosaic. Someone out there, I reasoned, had to know more—had to know the whole story.

So I went looking for the one Rosenthal relative that nearly everyone told me *not* to look for—my uncle, Leonard Rosenthal.

All the stories I heard about him had the same unnerving message—stay away from him, he's dangerous. Angry, abusive, disruptive, violent. I heard from one relative that Leonard once punched a child in the face and broke her nose. I heard that he killed family pets for fun. That he would stalk and haunt you for weeks and months, maybe even years, if he had some bone to pick with you. His ex-wife told me it took her ten years after finally escaping him to even begin to feel like a human being again.

"Leonard doesn't worship the devil," his daughter told me. "The devil worships him."

Leonard's daughter was reluctant to even talk about Leonard, as if merely invoking him would somehow bring him back into her life—her greatest fear. She told me she would not go into the details of Leonard's abusive behavior, because "it takes me to a place where I don't want to be. Certain things, I just can't repeat." She assured me "it's not a daddy-daughter thing, it's about one person who is evil. He was born with evil in him, and he hates everyone. I grew up in a house of horrors. The more he could abuse you, the better. And nobody could stop him."

Her shaky voice betrayed the scars she bore from her life with Leonard, and she spoke of that life in terms I could hardly comprehend. I hadn't ever encountered anyone who could be capable of the types of atrocities attributed to Leonard, or who could inflict the kinds of wounds Leonard seemed to relish inflicting. In my mind, Leonard took shape almost like a fictional villain—a wild caricature of unbridled evil and sadism.

But no—he was real. All too real.

And—he was my blood. My uncle. My father's brother, born of the same stuff, inheritor of the same traits. He was a Rosenthal, and so was I, and we were just a branch apart. What ran through him, I had to assume, also ran through me, at least partly. There was no escaping this fact; it was written in the DNA. This living embodiment of evil was my very close kin.

"I got it in me too," Leonard's daughter told me. "I have to fight to keep all that evilness away from me. I believe I have the ability to do all the things he did—I really believe that. Only I never would. Not in a million years. But I can feel it.

"I can feel the evil coming."

It was a chilling thing to hear, and it left me with a lingering bad feeling. I'd never known what I would confront along the way to learning my true identity, and I don't think I created any kind of rosy fantasy of what my biological family might be like. But neither did I consider that one of them would be described in the stark terms people used to describe Leonard.

I mean, I never felt like I had anything remotely evil inside me, waiting to surface. But was it there inside me nonetheless? Had I just been really good at suppressing it? Or had nothing happened in my life to activate it, as something might have in Leonard's life? I heard that when he was a child, Leonard had really bad skin, and the other children teased him mercilessly. Was that the event that made Leonard feel like a freak or a monster, allowing him to tap into his resource of hate and evil?

These were questions I didn't want to consider, much less try to answer. But the bad feeling inside me remained for a long time. Solving the riddle of my identity—and finding my missing twin sister

Jill—would necessitate confronting a certain kind of dysfunction and bitterness and, yes, even evil, that ran through both sides of my biological family. This was the reality of my family situation. To get to whatever ultimate truth I was so determined to learn, I would have to go through this gauntlet of rough characters, ruined dreams, and broken personalities. There was no other way. To find Jill, I had to team up with the Rosenthals, dead and alive. They were the only ones who could take me to the place I wanted to go.

Leonard Rosenthal was not easy to find. Many years earlier, he'd gone off the grid. His ex-wife and daughter occasionally got a phone call from him, but after a while, they no longer picked up when they didn't recognize the number. He lived in Florida for a while, but the last place they remembered him frequenting was the southern part of New Jersey, likely along the shore—either near or around the place he grew up, Atlantic City.

I tried my best to locate him, but I knew I would need help. So I hired a private investigator named Nino Perrotta. Nino turned out to be an incredible person, and a good friend, and a huge part of my journey. He'd worked in law enforcement in the District Attorney's office in the Bronx, and he'd also been part of the Secret Service. After 9/11, he was recruited by the Department of Homeland Security. For a while, Nino provided security for a White House cabinet member. His greatest attribute as an investigator, from what I could tell, was his unfailing street savvy. He truly understood the typically lowlife characters he was hired to catch; he could get into their heads and figure out what they were thinking. Someone like me would always be six or seven steps behind someone like Leonard Rosenthal. But Nino? He was always only a step or two behind, until, eventually, and inevitably, he would end up one step ahead.

Nino responded to the story of my missing twin, and before long, helping me find Jill became a personal obsession for him. I could never pay him more than a fraction of what he was worth, yet he gave up hours and hours of his time to the pursuit of Leonard, who, Nino had to admit, was an especially slippery target. Yet the more elusive a target he was, the more zealous Nino became. He interpreted someone's evasiveness as a direct insult. Within two or three weeks, Nino managed to track Leonard down to a series of dingy hotels along the Jersey shore. He'd call a hotel manager and get a tip that Leonard had moved on to a different hotel, only to find, when he called that manager, that Leonard had just checked out. One short step behind.

Until finally, Nino caught up. He found Leonard in a forty-three-dollar-a-night room in the Red Carpet Inn in Hammonton, New Jersey, thirty-one miles northwest of Atlantic City. Nino posed as a woman and called Leonard in his room, and flirted with him to confirm that it was really him. All I had to do, Nino told me, was get on a plane, drive to Hammonton, and knock on his door.

At the time, I was working at a job that didn't allow me much free time. In the end, I had to wait nearly a full week before I flew from Las Vegas to New Jersey and drove south to the Red Carpet Inn. By the time I got there, predictably, Leonard was gone. Had he been spooked by Nino's call? Or was this his usual game of cat and mouse to avoid detection? I had no way of knowing, but I felt like, by hesitating, I'd let Nino down. I also felt, for the first time in my long journey, that I was in over my head.

Nino told me not to worry, that he would find Leonard again. And, remarkably, he did, this time pinning him down in a hospital in Atlantic City—the very hospital where I was born in 1963. The very day he called me to tell me he'd found Leonard, I took an overnight flight to New Jersey and was in the hospital by noon the next day. I asked an attendant on the first floor for Leonard's room number, expecting to get kicked out at any time for being an unauthorized visitor. Ironically, Leonard and I *were* family, but I had no way of proving that to a hospital orderly.

Somehow, I was let through all the way to the third floor, where I found Leonard in Room 31-17 of the hospital's trauma wing. It was a large private room, and when I walked in, Leonard was sitting in a chair in the middle of the room, with blood pressure cuffs on his arms and legs and an IV plugged into him. His eyes were closed, and I had the chance to take a good look at him. From all the build-up, I'd expected to meet a monster.

In fact, Leonard looked like any other sickly old man.

He was in his eighties. His arms were bruised purple from having been needled for IVs and shots. He was bald, and his skin seemed perfectly fine. A monitor showed his blood pressure was 185 over 76. When he stirred in his chair and finally saw me, his eyes were watery but also brightly alive, suggesting there was plenty of life in him yet. I remembered something his daughter told me when I asked if she thought he was still alive.

"Sure he is," she said. "God don't want him yet."

I sat in a chair across from Leonard as he struggled to place my face. I told him I was Jack Rosenthal, one of his brother Gilbert's twins. It took him a few seconds to grasp the concept, but eventually he did. He said he remembered the twins. I asked him point blank if he knew what had happened to them.

"Why was I given away?" I asked.

Leonard looked away from me, down at the floor.

"It's so sad," he said in a whisper. "I'm heartbroken that our family fell apart. I would have raised the twins myself."

"But what happened, exactly?"

"I don't know."

"But you were there. You were there when it happened."

"Sometimes you're too close to the pie to smell it."

"Try to remember," I said. "You saw the twins. You would visit the twins. Why did Jill suddenly disappear?"

"I don't know," he said again, shaking his head. "It's so sad. Family is the most important thing."

Leonard blamed his spotty memory on the drugs he was receiving ("They're trying to turn me into a junkie," he said). I was just about ready to give up when something seemed to stir inside Leonard. He sat up a little and said, "Now that you're asking, you're taking me back. There is one story I remember."

Then Leonard told me the story. It was about a surprise visit he and some other relatives paid on Gilbert and Marie one afternoon in their home. Marie, Leonard said, did not seem happy to see everyone there. When someone asked to see the twins, Marie said she would bring them out.

"She went upstairs, and she came back with the twins in her hands," Leonard told me. "One in each hand. She was holding them by the... by the wrist, like you'd hold a chicken by the neck. Just dangling by their wrists. The boy didn't have any clothes on."

Then, Leonard said, Marie began to walk down the stairs.

"When she got to about the fourth step, she dropped them," he said. "She dropped them and said, 'Here are the twins.'"

Leonard remembered that the boy—me—got up and ran over to him and hugged him tightly. "He held on to me, you know?" Leonard said. "Like you would hold on to someone if you were scared." But what about Jill? Did she get up and run to him too? Did she get up at all?

"I don't know," Leonard said. "I don't remember."

And that was that. Leonard drifted away again, into some reverie about a singer he used to know, and then into a hushed tirade about how his nurse was trying to kill him. Clearly, whatever drugs he was on were scrambling his grip on reality. I remembered something else his daughter told me, as a warning.

"Everything that comes out of his mouth is a lie," she said. "Everything. That's what he does—he lies and makes things up."

I spent about an hour with Leonard before I hugged him goodbye and left. His doctor told me Leonard had blood in his stool, a complication from a previous aneurysm surgery. He might have to have a good part of his large intestine taken out. At the same time, Leonard's vital signs were, against expectations, improving. There was a chance, the doctor said, that Leonard wouldn't need any further surgery at all, and would be able to walk out of the hospital in a day or two.

"God doesn't want him yet," I thought.

Leonard's story about the twins aligned with others I had heard about Jill being dropped, and his was the most specific recollection about the incident I'd heard from anyone. Still, how could I know if any of it was true? And if it was, what did it mean? Did it mean that Jill died when she was dropped, which forced my parents to get rid of me, under the theory that it's easier to explain away the disappearance of both twins rather than just one? Or was the dropping story just a cover-up for something more sinister, recited like lore and ingrained in Leonard's brain like an actual memory fifty years later? I didn't know. I *couldn't* know.

All I had, really, was a bunch of stories.

The time I spent with Leonard seemed like the end of a certain leg of my journey. I'm not sure why it did, but it did. It felt like I'd exhausted my most readily available resources in the search for my missing twin—the memories of family members who had known about us. Surely one of them, I thought, would have known the whole story and also have been willing to share it with me. But that was not the case. Many relatives knew bits and pieces, but no one I spoke with seemed to know the whole tragic truth—or if they did, they were pretty artful about making me believe they didn't. Whatever happened way back in 1965 had, by design, been lost to time—whitewashed early and often, so that only streaks of the covering layer remained. What was beneath it all was now, nearly half a century later, too faded—or too terrible—to emerge again as anything coherent or even recognizable.

There were just pieces of story, and perhaps that was all there ever would be.

I decided to take what little I'd learned and try to reach some conclusion about the fate of Jill. The theory that seemed most plausible to me was that something bad had happened to her, which led to her death and, along with it, my abandonment. Maybe the pressure of having five young children and a husband who had just run out on his family was just too much for my mother Marie to stand, and she either deliberately, or through an alcoholic haze, brought some kind of harm to Jill. Maybe she thought the only way she could ever get her husband back was to somehow lesson the load at home—to get rid of the twins. Maybe, in the end, Marie *had* accidentally, or semi-accidentally, dropped Jill down the stairs, just as Leonard remembered it.

In any of these scenarios that seemed most plausible, my twin sister Jill was no longer alive.

I felt that I owed Jill at least one last big effort to find out the truth of what happened to her. So, I looked back over my family's records to figure out where they had lived at the time the twins disappeared. My best guess was that they had just lost the house they had owned together, and were forced to move in with Gilbert's mother, Bertha, in the house she shared with her second husband, Auggie. That house had been at 278 N. Georgia Avenue in Atlantic City. I went looking for the house, but it was gone. All that remained was an empty lot overrun by weeds and trash.

But in the back of the slender lot, what had once been the Rosenthals' fairly private backyard remained unpaved and uncovered. What if, I wondered, the Rosenthals had indeed brought harm on their daughter, Jill, and then, in the panic, buried her little body in the ten square feet behind Bertha's house?

What if the truth I was looking for was there, under the dirt?

I hired a man with an SIR-3000 ground-penetrating, radar-processing unit with a four-hundred-megahertz antenna to roll his ungainly machine over the empty lot, bouncing waves off whatever lay beneath the surface and sending back patterns that indicated any disturbances in the smooth soil.

Buried things.

The man found several small disturbances, as well as one larger one, right where the Rosenthals' back porch might have been. I marked the spot by spray-painting a big *X* on the dirt and weeds. Several weeks later, I went back to the empty lot with four sixteen-dollar fiberglass shovels from a local Home Depot and a canvas tarp on stilts to block the harsh summer sun. Then I hired a freelance construction worker named Shane to help me dig up the spot.

The *X* was gone, but I had a photo that showed exactly where we wanted to dig. Together Shane and I shoveled out the first three feet of dirt, until there was room for only one of us in the hole, at which point Shane did all the shoveling. It took a couple of hours, but by the end of it, Shane had dug a four-foot-wide by six-foot-long by six-foot-deep hole in the empty lot that had once been home to the Rosenthals.

In that hole, we found several small bones. Something that looked like a femur. Something that looked like a vertebra. Random pieces from someone or something's skeleton.

I asked a forensic anthropologist at New York's American Museum of Natural History to take a look at the bones. Within a few hours, the anthropologist knew what he was looking at.

"We are ninety percent certain they are all animal bones," he said.

A cow's distal humerus. A young pig's femur. Perhaps the same pig's calcaneus, or heel bones. All the fragments showed evidence of having been roasted.

Soup bones. We had found soup bones. I remember not being sure if that was good news or bad news.

The anthropologist had one last thing to tell me. Most likely, he said, a child's fragile bones buried that long ago would no longer exist. They would have long since crumbled to dust. Even bones, I learned, can vanish without a trace.

It was around that time, four years into my journey of self-discovery, that I took a little break from it all. I had learned much, including my own identity, but I had left much more undiscovered—principally, the whereabouts of my twin sister, Jill, and also the story of the real Paul Fronczak. I was tired and also dispirited, and I needed to take stock of all that the journey had cost me. It came at a much steeper price than I'd expected.

During my search, my adoptive parents Dora and Chester Fronczak did not speak with me for more than two years. They were so angry about my decision to reopen the long-buried case that they completely froze me out. So did my adoptive brother, Dave, who sided with my parents and turned his back on me.

By the time I was able to reconnect with my parents, my father had already begun his slow descent into dementia. Essentially, the father I knew from before our feud was gone. That was an incalculably high cost for me to pay. The precious time we lost was something I could never, ever reclaim.

My marriage to Michelle also fell apart, largely because of the time I spent searching for my identity and my family. Michelle had watched it all happen, and she had warned me of the horror of what was slowly unfolding—by trying to get closer to a family that had rejected me, I was drifting further away from the family that loved and accepted me, until, at a certain point, it was too late for me to find my way back. Michelle and I divorced but vowed to always stay friendly in order to co-parent Emma, the love of both our lives. The end of our marriage is something that still weighs heavily on me, and sometimes it makes me wonder if my search was even worth starting. But I know this is a pointless question, because it implies that I had a choice in starting my search or not. Of course, I *did* have that choice, but for all the world, it did not feel to me like I had any choice at all. Once I knew I wasn't the real Paul Fronczak, I simply could not conceive of doing nothing.

Instead, I felt I had to begin the long search for the truth.

And then, when I failed to find Jill or the real Paul, I took a break. I rested. I tried to reprogram my brain so it wouldn't be dependent on the next clue. I tried to slow things down and concentrate on being a good and attentive father to Emma.

The reprogramming, however, didn't work.

Many months later, I opened an email on my website, as hungry as ever to see if it might hold the next tantalizing lead. The subject, mysteriously, was simply "Ducktown."

"Jack, I was a babysitter who watched you and Jill when you were little," the letter began. "It was shortly after I watched you that you both disappeared, and it may be my fault."

My break was over. It was time to get back to work.

CHAPTER 10

What if something we do in the present can influence, or even alter, the past? What if our actions today can change what happened long ago? If this were possible, it would mean that time flows forwards and backwards, and not just towards the future, which, most people would argue, is pure science fiction.

But what if it isn't?

I've thought about this a lot since I started looking for my twin sister Jill. I thought that if I could somehow find her, and reunite with her, and become her twin again, I could undo her past—the past that said she wasn't a twin and had no family, which is the same past I had for the longest time. If I found her, I reasoned, then she would never have *been* a doomed foundling. Instead, she would always have been my twin, someone who belonged with someone, someone who belonged *to* something. The very act of immersing myself in the search for her would transform the reality that was created when she vanished. What I was doing was nothing short of manipulating the rule of cause and effect, so that the effect of Jill's disappearance was no longer bound to its cause. I was going back in time to reclaim my twin.

If that sounds crazy, I can say that it's not entirely out of left field. There's a theory called retrocausality that attempts to explain this possibility. Retrocausality, put simply, is the ability of present actions to change actions that happened in the past. A physicist named John

Wheeler conducted what is known as Wheeler's Delayed-Choice Experiment, and produced a result that amazed and baffled other prominent physicists. Richard Feynman, the famous American physicist, called the results "the mystery which cannot go away."

Wheeler shot photons towards a detecting apparatus at the other end of a test field. The photons passed through a panel with a double slit, and then either hit the end of the field or hit a screen, depending on whether or not the screen was there.

The tester determined if the screen would be put in place—but only made this decision *after* the photons had already passed through the double slits.

If the screen was there and the photons hit it, they were detected as waves. If there was no screen, the photons were detected as particles.

That meant the decision to lower a screen or not *changed the physical characteristic of the photons*, even though they had already been defined when they passed through the double slits.

A later event changed a previous event.

Now, retrocausality is just a theory. If it were proven to be an actual phenomenon, it would mean the concept of time as we know it is meaningless. It would mean time does not march forward. Instead, the past, present, and future exist all at once, momentarily, in a situation that is neither "then" nor "now," but simply "is."

I bring all this up because, in a way, it helped me sort through the meaning of my search for Jill.

Jill was either alive or dead, but she could not be *proven* to be either one, since not a soul was looking for her, or cared about the result. It was as if she had never existed, and thus her fate was irrelevant. It felt to me that, by committing to learning where she was and what happened to her, I was, in a way, bringing her back *into* existence—as opposed to the netherworld she was in when there was no one to acknowledge that she had ever lived or mattered. I was *willing* her to be Jill, my missing twin, out there somewhere, waiting for me to find her.

And if I found her—if, somehow, I found her—I could break the death grip the past held on me, and allow for a new past, and ultimately a new present, to emerge.

CHAPTER 11

The email was from a woman named Susan. She said she'd recently watched an old *20/20* show about my case, and seeing me as an adult on TV triggered something in her—a flicker from her past. Finally, she remembered where she'd seen me.

She claimed to have babysat my sister Jill and I in Ducktown when she was a teenager.

Ducktown was an Italian neighborhood in Atlantic City, roughly between Missouri and Texas Avenues, and close to Little Bay. The immigrants who settled there in the early 1900s built shacks and coops along the water for their ducks and chickens, leading to the nickname. By 1965, when my family lived there, the neighborhood was pretty much run by Little Nicky Scarfo and the Philadelphia mob. Scarfo was, as I mentioned, a remorseless killer, but his presence in the neighborhood, many residents will tell you, made them feel safe in Ducktown.

Some of the relatives I found after learning my identity in 2015 remembered my parents living there. My mother's brother, Frank Duncan, even remembered visiting her and seeing me and my twin sister, Jill. But that was all he could remember—*seeing* us. Not what we were like, or how we were treated, or anything about our lives. His memories, like nearly everyone else's, were maddeningly sparse.

Would Susan's memories be any better?

First, I had to do my due diligence to establish that Susan was a real person who was around Atlantic City back in the 1960s. I dug around a couple of websites, and I learned that Susan graduated from Atlantic City High School in 1966, which would have made her a junior in 1965, the year I was in Ducktown. That fit. That was enough for now. I replied to Susan's email and told her I wanted for us to talk.

On the phone the next day, Susan was sweet and kind. She sounded upset, almost embarrassed, but she was also very sure of what she wanted, what she *needed*, to say.

"All I can do is tell you what happened that night," she began. "It has been haunting me my whole life."

Then Susan told me an incredible story—a story that was difficult for me to hear.

She took me back to Atlantic City in 1965. She was fourteen, and she had a regular babysitting job with the Pileggi family on North Mississippi Avenue, in a housing development not far from the boardwalk called Pitney Village. Susan lived there, too, a few houses away from the Pileggis. One afternoon, while she was watching young Ralphie and Paulie Pileggi in their backyard, a woman came out of the house next door and approached her.

"She asked me if I could watch her daughters that night," Susan said. "I'd seen her before with her family, and she was very elegant and well dressed. I knew she had two young daughters that she doted on. If you saw her and her husband and their children in the backyard, it was like the ideal family you'd see in a 1950s magazine. They just looked like the perfect family."

The woman who approached her was my biological mother, Marie Rosenthal.

Ideal family? Perfect family? I'd heard just the opposite. But from the outside, Susan said, they did indeed resemble a typical middle-class American family. Elegant and well dressed. Right out of a magazine! I was enchanted by that detail. I wanted to be able to imagine the Rosenthals looking like that as they strolled through town with their equally well-dressed children. But I couldn't, because I already knew that such an appearance would have been, at best, a façade.

Susan went back to her story. She said she told Marie that she would love to babysit her daughters, and that evening she showed up at 278 North Mississippi Avenue, the Rosenthals' address in Pitney Village. They lived in a two-story brick row house that shared a front porch with their neighbors, the Pileggis. The front door opened onto a staircase, and to the left were the living room, the kitchen, and a big pantry closet. The bathroom was at the top of the stairs, along with three bedrooms. It was a small house, but it was, Susan remembered, immaculate. And the Rosenthal girls, Karen and Linda, "were just so beautiful," Susan recalled. "They were itty bitty, just three or four, but they were pristinely dressed. Everything in the house was perfect."

My mother was wearing a fancy outfit, and my father, Gilbert, was in a fine suit. They were going somewhere special, but they didn't say where, though they did say they wouldn't be back until the following morning. According to Susan, overnight babysitting jobs were not uncommon back then. A couple might go out for dinner, take in a show, and treat themselves to a hotel stay. Susan assumed the Rosenthals were doing something like that, but she didn't ask, because it wasn't her business.

Just before my parents left, Marie gave her some final instructions.

"The girls can sleep downstairs wherever they want," she said. "Oh, and the twins are upstairs, but you don't have to bother with them. Just leave them alone upstairs."

With that, my parents left for the night.

Susan was stunned. Twins? No one had mentioned twins. She quickly called her sister, who was also a babysitter in the neighborhood. "You've got to come over right away," Susan said. "There aren't two kids, there are *four* kids! They have twins too!"

As soon as her sister arrived at the house, Susan asked her to watch the girls on the first floor. Then, slowly, she started up the narrow staircase, to the dark second floor.

At the top of the stairs, Susan held her breath and looked around. On the right side of the hallway, she saw my parents' bedroom and a bathroom. On the left, two closed doors. She listened closely but did not hear a sound. It felt to her like no one was upstairs at all.

Finally, Susan stepped forward and stood in front of the first closed door. She turned the knob, leaned, and looked inside.

"What I saw," she told me, "broke my heart."

The room was dark. One window let in the last bits of evening light. In the back of the room, by the window, she saw a crib. She saw movement. It was a boy, small and skinny, maybe one year old, she guessed. Through the dimness, she could see he was in pajamas, and he was holding a baby bottle. He had a black eye.

"When he saw me, he whimpered and cowered in the back corner of the crib," Susan told me. "It was like he was afraid of me, and that's what broke my heart."

The little boy was me, Jack Rosenthal.

There was another crib in the room, as far apart from my crib as possible. In it was my twin sister Jill, also small and frail, though she didn't whimper or cower. She just stood up in her crib, watching. Susan walked slowly up to me, whispering soft words. "The milk in your baby bottle had curdled," she recalled. "It was solid. Your sheets and your pajamas were filthy. I looked at Jill, and she was just as bad. I was just a teenager, but even then I knew that something was terribly wrong."

Some instinct told Susan to take care of me first. She gently touched my hair and patted me on the head, like a cat. She took me out of my crib and held me, and felt me trembling. She held onto me for a few minutes and could feel me calming down in her arms. She took me out of my pajamas and walked with me to the bathroom and cleaned me up, and she did the same for Jill.

"Your diapers were dirty, and you both had rashes and blisters on your butts," Susan said. "It looked like no one had changed you for a long, long time."

Susan looked around upstairs and found clean sheets to put in our cribs. Then she gave us fresh milk, and she held us and stayed with us through much of the night. She studied Jill and I to see if there was anything that might explain the way we were being treated. She'd never heard that we existed, never seen us in the backyard, which suggested our parents were deliberately trying to hide us. But why?

"I couldn't see anything wrong with you besides the abuse and neglect," Susan said. "You weren't sick or ill or not functioning or anything like that. You were healthy babies, except for the neglect and the black eye. None of it made sense."

Early the next morning, my parents Marie and Gilbert came home. Susan met them at the front door and told Marie how she'd bathed and fed the twins.

My mother's face went white.

"I told you not to do that!" she screamed. "I told you not to go upstairs, you shouldn't have gone up there!"

"But..."

"I told you not to bother the twins! Obviously you don't listen very well!"

"I do listen!" Susan yelled back. "But they're just babies!"

With that, Susan grabbed her coat and ran out the front door, not even waiting to be paid her fifty cents an hour.

"I just wanted to get out of that house as fast as I could," she told me. "I was scared. I thought I did something wrong."

She took a long pause before continuing.

"But you see, that is what haunts me to this day. That I left you there. That I left you both behind. I think of your faces, and how scared you were, and then I think of leaving you there to deal with it all. And it haunts me. It haunts me every day."

Just a few days after that night, Susan recalled, a friend in the neighborhood told her the Rosenthal twins had disappeared.

I'd heard little snippets of stories about the twins being abused. One relative thought she remembered seeing a cigarette burn on my arm when I was one. Another remembered seeing Jill and I locked up in wooden cages in an upstairs bedroom. My uncle Leonard Rosenthal, of course, told me the story of my mother deliberately dropping Jill and I down the stairs. None of these stories had any context, other than a general observation that my mother was extremely stressed after having had four babies in three years. The only other partial explanation for my mother's behavior towards the twins was that she drank. Her brother told me that, and so did Leonard. Even Susan the babysitter remembered smelling alcohol on my mother's breath before she went out for the night.

Susan's story, however, was something new. If it was true, it meant my parents—for some reason I still couldn't comprehend—so disfavored the twins that they neglected them and abused them and hid them away from the public before, finally, getting rid of them altogether. It implied a level of cruelty and madness that hadn't been part of the story before. How could any parent do to their child what my parents did to Jill and me? Leave us in our own filth for hours and hours, maybe even for days? And the black eye? Did I fall out of my crib, as children sometimes do? Or was it something worse?

I asked Susan about her impression of my parents in the brief time she spent with them. "Your mother was well dressed and acted very elegant, but it was like she was putting on a persona," she said. "Like she was trying to present an image of herself as perfect. Your father was very quiet, but you could tell he was the boss. It was very clear that he was the man, and she was the woman, and she took care of the children, not him. Sort of like a lot of families back then."

The morning Susan raced back home after taking care of the twins, she immediately told her mother what she had seen with the twins. Her mother's response was clear and direct.

"Stay out of it," she said. "It's not your business."

And that was that. Susan never told anyone else about the twins, until she told me.

"I've carried that guilt around with me for a very long time," she said. "The twins disappeared, and I could have stopped it. But there was no place for me to turn back then. There weren't resources like we have today. Even so, I feel so guilty for not telling someone about the twins locked away upstairs."

I assured Susan she had nothing to feel guilty about. Her coming forward now, I told her, was more helpful than she could possibly know. For me, finding someone who had been in the same room as Jill and I—who had actually *held* us—was a gift beyond imagining, a chance to peer back through the years, even if it had to be through a smudged lens. I asked Susan something I'd wanted to know the answer to from the moment I learned I had a twin sister several years earlier.

"Did Jill look like me?" I asked.

Susan did not hesitate.

"Jack, she looked *so much* like you," she said. "I know boy and girl twins can't be identical, but that's what it looked like with you two. She was just a little more feminine version of you. It was an amazing thing to see."

I felt myself start to tear up. This was the first time anyone had told me *anything* about what my twin sister looked like, and the news was that she looked just like me! I don't know why that should seem so important, so crucial to me, but it did—*my sister looked like me.* For years, I'd been trying desperately to nourish the fragile bond I felt with Jill—a sister I couldn't even remember—and every year it got harder to picture her in my mind, as a girl, as a teen, as a woman, as anything. She was slipping away from me a bit more every day.

But now, I had something to go on. A description, a mental picture. Susan's recollections made me feel bound to Jill more deeply and strongly than ever before. My sister and I shared a face, and to me that meant we shared a soul too. We were connected, profoundly, no matter how far apart we were.

And suddenly, as I spoke with Susan, I was filled with a sureness, a certainty, as if someone had come up behind me and whispered an indisputable truth in my ear.

Jill is alive, I thought. *Jill is out there. And I need to find her.*

Susan had another observation about my sister that heartened me greatly.

"It was something that happened, or didn't happen, when I first walked into your bedroom," she told me. "When you saw me, you whimpered and backed up into the corner of your crib. But Jill didn't do that. She didn't react the way you did. She just stood there, almost like she was saying, 'I'm fine. Take care of him.' And when I picked you up, you were trembling. I could feel your legs shaking against me. But not Jill. Jill wasn't trembling. I don't know if you got more of the abuse than she did, but there was just something about her. Almost like she was defiant."

Based on that, I reached a conclusion—Jill was strong. Back then, she was only a wisp of a thing, a nearly-two-year-old girl who looked like she was only a year old, skinny, malnourished, neglected—but she was tough. She couldn't be so easily broken. She had some kind of innate survival instinct.

Jill was the stronger twin.

I had no idea if this was true. But from what Susan told me, it very well *could* be true. And if Jill was the strong one, mentally at least, then maybe she'd been able to handle whatever misfortunes befell her, both at the hands of my parents and—if she survived—at whoever's hands she wound up in.

I can't tell you what a heartening thought that was—that if Jill had indeed been cast out into the world as I had been, she might have had the toughness, the resourcefulness, to survive. I held onto that notion like I'd hold onto a rope dangling from a cliff, with all my might, and for dear life. I needed to believe that Jill had a protective layer, a built-in willfulness that would enable her to make it through the darkness in one piece. The alternative—to imagine that she was broken and fragile and doomed—was too grim to contemplate.

Susan had one last important detail to share. "It was going around the neighborhood that the Rosenthal twins had vanished," she remembered. "And what I heard was that one of them got sent to Ohio, and the other to Newark. But that was all I heard. No one knew anything for sure. All we knew was that the twins were gone."

Other relatives had told me they'd heard about the twins being sent to live with their extended families. Obviously, this was a lie, given what happened to me. But it was enough to satisfy anyone who dared ask about the twins, and the cover-up worked until finally people stopped asking about the twins at all. "As kids, we were all told never to bring up the twins, so we only whispered about them to ourselves," one of my biological aunts told me. "We were all curious, but we knew never to mention them, so we didn't."

But what Susan heard was more specific. She heard that one of us went to Newark—which, in fact, is where I was abandoned—while the other went to Ohio—which is where my mother Marie's family lived. The Ohio part made sense—this was my mother implying that one of the twins was with her family two states away. But Newark? We had no family in Newark. Why would my parents cite the very city where they had left me on a sidewalk? I filed the detail away, not sure what to make of it. By that time, I understood that the truth about Jill would not come to me whole, in one blinding revelation. It would come to me in pieces, scraps of information, tiny puzzle parts. But that was okay. I was used to that. I had an eye for small details now. I knew the truth was prone to concealment.

Susan also gave me the names of some of the neighbors and friends she remembered from her days in Ducktown. With any luck, I thought, some of them might still be around and remember something about the twins. I spoke with Susan for a long time, and I tried my best to assure her she had nothing to feel bad about. In fact, I told her, it was possible that she might have given the twins their only real moment of human warmth and connection and affection in all their young lives. I told Susan she was my hero for stepping forward now.

"Everyone has an idea of how their parents should be," she replied, her voice heavy with sorrow. "I'm just sorry I had to tell you these things about yours."

At the end of our talk, Susan had only one request. But she was emphatic about it.

"Promise me, Paul, that if you do find Jill, you will let me know," she said. "Promise me that. I need to know."

I promised Susan I would let her know, no matter what I discovered. We said our goodbyes, and I hung up the phone.

My time in the Ducktown of the past was over, at least for now.

CHAPTER 12

Susan's memories about the twins left me with a sad, hollow feeling. It was hard for me to imagine that anyone could have been that cruel to two innocent children, much less that it could have been my own parents. I already knew from other stories I'd heard that the arrival of the twins put enormous pressure on my mother, and most likely led her to resent them for their very existence.

But what Susan described was not resentment. It was more like revulsion. Something drove my mother to look at Jill and I as less than human—as burdens to be ignored, avoided, forgotten, hidden away. To be left in our cribs upstairs all night, with no food or water or attention, while our sisters frolicked downstairs. How could anyone be that inhuman and uncaring?

It was the darkest turn my journey had taken yet.

Susan gave me the names of three families she remembered from her days in Pitney Village. I couldn't find any contact information for two of them, but for the third—a woman named Joan Pileggi, who according to Susan had lived right next door to the Rosenthals—I found a working phone number. I left a message for her and for one of her sons, Ralph Pileggi, who like Joan still lived in the Atlantic City area. I noticed Ralph's age and figured he would have been four years old the year the twins vanished—the same age my sister Linda had been in 1965. Could he possibly remember anything from those days? Could he remember having seen the twins, or having heard about them? I could only hope.

None of my messages, though, were returned. I tracked down Joan Pileggi's daughter, Ann, and called her, and to my surprise she picked up. At first, I explained that I had grown up next door to her parents and wanted to get more information about the old neighborhood. Ann assured me that her mother, who was in her eighties, was still sharp as a needle and remembered quite a bit about her time in Pitney Village. Then I brought up my parents, the Rosenthals, and explained what I was really looking for—any information about the twins that disappeared.

Ann went silent on the phone. When she finally spoke, she said she would give my number to her mother, Joan, but it was clear she no longer had any interest in speaking with me. Just the mention of the twins, it seemed, had been enough to shut her down. Not surprisingly, I guess, months passed and I never heard back from Joan or Ralph or Ann. Even so, every few weeks I would leave another phone message. If Joan Pileggi really did remember her time in Pitney Village, how could she not remember the Rosenthals, or the twins they had for two whole years before, mysteriously, they vanished? A next-door neighbor was precisely the kind of source I wanted to speak with—someone who had been there, heard things, seen things. I was determined to find a way to sit down and talk with Joan Pileggi.

Susan's story also made me think about my biological sister, Linda. Linda told me she had no memories of the twins, even though she had been four years old when they disappeared. Do we retain memories from when we were four? The common thinking is that we don't really form what are called explicit or experiential memories until we are five years old or so—but, we can remember events or images from when we are three or four. Surely Linda must have seen the twins in her two years with them. Wouldn't that have been enough to form some kind of memory of them? After speaking with Linda, I got the impression that she knew more than she was willing to tell me.

It was Susan's story that convinced me I was right. How could Linda not recall playing with Karen downstairs while the twins were locked away all night one floor up? Had she blocked out the memory?

And if so, could it be retrieved? After speaking with Susan, I knew I had to try again with Linda. I'd honored her apparent wishes and not bothered her for nearly two years. But now, I needed her help. I needed to know what she knew. Somehow, I had to find a way to get her to speak with me again.

It was around that time, ironically, that Linda reached out and spoke to me.

Not directly, mind you, but on a chat board that I happened to look at. And on that chat board, she made her feelings about me very plain.

I found the discussion on Goodreads, a site that allows readers to form groups and leave reviews of books they've read. My first book, *The Foundling*, had recently come out, and I came across a group discussing it. The woman leading the discussion enjoyed the book but criticized me for what she called my "obsession" with finding the truth. My decision to keep digging, she wrote, was "not necessarily a bad thing, except the author obviously has trouble living in the present, and finds more meaning and happiness discovering and dwelling on the past and anxiously awaiting future news about the case."

I had to admit there was some truth to that, in that the search for my identity did indeed intrude on my present life in ways that weren't always positive. But I don't think anyone can truly comprehend the dilemma I faced without actually living through it, and feeling the giant emptiness of not knowing who you are or where your missing twin is. Like I've written before, it never really felt like much of a choice to me. It was simply something I had to do—learn the truth of my life.

A bit further on in the discussion, someone commented that the book was nonfiction, meaning that everything in it really happened the way I described it. The very next comment was:

Not everything is fact.

The person who posted the comment was named Linda.

I kept reading. Someone asked Linda what she meant, to which she replied:

> *[The author] slandered a lot of people in this book...especially my deceased parents as they are unable to defend themselves. He took everything that was told to him and lied. I found that he twisted everything to help sell a book. When he didn't get the answers he wanted, he went on to make up ones.*

I was shocked. I had been scrupulous in writing my book, and I only included details people told me in our discussions, without any embellishment. When we spoke in her trailer, Linda told me that our father Gilbert was "not a nice person," and that my mother was relieved when he passed. She told me not a single person had attended his funeral. I included these comments in the book, even though I knew they made the Rosenthals look bad. What was the point of sharing my story with the public if I was only going to include half the story? And anyway, how much worse could I make the Rosenthals look once the reality of them abandoning me on a sidewalk became public?

Even so, it hurt me that Linda was so offended by what I'd written. I understood that in the process of searching for the truth, and making that search public so I could help other people in similar situations, I would have to make decisions that wound up hurting someone. After all, I was trying to uncover long buried secrets, and there were people still alive who wanted those secrets to remain buried forever. This was something I wrestled with every time such a decision came up.

What information was part of my story, and thus okay for me to share? And what information wasn't?

These are not easy decisions to make. People are entitled to their privacy, and no one has a right to lay bare someone else's life story without their consent. But in no way was I telling Linda's story. I was telling my own story, and Linda became a part of it. Her parents were also my parents, and we obviously had very different experiences with them, and wasn't I entitled to share my own experience—including whatever other relatives told me about the Rosenthals? I honestly did not feel like I had somehow invaded Linda's privacy by including comments she freely gave me during our discussion.

And certainly, I did not lie. I did not invent stories about the Rosenthals. I didn't have to. The stories I heard were fairly uniform in their assessment of the Rosenthals' marriage and family life—it was not like I was "spinning" their memories by suggesting my parents had a very tough time of it. Nor was I inventing that my father was a difficult person; I heard that from several people. I never intended to slander my biological parents, or depict them in a harsher light than I had to. But I did intend to tell the truth, the whole way through. And the truth, I would learn over and over, can be an extremely destructive force.

Linda had one other thing to say in the Goodreads discussion. It came without prompting of any kind:

I'm sure his twin is alive and happy and wants no part of this.

"I'm sure his twin is alive and happy." I read that line several times. No one asked Linda about Jill, or even mentioned her in the discussion. Yet she volunteered that she was sure Jill was still alive. Did that mean she *knew* Jill was still out there somewhere? Or was this her dismissing my assumptions that something bad had happened to Jill? It was impossible to know, but the certainty of her statement convinced me even further that Linda knew more than she had let on to me.

I even called Nino, my friend and investigator, and asked him how he would have interpreted such a statement, should he have come across it in an open missing persons case.

"I would think Linda knows what happened to Jill," Nino replied, "and that she wants to tell someone about it."

I knew that "someone" would not be me. I'd badly damaged any chance I had at a trusting relationship with Linda by including her in my book, and it would take a long time for me to repair whatever trust I'd betrayed, and to cultivate a friendship that was real and meaningful. Even without the notoriety of the Fronczak case, and the widely watched *20/20* reports, and the book that struck Linda as a hit job on the Rosenthals—even without all that, establishing a relationship with my sister would require lots of patience and tenderness and commitment, given that we were basically strangers. Nor was there a guarantee that we would ever truly bond. Much of that would depend on Linda and what she wanted. It wasn't anything I could control, only attempt.

And obviously, I'd gotten off on the wrong foot with Linda by including her in the book.

It came down to priorities. What was my primary goal? Was it to find my biological relatives and establish relationships with them? Or was it to get to the bottom of the mystery of why I was abandoned, and what happened to my sister, Jill?

In the first scenario, I was the wayward son trying to find his family. In the other, I was the investigator, ruthlessly pursuing the truth. The two roles—outcast relative, and investigator—were not complementary. They were in opposition to each other. One required a kind of gentleness and a willingness to forgive.

The other required hardness and a lack of sentimentality.

So which was I? Was I Linda's brother, or her investigator? Was a relationship with her my priority?

Or was it learning the truth about Jill?

Imagine, for a moment, if that was the decision you had to face. Which would you choose?

You may see this as a cop-out, but once again it didn't seem like I had much of a choice.

How could I have any kind of relationship with Linda if I suspected her of knowing the truth about Jill, and withholding it from me? Was I supposed to just forget about Jill, accept that she was gone, and make the best of it with the two biological siblings who I still had? That hardly seemed possible to me, or desirable. It would be a relationship based on a lie, and that was precisely what I was trying to escape when I started my search in the first place. I didn't want to live with buried lies anymore. I wanted to know who I was, where I stood, what I had lost.

There really was no choice for me.

I had to be the investigator.

I called Nino and asked him if he could travel to Atlantic City and approach Linda on my behalf. Nino was very, very good at gaining people's trust, and my fondest hope was that he would be able to convince Linda that if she knew anything about Jill, the time for her to talk was now. That it was time for all the secrets to end, and for her to play her part in bringing it all to the surface, confronting it, finding a way to move past it, and, ultimately, pursuing any solace and redemption there was to be had in finally knowing the truth.

Nino agreed to give it a try.

On an overcast summer day, he drove north two hours from his home in Maryland and arrived at Linda's trailer on the outskirts of Atlantic City. Same as me, he walked gingerly up the four steps to her trailer and knocked on the outer door. And, same as me, he waited and waited for a response. Several minutes passed before Nino saw movement through the small, curtained window above the door. The front door opened just a bit.

"Who is it?" someone called out.

"My name is Nino Perrotta. I'm an investigator, and I'm here on behalf of Paul Joseph Fronczak. Linda, if it's possible, I would like to talk to you about Jill."

The next thing Nino heard was the door slamming shut, a stream of curses, and a loud voice telling him to leave and never come back. Nino tried again, but the same message came back.

After a minute or two, Nino got back in his car, drove away from the scattered casinos littering the Atlantic City skyline, and made his way back home to Maryland.

CHAPTER 13

Finding Jill was always going to be hard. But finding the real Paul Fronczak, many people told me, would be impossible.

As cold cases go, the Fronczak kidnapping case was about as cold as you could get. Yes, the FBI reopened the investigation in 2014 after I came forward and announced I wasn't the real Paul. But as far as I knew, there wasn't a single new clue or lead that might help break the logjam that led to the case being shelved more than fifty years earlier. The FBI did have all the original police and bureau paperwork from back in 1964, but really, how useful could that be? Old witness statements? Descriptions of people who were now old or deceased? No primary suspect, or any suspect at all? It seemed to me that it would take a genius-level investigative mind to pore through all the casework and come up with something fresh.

As for me, I didn't even get to see the old paperwork. Because I wasn't biologically related to the Fronczaks, I was kept out of the loop as far as the kidnapping case went. I was free to call the FBI Special Agents in charge of the case, to ask how things were going, but their response was always the same—they weren't allowed to give out any information about an open investigation. Basically, in my search for the real Paul, I was out there on my own without any law enforcement resources. I knew it wouldn't be easy.

I also understood that my best chance of finding the real Paul would likely come in the form of a random DNA connection on a genealogical website. The real Paul, in other words, had to not only still be alive, but also be curious enough about his family history to take a DNA test. At the time, about seven million people in the U.S. had submitted DNA samples to genealogy sites, out of an adult population of some 247 million people. That meant only 3 percent of eligible adults went to the trouble of taking a DNA test and mailing it in. The odds of the real Paul being among them were not that great.

In other words, I needed to get lucky.

Then, in early 2019, I got the email with the tantalizing subject line:

This is the baby you're looking for.

Of course, I'd heard that before. Many people contacted me to say the child of a middle-aged man somewhere looked *exactly* like the hospital photo of Baby Fronczak, and therefore the father *had* to be the real Paul. Other men were said to be identical to the age progression image we made of the real Paul. I followed up on all of them—dozens and dozens over the years—and at first I convinced myself to stay positive, and to always believe that this guy *could be the guy*. But as time passed and the DNA eliminated one potential Paul after another, it was harder and harder to stay positive.

And yet, I had a strange feeling about this latest tip before I even opened the email. I don't know why, I just did. Something about the directness of the sentence in the subject line, the certainty of it. *This is the baby you're looking for.* I opened the email and read the rest of the short message.

He doesn't know his daughter's DNA matched your brother's through a national database. She is too scared to tell him.

Now I was really intrigued. I wasn't aware that my non-biological brother, Dave Fronczak, had put his DNA on a genealogy site. I knew I'd asked him to—begged him to, really—when I first started my search for the real Paul and needed Fronczak DNA. But he refused to do it and joined my parents in not speaking to me for years. I couldn't imagine why he would suddenly take a DNA test and submit his sample now.

But, okay, perhaps he had. And perhaps he'd then matched with this potential Paul's daughter. Had they contacted Dave? Did Dave know? And if he did, why hadn't he told me? At the time, Dave and I weren't getting along—barely speaking, really—the result of the fallout from me starting the search in the first place. But if Dave had stumbled across the real Paul, I felt reasonably sure he would have let me know. I thought about just calling Dave and asking him if there had been a match, but I anticipated the argument that might lead to, and I decided not to. Dave and I just weren't in a place where we could work together on anything, though I would have loved it if we could have. But that wasn't our reality. If there were any truth to the tip, I'd have to prove it on my own.

The person sent the email anonymously, but I still had their email, and I had a way to trace it to its owner, which I did. I also responded to the email, and I asked the person—I'll call them the Tipster—how they knew all of this, and why they were reaching out to me. I got a fairly quick reply. The Tipster revealed the original source of the information—someone close to the man's family—but insisted that the source, as well as the Tipster, remain anonymous. I agreed to keep their identity secret. I was just happy they were willing to talk to me at all.

The Tipster followed up with more details.

> *What I know is that his daughter took a DNA test and matched to a man who was likely her uncle. There was some contact with this match, and the daughter obtained enough information to indicate that her father is likely the missing child. I know her father, but have not had contact with him in years. I have no idea why his daughter hasn't told him [he might be the real Paul], but I think he needs to know.*

The Tipster also told me the father's name—Kevin.

As much as I wanted to assume the Tipster was being truthful, I knew I couldn't. Before I could allow myself to get excited by the idea that the real Paul might have been found, a half century after his abduction, I had to find a way to prove that Kevin was, indeed, the kidnapped child. I had to be certain. And there was only one way to do that. It had to be through the DNA.

Even so, I was disappointed. I was tired of being rejected. Now I had to prove Kevin was the real Paul without any help from him or his family, or from Dave, and how was I going to do that?

Years earlier, I had asked a woman named Linda—who was related to the Fronczaks at the first or second cousin level—to put her DNA on all the major genealogy sites, just in case the real Paul ever submitted a DNA test. That way, if there were a match, I would hear about it from Linda.

But Linda's membership to the site Kevin's daughter used lapsed sometime before the daughter's match with Dave, so I never knew it happened until I heard about it from the Tipster.

After the Tipster's email, I called Linda and asked if I could help her renew the membership and have access to her tree again. If Linda's DNA went back on the site, and she matched with Kevin's daughter, that would be a huge step in confirming Kevin was the real Paul. Linda agreed and sent in another DNA sample, which meant we had to wait about three weeks for the results.

When you're waiting on crucial DNA test results, three weeks can seem like three years.

Finally, Linda got a notice about her test. The sample was faulty, and she'd have to submit another one. More waiting.

It took about six weeks from when I contacted Linda, but her DNA was finally loaded on the site. I got a notice that her matches were up, and I felt my stomach tighten. *If Linda matches with Kevin's daughter, this could be it*, I thought. *This could be Paul.*

I logged on and quickly checked Linda's matches.

I saw that Linda did *not* match with the daughter.

I sat there in something like shock. Every gut instinct I had told me this was the one—this tip was the real deal. I emailed the Tipster about the non-match, but the Tipster was insistent. "I am thoroughly convinced that Kevin is the real Paul," they wrote back. But how could he be, if his daughter didn't match with someone who would be the daughter's second cousin or even closer? DNA doesn't lie. No match meant no match.

I was confused. Something had to be wrong. I sat down and thought about all the pieces of the puzzle. Of course, the Tipster could be flat wrong. Or was the whole thing a scam? But why would anyone run this kind of a scam? There was no fortune at the end of the rainbow. No, the Tipster had struck me as completely sincere. So why wasn't there a match?

I could have given up right there, and just moved on from what had to be another false lead. But that didn't feel right. Something told me to keep thinking, keep questioning. What was I missing?

I went to Google and typed in: *Can you erase your profile from a genealogy site?*

I learned that if you wanted to, you could. You could remove your DNA data and your profile, and make it look like you'd never even been there.

Is that what Kevin's daughter did?

I went back to Linda's matches and saw that Linda hadn't matched with my brother Dave Fronczak either. That made even less sense. The Tipster said Kevin's daughter matched with Dave, which meant both of their DNA had to be on the site. Had Dave also taken down his DNA data and profile?

I bore down on Linda's matches, hoping for inspiration. Her closest match was her father, but after that her second closest match was a user named Julie L. They shared a little less than 6 percent of their DNA, which I knew from working with the genetic genealogist CeCe Moore was a fairly substantial amount. Perhaps Julie L. was a cousin of Linda's from the other side of her family, not the Fronczak side. I quickly emailed Linda and asked if she knew who Julie L. was.

Linda told me she had no idea.

So I emailed CeCe and asked her what the likelihood was of someone matching 6 percent of your DNA, and you having no idea who they were. Was that a common occurrence?

"Absolutely not," CeCe wrote back. "That's a lot of DNA to share with a total stranger. You should at least have some idea who this person is."

Okay, then, here was an anomaly. And in the field of genetic genealogy, anomalies are good. Who was Julie L., and how did she fit into the puzzle?

The Tipster only told me about one of Kevin's daughters. But did Kevin have any other daughters? I plugged into my public database and searched for more information about Kevin and his family. I learned that in fact he had *three* daughters. There was the one who took the test, Tillie, and another daughter named Mollie.

The third daughter was named Julie.

Julie's last name began with the letter *L.*

Now I had something. Unless it was an incredible coincidence, the Julie L. who matched with Linda *had* to be the same Julie L. who was Kevin's daughter—which would prove the Fronczak connection. What were the odds there were two different Julie L.'s, both somehow linked to Linda?

Even so, I knew I had to *prove* that they were the same person. Without more proof, all I had was an educated hunch. "If you can determine the Julie L. on the site is Kevin's daughter," CeCe told me, "you can be ninety-nine percent sure that Kevin is the real Paul. There would be no other explanation."

Right away, I emailed the Tipster and asked if they knew, or could find out, if Tillie's sister Julie had also submitted her DNA to the site. The Tipster poked around and learned that, yes, Julie joined the site after Tillie matched with Linda, as a way to double-check the results. That was good news, but I still needed to find more data points that would link the two Julies. For instance, I knew Kevin's daughter Julie was thirty-six years old and lived in Michigan. Somehow, I had to find out the age and location of the Julie L. who matched with Linda.

The genealogy site provided a way for matches to communicate with each other, to presumably begin sharing their family trees. I asked Linda if she could send Julie L. a message saying they had matched, and—essentially—fishing around for more information. Linda agreed, and sent a note that had her own age and geographic location in the first sentence. We were hoping Julie L. would respond with the same details.

A full day went by with no response. Then another. And another. Five days passed, and still no answer from Julie L. If she didn't get back to Linda, we had no real way of finding out more about her. She would remain anonymous beyond her first name and last initial. I forced myself to be patient and not let my mind dwell on bad breaks and worst-case scenarios.

And then, toward the end of the fifth day of waiting, Julie L.'s response to Linda appeared on the site.

Hi! It's nice to meet you! I'm 36 and live in Michigan.

There it was! Same age, same location—the two Julies had to be the same person! The response had another line in it that seemed to confirm we had the right person. "I'm sorry, but I can't tell you anything about my paternal side because of an unusual family situation," Julie wrote. An unusual situation on her paternal side? That *had* to be a reference to Kevin being the real Paul. I was about to call CeCe with the news when a speck of doubt tumbled annoyingly through my brain. If this was in fact Kevin's daughter Julie on the genealogy site, why hadn't she—like Tillie—scrubbed her DNA data and profile?

I had no good answer for that.

"Okay, then let's go one more step," CeCe said when I called her and told her about my lingering doubts. "See if you can get Julie to send us the names of any grandparents or great-grandparents, and we'll see if they match the other Julie."

We knew not to ask about anyone on her paternal side, so we had Linda write back to Julie and include the names of her maternal grandparents and great-grandparents, in the hopes that, once again, Julie would respond in kind.

Luckily, she did, and in her note, she volunteered the last names of two of her ancestors—Monroe and Wicks.

Now it was time to investigate *our* Julie L.—Kevin's daughter. CeCe dug around for public records that could help her build a quick family tree, and I sat down at my laptop and did the same thing. We were looking for relatives who turned up in obituaries, or on Facebook pages, or wherever. Sometime around midnight, I found a group photo on a social media page that featured Julie's other sister, Mollie. I looked for the name of the person who posted the photo. It was a name I didn't recognize. Just beneath it, though, in parentheses, was the woman's maiden name.

Monroe.

At almost the same time, I got a text from CeCe saying she'd found a local obituary for the mother of Kevin's ex-wife—Tillie and Julie's grandmother. The article mentioned several other ancestors.

One of them had the last name Wicks.

Monroe and Wicks.

I told CeCe about what I'd found, and she texted back a two-word message: *Slam dunk.*

We'd proved Linda was closely related to Kevin's daughter, which meant, according to CeCe, we could be 99 percent certain that Kevin was the real Paul. The only way to be 100 percent certain was to have Kevin take a DNA test. But even without that, CeCe assured me, we should proceed as if we had our man.

Fifty-six years after a woman dressed in a nurse's uniform entered Dora Fronczak's room at Michael Reese Hospital and took her one-day-old infant out of her arms—and fifty-four years after I was presumed to be that kidnapped baby and handed over to the Fronczaks—we found Dora's biological son.

We found the real Paul Fronczak.

The very next day, Julie L.'s profile disappeared from the genealogy site.

CHAPTER 14

The first person I thought of in that moment was my mother, Dora. Reuniting her with Paul was the reason I started my journey eight years earlier, and all I wanted was to tell her we finally found him. But I had no idea if Dave had already told her about Kevin, or if she knew for sure that he was her biological son. As far as I could tell, Kevin himself wasn't even aware that he was Paul. So I had to be careful and think things through. I'd learned not to be too casual with the truth.

I reached out to the Tipster to find out more about Kevin. I was curious about his life. Who had raised him? Did he have a hard childhood? What kind of life did he end up living? I'm not sure what I expected to hear, but the Tipster's portrait of Kevin was pretty rough.

"He was a drinker," the Tipster said. "His personality was just different. We always passed it off as shyness, and maybe that's why he drank, because he would come out of his shell a little when he drank. But then sometimes he drank too much and he got into fights. I remember him fighting his stepbrother in a bar, and his stepbrother knocking him out."

The root of his problems, the Tipster said, might have been the woman who raised him. Her name was Lorraine, and she passed away in 2004. Lorraine "was a very angry woman," the Tipster said. "That's why Kevin is the person he is. She never showed up at any of his games, and he was always afraid of her."

Kevin's life had apparently been derailed by a streak of sadness or anger or both that ran through him. "He had a lot of psychological issues throughout his life," the Tipster said. "He was an alcoholic, but a true-blue, mean-drunk kind of alcoholic. After his wife left him, he threatened suicide on multiple occasions. And he was estranged from his three daughters."

I was horrified to hear this sad litany of Kevin's problems. My heart broke for him. All along, the hope had been that the Fronczaks' kidnapped child wound up with people who loved him and cared for him and steered him towards a happy life. It didn't look like that had happened. I wondered if he bore any scars from the kidnapping, which happened when he was too young to comprehend anything—just like I may have been lastingly affected by the abandonment I couldn't recall.

My impulse was to reach out to Kevin directly. I'd done that with other potential Pauls, but the difference was, they'd all known about my case and willingly came forward. Kevin, apparently, knew nothing about it, and his daughter had yet to tell him about the DNA test. I didn't feel like I should be the one to break the news to him, so I decided against any contact.

But I did search for and find his daughter Tillie's email. I wrote to her and told her who I was, how I'd been searching for the real Paul for eight years, and how I'd heard she discovered her father might be him. I told her all I wanted was to be able to speak with her about it—that was it. I had no interest in disrupting her or Kevin's life in any way.

Tillie did not respond.

After two weeks, I sent her another email, but she didn't answer that one either. I sent her a third email, and, finally, she replied. Her answer was short and to the point.

Please leave me alone.

I can't say I was surprised by the reaction. Tillie, the Tipster told me, "is afraid to discuss this with her dad, since trying to predict how he will react is difficult. Kevin is a tough one to read." In fact, I'd received the same response from so many people in the course of my search for the real Paul, as well as for my own family. I'd been told to go away a whole bunch of different ways.

There was another reason Tillie might not wish to speak to me. If her father Kevin was indeed the real Paul, as it appeared, that meant whoever raised Kevin could be the person who kidnapped him from Reese Hospital in 1963. Imagine an innocent DNA test revealing to you that your father is at the center of the oldest kidnapping cold case in U.S. history—and that your grandmother could be a wanted kidnapper. To learn all that, all at once, would be, I knew as well as anyone, a very heavy thing. I understood why Tillie wasn't anxious to talk just yet.

My email, however, alerted Tillie to the fact that someone else knew about Kevin's real identity. That changed things. Now, the Tipster told me in a later update, "Tillie is concerned her dad will be contacted by someone before she is able to tell him what's going on." Though I hadn't meant it to, my email accelerated everyone's plans. Soon, Kevin would know the truth.

After that, I waited and did nothing. I sat on the biggest discovery of them all—the real Paul. Once again, I found myself in a conflicted position. Of course, I respected Tillie's privacy, and Kevin's privacy, and their need to move at whatever pace they felt was best. At the same time, I was impatient. This secret had been buried for more than fifty years, and I was anxious to unearth it and have it not be a secret anymore.

Some will say I overstepped by emailing Tillie and inserting myself into her situation. Perhaps they are right. But Kevin and his daughters were not the only players in this drama. There was also my mother, Dora, who had suffered long enough not knowing what became of her son; and my brother, David, who'd been deprived of a brother; and even me, the man who ended up living Paul Fronczak's life. We had our own emotional investments in the story—and our own claims to the truth. The secret, I felt, was not necessarily anyone's to keep.

About two weeks later, the Tipster had an update for me. Tillie had finally informed her father about his real identity, and also traveled to Chicago, along with her two sisters, to meet with Dave and Dora Fronczak. What's more, Tillie called the FBI and let them know about Kevin too. It was the FBI that advised her not to share the news with anyone, including me.

It wasn't much later that I got a call from my mother, Dora.

"I have some important news to share with you," she said in a serious tone. "Paul was found."

"Mom, I know," I replied.

"You know? How do you know?"

"Someone close to his family sent me a tip."

And then we started talking. It was a conversation many, many decades in the making. My mother, I was happy to hear, was excited about the discovery. After so many years of never speaking with her about the kidnapping, it was remarkable to hear her talk so freely about Kevin, and even say she was looking forward to meeting him. I didn't know how she'd react to her son being found, and I feared it might upset her and drive her away from me again. In fact, she could hardly stop talking about him.

Frankly, neither could I. Something that seemed so unlikely to happen now had a very good chance of happening—a reunion between my mother and the boy who was taken from her.

There was one thing the Tipster told me that I did not share with my mother, because I didn't know what to make of it, and I didn't want my mother to have to worry about it.

"Before Lorraine died," the Tipster said, "she told one of Kevin's sisters that there was a box in her closet she didn't want anyone to get ahold of. But no one has any further details of the whereabouts of the box, or its contents."

We weren't done yet, it seemed, with secrets.

Now that I knew Kevin was aware of who he was, I sat down and wrote him a letter:

Hello Kevin:

My name is Paul Fronczak, and I'm the guy who's been living your life.

I learned that you might be the real Paul Fronczak, and I wanted to reach out to tell you that I've been looking for you for seven years. I think I understand what you might be feeling these past few days and weeks, because I went through something similar, when I took a DNA test and learned I wasn't the real Paul Fronczak—even though I spent my whole life being told that I was. I understand what it's like to have your identity taken away from you in the blink of an eye.

Pretty much every day since then, I have hoped that the real Paul was still out there somewhere. I had the feeling that he was. I always thought he might be the only person who could really comprehend the strange adventure I've been on. I imagined meeting him and having a beer or two, or three, and just sitting around and talking about our lives.

As for me, I'm 54 now. I've been divorced twice, and I have a beautiful daughter, Emma, who is 10. I'm kind of a wanderer, and I seem to float in and out of jobs. I've probably held 100 different jobs in my life. I have a Harley Davidson motorcycle and I love The X-Files. For most of my life, I have felt like I didn't belong—like maybe I was an alien myself.

Kevin, I know that adjusting to this revelation is a very personal matter, and you deserve all the time in the world to make any kind of decision about yourself and your future. So I won't reach out to you again, because I don't want to bother you.

But I will leave you my email and phone number, and I'll hope that one day you will contact me, when you're ready, so we can go to your favorite bar and have a few beers.

Thanks for reading this, Kevin, and I sincerely hope you will find all the peace and love and security you need, now that you know the truth.

Be well. Paul

The truth was that I really wanted to meet Kevin. I felt we had a deep connection despite never having spoken or been aware of each other. I thought he might be uniquely suited to understanding what I had gone through, and vice versa. But if it turned out he didn't want to meet with me—that the whole thing was too much for him to handle, and he needed more time—I would have been fine with that. Meeting Kevin would be a bonus for me. But it was not my primary goal.

What drove me to keep going over the last seven years was getting my mother and her son back together again.

In fact, I couldn't imagine a scenario where Kevin—despite all his challenges—would *not* want to meet his biological mother. That just wasn't comprehensible to me. Was I projecting some of my own obsession with the case onto other people? Possibly. But to me, reuniting Dora with her long-missing son was something that absolutely *had* to happen. It wasn't that I thought such a reunion would fix anything, or heal anyone, or anything like that.

It was that I believed with all my heart that Dora was *meant* to be able to hold her son again.

I believed that reuniting Dora and Kevin would, in a way, rewrite the past and turn their story into something different from what it was. I saw the reunion as a brief but crucial moment of redemption, of triumph—a testament to the endurance of family through the longest of odds and the harshest of fortunes. I felt that Dora and Kevin being together, even if only for an hour or a day, could undo some of the pain and torment of the last half century—a final trick of fate that sets the world right again.

Of course, I was silly to believe that fate was some kind of benign force, rather than the indifferent sledgehammer it is.

In April 2019, three months after we confirmed that Kevin was the real Paul, I got another update from the Tipster.

> *I found out yesterday that Kevin was in the hospital last week for an extended stay. He was diagnosed with lung and kidney cancer. He will begin chemotherapy treatments next week.*

Further tests revealed Kevin also had four distinct tumors on his brain.

CHAPTER 15

Locating the real Paul energized me in a way that even learning my own identity hadn't. So many people told me I would never find him, and yet—through luck, through providence, through whatever you want to call it—we did find him. And if finding him was possible, then so was finding my sister Jill.

I honestly thought that Nino, our great private investigator, would be able to persuade my sister Linda to share some more of our family's history with me, and possibly tell me what happened to Jill. Nino has an uncanny ability to ingratiate himself with anyone, even people who are dead set against being found, much less interviewed. Yet Linda chased him away with obscenities in under a minute. I realized I wasn't dealing with just anyone. Linda was a Rosenthal, and the Rosenthals, I was learning, were a tough breed.

I asked Nino if we could dig up more information about Linda. I'd come to believe she was my very best hope for finding out about Jill. She was there when the twins disappeared, and she was there in the following years, when the Rosenthals somehow managed to keep their terrible secret. Yes, she'd only been four years old at the time, but surely she had to have some memory, some saved mental picture, some information that might help us unlock the mystery. Finding out more about her, I hoped, would give us an idea about how to get her to talk.

Nino did his usual quick work and located Linda's ex-husband. His name was Alfonso, and sadly he was battling cancer, and in a hospital in New Jersey. Even so, he agreed to talk to us about Linda. Nino told him the story of Jill, and Alfonso said he wanted to help in any way he could.

"I guess you heard I have a little touch of cancer going on," Alfonso said cheerily when we got on the phone. "Good days and bad days. Today I'm doing okay."

Then he said, "One thing you're going to realize from our talk today is that your family was so good at hiding family secrets, it was ridiculous."

Alfonso explained that, though he'd been with Linda for eight years, he had no idea the twins ever existed. He never heard about them, never saw a picture of them, never even got the sense that Linda was keeping such a huge secret from him.

What he did notice, as he would explain, was that something was wrong with the Rosenthal family. "What I came to realize was that these were not good people," he said, echoing what other relatives had told me. "You didn't want to spend time with them. They were very secretive, you know, stay in the house, keep to themselves. There was no—how do I put it—no spirituality with this family. None at all. Even Christmas wasn't a warm time with this family. I don't know what it was."

Every time I heard that about the Rosenthals, my heart would drop. It was clear they were a haunted family. Were they haunted by something that happened before the twins were born? Or was it the twins and their disappearance that turned them into the family they became? I felt enormous sympathy for Linda and Karen and Fred, my biological siblings, for having to grow up in such an atmosphere. It helped me understand why Linda and Fred were so reluctant to relive the past.

More than anything, it confirmed for me that the destructive power of a long-hidden secret can be catastrophic.

Alfonso told me how he and Linda met somewhere on the Jersey Shore, hit it off, and started dating. He said he saw some warning signs in her personality but proposed to her anyway. "When I told my father I was going to marry her," he said, "my father offered to buy me a house if I called it off."

Linda, Alfonso said, "just had a really dark personality. I don't know what to tell you. She didn't believe in anything, you know? It was like she had hatred in her heart towards humanity. When Nino told me she slammed the door on him, I wasn't surprised. I saw her slam the door on fifty people like that! That's just the way she was. She was not a good person."

Alfonso shared the story of bringing home a Rottweiler puppy—"the cutest thing you ever saw," he said. "I was crazy about the pup, but not Linda. One day he gets out, and do you think she went out after him? No. A neighbor told me he saw her watching through the window as somebody came along and took the baby. Just watching through the window."

The story of the puppy gave me chills. The image of Linda watching through the window as someone took her dog away—I couldn't help but connect it to what might have happened when the twins disappeared. Did Linda watch helplessly then, too, as someone took me away to leave me on a sidewalk? Had she watched powerlessly when my mother dropped Jill down the stairs? Was that the event that haunted Linda through what seemed to be her whole life?

At that moment, I felt deep sympathy for Linda again. She was just a child herself when the twins vanished. She would have had no way of stopping it from happening or doing anything about it. In a way, she was a victim of the same tragedy that separated Jill and I from our family. Linda lost two siblings in the blink of an eye, which had to have been a significant and lasting trauma in her life. Suddenly, I felt rotten for treating her like the subject of my investigation, rather than as someone who was wounded, like me, and doing whatever it took to survive.

It was the inescapable conflict at the heart of my search—was I searching for a family, or was I searching for the truth? Finding both, it seemed, just wasn't possible.

Alfonso told me stories about my parents. Gilbert, he said, was a serious man who never went outside in less than a spiffy shirt and tie. He could also be playful and crack jokes, until nearer the end of his life, when he was on heavy medication for his back pain. "He was running security at Pitney Village back then," Alfonso said, "and he had girlfriends throughout the complex. He was cheating on your mom pretty heavily."

As for my mother, "she was a heavy drinker," Alfonso recalled. "She hid her alcoholism pretty well. She was very functional. At dinner she could be hammered and there was no way to tell. But sometimes I would call Linda at their house, and I would hear your mother screaming and hollering and throwing stuff in the background, stuff breaking into pieces."

At one point, Alfonso paused for a long minute. It seemed like he was overwhelmed by all of his troublesome recollections of the Rosenthals. I was too. But something else was bothering him—the fact that he and I were talking at all.

"What I don't understand is, how could I have spent eight years with the Rosenthals thinking I am an intelligent human being, and not known about two other children they had who had been abandoned? I mean, not even an inkling that they even existed? It's insane. I can't get over it. The whole thing is very upsetting. If I can do anything to help you find Jill, I will."

I thanked Alfonso for being so generous with his time and his memories, and I told him I was rooting for him with all my heart to get better. Just before we hung up, Alfonso had one last thought he wanted to share.

"You know what, Paul?" he said. "You would have been my brother-in-law. It's good to finally be talking to you."

I told him it was really good to talk with him too.

Ever since I learned I had a twin sister in 2015, I'd resisted doing the most obvious thing I could have done in response—filing a missing persons report with the police. I hadn't been able to find any official paperwork regarding the disappearance of the twins—with police departments, with foundling hospitals, with institutions, anywhere I checked—so I felt reasonably certain no one ever reported that Jill Rosenthal suddenly vanished from her home. In terms of records and documents, Jill simply didn't exist anymore.

Filing a report with the Atlantic City police would mean, at the very least, that someone somewhere was aware that Jill was missing, beyond just me.

Still, I didn't do it. I didn't want to do it. Part of it had to do with my experience with the FBI in the years after I proved I wasn't Paul Fronczak. When the FBI reopened the long-cold case, it was effectively the end of my official participation in the search for the real Paul. I was completely shut out of the investigation, other than a preliminary interview with two FBI Special Agents and a couple of quick follow-ups. No information was ever shared with me, and months would pass without any word from the FBI about their progress. It became hard for me to imagine the FBI was doing anything at all.

From that point, it wasn't too much of a leap for me to believe the FBI did not *want* to find the real Paul.

The original kidnapping case had not been a shining moment for the FBI. After all, they handed over the wrong child to the Fronczaks, and—as my research showed—they did so knowingly. They failed to make any serious inroads in the case in the two years it was actively worked on, despite what was then described as the biggest and broadest manhunt in the history of Chicago. No leads, no suspect, and certainly no kidnapped child. And then, when I came along, the FBI suddenly had a nice, tidy way to button up the whole case.

To have to reopen it fifty years later, and to have to confront the botched handing-over of the wrong Paul, could not have been high on the FBI's wish list.

My fear was that if I opened a missing persons case with the police for Jill, the same thing would happen—I'd be shut out of the official investigation and hampered in my own search for Jill. I could not, for instance, try to interview Linda again—not if she wound up on a police list of potential witnesses. I feared a situation where all I'd be able to do is sit and wait and twiddle my thumbs. I just didn't want that to happen.

But after five years of searching for Jill, I knew I needed help. There were two big national organizations devoted to finding missing children—the National Center for Missing and Exploited Children (NCMEC) and the National Missing and Unidentified Persons System (NamUs)—which could lend enormous resources to the search, provided they were willing to devote themselves to such an old, cold case. But for them to begin to help me, they would need a missing persons case number from the investigating police department. I had no choice but to open such a case.

And anyway, after Nino and I both failed to persuade my sister Linda to talk, I figured the only person who could was someone with a badge. I still feared being shut out of the search, but to keep going at it alone just wouldn't be smart.

It was time to make Jill's disappearance official.

So, in March 2020, I flew from Las Vegas to Newark, New Jersey, drove south down I-95 to Atlantic City, and walked into the Clayton G. Graham Public Safety Building on Atlantic Avenue, across from the looming Tropicana casino. Nino told me the only way to ensure an investigator will take a case seriously and give it his or her best effort is to look them in the eye and get them emotionally invested in the missing person. I couldn't do that over the phone. So I went to the police station.

After I filled out a two-page report and handed it to the woman behind Window 1, I waited in the office's cramped outer space for whatever happened next. Through the window, I could see plain-clothed detectives walking around. I knew they were detectives by their holstered guns. Ten minutes passed before the woman returned and summoned me to step forward.

"I'll pass this along to a detective, and we'll get back to you," she said.

"Wait," I said. "I need you to give it to a detective now. I need a missing persons case number. I came all the way from Las Vegas to get it. Can you please give it to someone now?"

The woman did not try to hide her annoyance.

"I don't know if anyone is available right now," she said.

"Can you check? Can you explain the special nature of this case? All I need is the number of the report. Please. Please."

The woman got up and walked away. I didn't see her again for ten more minutes. When she came back, she still had my two-page report in her hand.

"Looks like everyone is busy right now," she said.

My sister had been missing for fifty-five years. Another week or two, I knew, would not make a difference. But I didn't want to wait. I was tired of waiting. I needed the case to be opened. I needed to know someone was going to join me in looking for Jill. The case would never be a priority—that I understood. There were tens of thousands of missing children who needed attention more urgently. But I couldn't leave without the case being opened, at least. I needed to know who I was handing the case to. I needed to look them in the eye.

I needed to plead the case for my sister, who couldn't plead it herself.

Just then, before the woman behind the window and I could resume our debate, the door to the inner station opened, and a man stepped out.

"I'm Detective Jenkins," he said, extending a hand. "I overheard you talking about your sister, and I want to help."

He looked to be about thirty-five years old, with a trimmed mustache and a friendly, open face. There was something boyish about him. My first impression was that I really liked him. Heck, I wanted to reach out and hug him.

Det. Jenkins explained that his father had been an officer with the Atlantic City Police Department and had sometimes taken on cold cases to pore over in his spare time. Jenkins said he had an interest in old true crime stories, especially ones set in Atlantic City. He said he'd be happy to take on Jill's case.

I couldn't have asked for a better scenario. Here was someone willing to take a personal interest in Jill's disappearance—and maybe even make it a mission, like I had. And the serendipity of a true crime aficionado walking by just when I was talking about a mysterious unsolved disappearance was, in my mind, one of those happy, helpful twists of fate. Det. Jenkins retreated to his office for a few minutes and came back with an official case number on a piece of paper.

ACPD Case No. 2003-0214.

I promised to send Det. Jenkins my book, and I shared what I thought was the most pressing priority in the case—interviewing my sister, Linda. I gave him background and contact information for anyone in the Atlantic City area I thought could help in the search. Det. Jenkins and I shook hands, and I wished him the best of luck.

"I'll be in touch soon," he said.

Now it was done. The search for my sister Jill had been joined. I felt better than I had in a long time about my chances of solving the mystery of my missing twin. The secret, I convinced myself, could not keep forever.

But twists of fate, I had to be reminded yet again, are not always happy or helpful.

It turned out I had handed the case to the wrong cop.

CHAPTER 16

I could not imagine what the real Paul was going through.

To learn his life had been a lie—that part I understood.

But to follow that up with a severe cancer diagnosis three months later, out of the blue—that I could not fathom.

Kevin wasn't old. He was my age, fifty-five. From what I was hearing, he'd had a hard life. Didn't he deserve a break? Hadn't he gone through enough?

I wanted so much to reach out to Kevin, to offer to help him get through his ordeal, but I knew I couldn't. It just wasn't my place. We were connected in the oddest ways—the same name, the same disruptive experience at roughly the same age, the absence from our lives of our biological parents—and yet we were strangers. There was nothing I could do for him but root for him to beat his cancer and keep him in my thoughts.

Actually, there was one other important thing I could do for Kevin—I could leave him alone and keep his story private.

So that's what I did. I didn't try to contact him or his daughters. I lied to all the reporters who called me from time to time, asking for updates. I didn't mention Kevin to anyone. I'd imagined that finding him would be a joyous moment—the most meaningful moment of my long, hard journey. But it didn't turn out that way. The moment was much more fraught, much more complicated, than I'd envisioned. And now I had to act as if it hadn't happened at all. My only option was to wait.

I asked the Tipster to keep me posted on anything they heard about Kevin's progress. Over the next month, I learned that, after Tillie told the FBI about her father's real identity, the FBI called Kevin and arranged a time to visit him at work to draw a sample for a DNA test. The FBI, of course, needed the test to be certain that Kevin was Paul, something I already knew. A few days later, they paid another visit to Kevin, this time at his house. But this second visit was unannounced, and it didn't go well. Kevin cursed at the Special Agents and chased them away.

"He told them he'd just received his cancer diagnosis and couldn't deal with this other stuff," the Tipster told me. "There is no right way to confront Kevin about the Fronczak case, since his mood is so unpredictable. But he definitely doesn't like unannounced visits."

My thought when I heard Kevin kicked FBI agents out of his house was—*good for you.*

I was always anxious to hear how Kevin was doing with his treatment. Obviously I didn't want him to die. Not just because I wanted so desperately for him to finally meet his mother, but also because his illness seemed so utterly unfair, after everything else that had happened to him. I wanted him to beat the hell out of his cancer, and I really wanted his life to have a happy, family-filled second act. The Tipster was kind enough to send me updates, and the positive ones made me feel optimistic. "I ran into Kevin at the gas station and he seemed pretty upbeat," the Tipster wrote. "He has lost his voice because of the treatments and he could only respond in a whisper, but he looked really good. He said the treatments were going well and he was crossing his fingers and hoping for the best."

On the negative side, word about Kevin's connection to an infamous kidnapping case somehow leaked out in his small town. Reporters from all over bombarded Kevin's daughters with emails, letters, and calls. Some of his relatives, it seemed, were happy to speak to the press, most likely in exchange for money. Almost certainly, it was a cousin or in-law who alerted the press in the first place. The pressure was on, but Kevin and his family refused to comment to anyone about the story.

And without Kevin, or a statement from the FBI, there was no way for reporters to confirm his true identity.

Eventually, things quieted down. Reporters stopped calling, and the story never broke nationally. I learned Kevin was thinking about contacting my mother but hadn't decided to do it yet. That was frustrating to hear, but I had to understand why he wasn't ready to make it happen. He was seriously ill and had lost his hair and his voice; he was literally fighting for his life. To ask him to face yet another intensely emotional, possibly wrenching confrontation was, understandably, too much to ask.

One day, the Tipster sent me a photo of Kevin from when he was a teenager. When I saw it, I immediately recognized him. I dug up a photo of my brother Dave from when he was around the same age and looked at the two photos with awe. Their faces, their hair, their smile, were identical. It was a stunning thing to see.

Whenever I posed alongside Dave for a photo, I would cringe when someone showed it to me, exposing yet again how different we looked. I mean, we didn't share a single feature. Then to see Kevin and Dave side-by-side at the same age, looking like twins (they were less than two years apart in age), was powerful. It was Kevin who belonged next to his younger brother Dave in those old photos, not me. Yet there I was, standing in for him—pretending to be him.

Seeing how closely Kevin and Dave resembled each other was a striking reminder of just how much had been lost.

Over the course of my conversations with the Tipster, I learned something remarkable about Kevin. After graduating high school, Kevin chose not to go to college, and instead went straight to work at a job. The place where he worked was a factory, and the profession he chose was machinist.

The same profession as his biological father, Chester Fronczak, who he never met or even knew about.

How amazing, I thought—a particular trait, a life-shaping aptitude, passed on from father to son, so that, although they'd been cruelly separated, the father's towering influence remained. The wolf stays connected to its family. The only shame was that my father, who had passed away two years earlier, would not be able to meet the son who carried his genes. They would have had something to talk about right away, something to break the ice. It would have been a nice conversation to have.

Knowing Kevin was a machinist made me want to learn more about him. Part of it was that I was curious about the extent to which the kidnapping had taken a toll on Kevin, as unaware of it as he was. Maybe I wanted to compare it to the effects my abandonment had on me. Or maybe I believed Kevin and I could help each other fill in the awful gaps created by being wrenched away from our families. I can't say for sure we could have helped each other; maybe it was just a hopeful thought.

The other part of wanting to know more about Kevin was wanting to know more about the mother who raised him.

Or, I should say, wanting to know if the woman who raised him was also the woman who took him.

I did some research, made some calls, and began asking around. Thanks to several different sources, some who knew Kevin well, some who knew him from around town, I was able to put together a fragmentary sketch of his life.

Most of the sources confirmed the little I knew about Kevin already—that he'd had a difficult life. He grew up fully believing that the woman who raised him, Lorraine, was his biological mother, and kept that belief until Tillie's DNA test proved otherwise. Lorraine told him his father was a football player with the Detroit Lions who wanted nothing to do with the family. She told other people in town the same story.

Lorraine's parents came to the United States from Russia and Lithuania and settled in the city of Chicago. I later learned that Lorraine's mother, Blanche, was, at one time, a nurse's aide, which may have been where the kidnapper's nurse uniform came from. Lorraine spent many years in Chicago—including 1964, the year Baby Fronczak was kidnapped—and bounced back and forth between there and Michigan. From what I could tell, she had three children: a natural son and daughter, who grew up in Michigan, and then, nearly twenty years later, Kevin. She moved to Michigan with Kevin when he was already at least five years old, surprising even her own grown children.

"Who's that kid?" her daughter asked.

"That's your brother," Lorraine replied.

She got married in Michigan, to a man named Bob, and he became Kevin's stepfather. In high school, Kevin was "just a regular guy," said someone who knew him then. "He played sports, football, basketball, and hung out on weekends. He was quiet but other than that he seemed normal." Kevin skipped college, went to work as a machinist, got married, and had three daughters. The marriage ended in divorce, at least in part because of Kevin's drinking. "People knew that when Kevin drank, he was abusive to his ex-wife and then to his girlfriend after that," one source told me. "When he drank, it was like someone flipped a switch and you knew what was coming next."

Kevin could be especially dangerous because of his size: he was roughly six feet, two inches and 280 pounds. I heard that he sent one girlfriend to the hospital with broken bones. "When there wasn't alcohol involved, he could be a really sweet man," I was told. "But I seen him put away sixty cans of beer in a day. Sometimes more. When he did that, he was a nightmare."

I thought back to Dora and Chester Fronczak, Kevin's biological parents, neither of whom had been a drinker. As far as I could tell, alcoholism wasn't something that ran through the Fronczak line. How was it, I wondered, that Kevin became such a destructive drinker?

"It was Lorraine," a source told me. "His mother spoiled him. If he wanted to have a party, she bought the booze and let him party. That was way back in junior high."

I learned that Lorraine was a pretty heavy drinker, too, and so was Kevin's stepfather, Bob. It seemed like Kevin never really had much of a chance to escape the curse himself.

The more I filled in the picture of Kevin's life, the less I wanted to know. I heard very few stories about happy times he'd had, if any. It all seemed pretty bleak. So I stopped asking around about Kevin, and I began asking more questions about Lorraine. Was there any evidence to suggest she'd been the woman in the nurse's uniform who kidnapped Baby Fronczak? And if there wasn't—and Lorraine wasn't the abductor—how did she end up with Kevin?

I'd always felt an obligation to locate the real Paul and reunite him with my mother. But I also felt a kind of duty—especially after the real Paul was found—to do whatever I could to solve the crime of his kidnapping. I suspected the FBI wasn't really interested in identifying a kidnapper, which would only bring more attention to the case. If I didn't pursue it, I couldn't imagine who would. Was it important that someone be held accountable for the crime, all these years later? I felt that it was, especially since that person could possibly still be alive.

So I turned my attention to Lorraine, and to the mystery of who took Baby Fronczak, and why.

CHAPTER 17

Six years ago, towards the beginning of my search, I sat down with a psychic medium. It wasn't that I wholeheartedly believed in the power of a psychic medium to talk to the dead or anything like that. The truth was, I was skeptical. But early on, I made a commitment to leave no stone unturned in my search for the real Paul, and for my twin sister Jill. I knew that cops sometimes used psychics on difficult cases. And if hard-boiled cops could use them, surely I could too.

I arranged to have a phone session with Bobbi Allison, the same highly regarded, East Coast psychic I used six years earlier. I didn't know if she remembered our session, or remembered anything about my case, and I didn't ask. I just gave her my first name, which was all she asked for and all she had to go on.

Almost immediately during our session, Bobbi said she was sensing very unusual and powerful energy. "There is a whole hurricane happening around you, but you are standing outside it," she said. "It's like you have learned how to move into the energy when you need to, and then get out of it. Like you can control this energy, to a point."

That sounded right to me. I often tell people I approached my whole ordeal as if it were happening to someone other than me. As if I was on the outside of it, looking in—the investigator, not the victim. It was a way of coping with the intense emotions involved, to be sure, by shunting them off to the side. But it also allowed me to be more methodical and less sentimental in my search. I learned to toggle in and out of the hurricane.

In our first reading, Bobbi somehow knew I had a twin. This time, she brought up my twin again, and said she saw negative energy swirling around her. "It strikes me as abuse," she said. "Abuse for your twin, and also abuse for you. Abuse and neglect. It's almost like the mother is looking the other way, knowing something is going on, something bad, and not taking responsibility for it. Do you remember the abuse, Paul?"

"No, but I've spoken with people who witnessed it."

"I see tears," Bobbi went on. "Were your parents addicts or alcoholics? I'm getting unstable, erratic energy. Substance abuse, torturing themselves, no smooth energy. They were part of your hurricane, and what they did was horrible. Horrible. It makes me want to cry. It is like…it is like they gave your twin away to someone in exchange for something. Mental illness crossed with addiction, a very warped love, like swimming in an emotional abyss of disconnect. It was like they said, 'We can't raise her, so let's trade her.' And that's what happened."

That was a lot to digest. The idea that my mother looked on helplessly while someone else, presumably my father, was the one who harmed the twins. And then my mother somehow trading my sister away, in exchange for something? Like what—settling a gambling debt? Or did that refer to whatever bargain she had to make with my father to get him to come back home?

I asked Bobbi if she thought my twin sister was alive.

"I do not see her on the other side," she said. "I feel like she is still living. I feel like she is a prisoner to her past, a prisoner to her abuse, and it is very confusing for her. Like she doesn't know where or how to start to move away from it. I see her sitting at a table and being interrogated, but she's turning her head to the side, like she's bewildered. She doesn't understand what's going on, so she just sits there, without much emotion."

Bobbi paused for several seconds, then continued.

"Paul, I am hearing that you will know. You are the one who will know if she is still alive. I don't know how, but you will know. *You will be the one to know.*"

There was more. Bobbi began asking about any other biological siblings I'd found. I mentioned the name Linda.

"Linda knows what happened to the twins," Bobbi said firmly. "She knows where your sister is. She knows what happened and why. It is like your father did not want the twins and said he was not going to take care of them. He demanded that they not be there anymore, and then your mother had to figure out what to do with the twins. And Linda knows all this."

I was taking notes and scrambling to keep up with Bobbi, but she was talking fast. She said a man with a last name beginning with *M* would come into my life to tell me there was a break in the case, based on information someone came forward with. And, oddly, she mentioned a tree.

"A white oak tree. Not a lot of leaves. Not too big or not too thin. Just a normal tree is what they're showing me. That white oak tree is supposed to be part of your journey."

One of the final images that came to her was a clock or a watch. "Time," she said. "Time moving, time coming. It's a message to you, Paul. Don't give up. Do not give up. Keep going, because the answers are coming for you. The time for you to know the answers is coming. So keep going."

What did it all mean? Linda holding the key to the mystery; my father demanding that the twins disappear; the clock or the watch, ticking away; and the mysterious white oak tree? Of course, none of it was evidence of anything, and all of it was open to whatever interpretation I wished to impose on it. Some of you reading this now might think I should have just discarded it all as worthless speculation. But I didn't. I filed the information away. I put myself on the lookout for oak trees, and I strengthened my resolve to find a way to talk to Linda again.

And I took encouragement from the imagery of time. I was very aware that my search for the truth was now into its ninth year, and that I'd allowed it to basically overtake my life in that time. The search consumed all else. And that implied a question—how long would I allow it to do so? When should I set it all down, like a heavy suitcase I'd been lugging for years, and finally walk away from it? Had that time already come and gone?

More importantly, would I even know when it was time?

The reading with Bobbi made me feel that time had not yet come. Like there was more to the story, the most important part, just beyond the horizon, waiting for me to find it. *Keep going,* she said. *Keep digging. The time for you to know is coming.*

So I listened to the spirits, and I kept going.

Unfortunately, I wasn't having much luck. After filing the missing persons report with Det. Jenkins, I waited a few weeks before calling to check in with him. But I kept missing him and leaving messages that he never returned. One of the things I needed Det. Jenkins to do was to call both NCMEC and NamUs, the two national organizations devoted to finding missing children, and give them the number of Jill's open case. Neither group could do anything without the case number from Det. Jenkins. All he had to do was make two quick phone calls and pass along the number, but for some reason he didn't. Month after month, I left messages for him, none of which he returned. I had no idea what was going on, and no idea how to get a hold of Det. Jenkins to talk about it.

I convinced myself to be patient. Jill's case was long cold, and surely Det. Jenkins had many other more pressing cases to handle. *Just give him time, he'll come through for you.* But all the waiting was making me miserable, and, even worse, paranoid.

Was there some other reason why Det. Jenkins wasn't working on Jill's case at all? Had someone, perhaps, instructed him to sit on the case—to, essentially, stall the investigation?

I didn't allow myself to go too deeply down that particular rabbit hole, at least not yet.

Meanwhile, I kept chasing an interview with Joan Pileggi, the woman who lived next door to my parents around the time the twins disappeared. I'd spoken with her daughter Ann, who showed no desire to get her mother involved with me or with the Rosenthal case. When I called Joan Pileggi directly, and called her sons as well, none of them ever got back to me. Still, I needed to know if Joan had ever seen the twins, or if my parents had succeeded in hiding us completely from the outside world. I felt I was entitled to answers. A crime had been committed, a truly horrible crime. Two children had vanished, and one of them was still missing. The repercussions from these crimes still resonated more than fifty years later. I understood the Pileggis preferred to not get involved or have to dredge up old memories. I just wasn't sure if that should stop me from pursuing them.

I didn't know where Joan Pileggi lived, but I did have a current address for her son Robert. So when I flew to Atlantic City to file the missing persons report for Jill, I paid an unannounced visit to Robert's home along a broad, quiet street on the fringes of the city. Robert was roughly my sister Linda's age, and Joan's daughter had told me during our phone conversation that Robert and Linda used to play together when they were kids. I wanted to speak with him to see if he, too, might remember seeing the twins. Mainly, though, I wanted his help in connecting with his mother, Joan. I walked up the three concrete steps to his front porch, shook the cold rain off my light coat, and knocked on the front door.

There was no answer. The window shades were all drawn, and beyond them everything was dark. It certainly looked like no one was home. Still, I knocked again, and again. *Keep going. Keep digging.* Ten minutes later, I still hadn't heard a sound in the house, and there seemed absolutely no point in knocking again, but I did anyway, one last time.

Suddenly, the front door unlocked and opened. A young man with a thick beard and unruly hair stood at the door in his bathrobe, groggy and confused. It was two in the afternoon on a Saturday, but it was obvious he'd just woken up. I explained who I was and why I was there, and I asked if he knew Robert Pileggi.

"He's my father," he said, "but he's not here right now."

I had to take him at his word on that, but I asked if he wouldn't mind calling his father and letting him know I was there. "I really need to speak with him," I explained. "I wouldn't bother him unless it was really important, and I'm only here for today. I came all the way from Nevada to see him."

Robert's son, still only half-awake, agreed to call his father. He went back in the house while I stood on the porch and watched the rain pour through holes in the gutters. I heard the son talking on the phone, and after a minute he was back.

"My father said he is busy right now, but he will call you in twenty minutes," he said. "Just give me your number and I'll send it to him."

I knew right then I would not hear from Robert that day.

Still, I left my number, apologized to the young man for waking him up, and trudged back to my rental car. I pulled away from the street and found a quiet place around the corner to idle while I waited for my cell phone to ring. Just in case, I told myself. Just in case he does call. But, of course, he didn't.

With the Fronczak case, things were also at a standstill. After Kevin's cancer diagnosis, we knew we'd have to wait for anything to happen. But months passed without Kevin reaching out to my mother. So much time passed that Dora began to wonder if she even wanted to speak with Kevin anymore.

"Maybe he just wants to be left alone," she said. "Otherwise I would have heard from him already." I did not want her to lose heart, and I told her we both needed to be patient. Everything was in Kevin's hands now. We had to give him time.

A few weeks later, I got a message from the Tipster about Kevin's condition. Apparently, the chemotherapy had reduced the size of two of the four tumors on his brain, and he was improving. He was feeling better. Through their source, the Tipster even learned that Kevin was getting closer to finally contacting my mother. He wanted to talk to her after all.

I was elated by the news, and I allowed myself to get excited about the prospect of an actual meeting. I told my mother I'd be happy to pick her up in Chicago and drive her to northern Michigan, should it turn out Kevin wanted to meet but could not travel. Whatever was needed, I told her, I'd be there for her. My mother set aside her reservations about Kevin and promised to stay open to the possibility of a reunion.

For a while there, it felt like good things were happening.

What I didn't know at the time was that, several months earlier, in a city halfway around the world, a cluster of mysterious illnesses had been reported by medical authorities.

A few dozen people from Wuhan, in China's Hubei Province, were sick and no one knew why. Two months later, the World Health Organization declared the illness a global pandemic. Around that time, a patient in a hospital near Seattle died of the illness; just a month later, the United States led all countries in reported cases of the strange sickness. No one really knew what it was or how destructive it would be, and people were genuinely scared of what a worst-case scenario might look like.

Within two more months, one hundred thousand Americans were dead—on the way to some six hundred thousand American deaths.

By then, the never-before-seen deadly virus causing the illness had an official name—Covid-19.

The world came to a stop. Restrictions on travel were put in place. People were told to stay at home and avoid contact with other people. Only essential visits with others were advised.

The virus was particularly deadly among older people and people with underlying health concerns—people like my mother, Dora, and people like Kevin.

Any meeting between Dora and Kevin would now have to wait. For how long, no one could say. I hoped it would only be a few weeks. It turned into several months.

The reunion, I realized, might never happen at all.

CHAPTER 18

Sometimes there is an expectation among adoptees looking for their birth parents that, at the end of the rainbow, they will find a white picket fence—the loving, accepting, idyllic family they always dreamed of having but never had.

Sometimes they get lucky, and find that white picket fence. Sometimes they don't.

So many things can go wrong on an ancestral search, or may simply no longer be possible to accomplish. People die, records get burned. Stories are forgotten. And even if you make it all the way through and find your family, alive and healthy, there is no guarantee they will greet you with open arms. Or that they will even remotely resemble what you imagined them to be.

Sometimes, what you find at the end of the rainbow may be so awful and traumatizing, you never get over it.

There are other dangers lurking in such a search. If it goes on too long, if it takes years instead of weeks or months, there is the danger that what was once merely a hobby may well become an addiction. Or that what you liked to refer to as your mission becomes, in fact, an obsession.

My own search had lasted years—years nearly consumed whole by my determination to solve the mysteries at the root of my identity. Somewhere along the line, my mission became an obsession. And obsessions *always* carry a cost.

In my first book, I wrote about the toll my search took on my marriage to Michelle. At the end of the book, Michelle and I had agreed to separate and were living apart. We'd been married for six years, many of them extremely happy years, and in that time we had our daughter, Emma, who instantly became the beating heart at the center of both our lives. We had problems, as most couples do, but as a family, we were doing just fine.

Until the day I learned I was not the real Paul Fronczak.

Starting on that day, there was a new presence in our family. Before that, it had just been the three of us—Michelle, Emma, and I. Then, suddenly, there were four of us.

Michelle, Emma, me, and my search.

Almost from the start, the search was a disruptive force in all our lives. It was extremely time-consuming, which meant I had less time to spend with Michelle and Emma. Even if I came home right after work, I'd immediately jump on my laptop computer and spend hours searching the web for tips and leads and clues. In the beginning, Michelle was completely supportive of what I was doing. She was wary of where it all might lead, to be sure, but she loved me, and she knew it was something I had to do. So she was there for me, cheering me on, steadying me, helping me in any way she could.

But then, when I finally learned my true identity after three long years, Michelle realized that this momentous discovery was not, in any way, the end of my mission, but rather a new starting point for an even more intense search—the search for my missing sister Jill. And, of course, I hadn't found the real Paul yet either. In other words, the end was nowhere in sight.

Perhaps it was then, or around that time, that Michelle became aware I was tipping toward obsession.

"Is it ever going to stop?" she would ask. "Will you ever be able to walk away from it all?"

I had no easy answers for her, and sometimes I didn't answer her at all. I just walked away.

Before too long, I was sleeping in the guest room.

The stress continued to build, and Michelle and I fought more often. At times, we would yell at each other. Emma was still young, but the fighting and yelling affected her, and that was the hardest thing of all. Neither of us wanted Emma to be a casualty of our complicated feelings, but it was getting harder to shield her from the obvious and ever-present tension. What we had built together was, to our great sorrow, no longer functioning.

The only solution was for me to move out.

A few months after I moved out, Michelle and I agreed to file for a divorce. Michelle was heartbroken, and so was I, but we both knew it was the best thing for Emma, and for our family, for us to no longer be together.

Could I have prevented the divorce from happening by agreeing to give up my search? I don't think so. For one thing, had I quit the search, I might have begun to resent Michelle for forcing me to stop looking for Jill—even though she never once asked me to do that.

Also, the stress of the search exposed a problem that had been there all along—Michelle and I were two very different people. Michelle was a planner. She liked regimentation, and she liked to schedule her life down to the minute. I was the opposite. I liked to fly by the seat of my pants. Even before I started hopping on last-minute red-eye flights to Atlantic City, I was prone to whimsical decisions. I would quit a job without much thought and move on to the next one, never worrying about the possible downside. As a child, I dressed up as different characters and dreamed of new adventures, and that spirit of adventure ran through me still, and that was one of the reasons I jumped so enthusiastically into the search for my true identity—it satisfied the longing I had for some new, exciting escapade in my life.

The truth is that the greatest adventure I would ever have was my role as Emma's father. In fact, before I took the DNA test that proved I wasn't Paul, I'd begun to settle down and feel more comfortable in that role. The urge to find a new adventure became less pressing, until it was hardly pressing at all. Instead, I found great peace and comfort in the security of my family. At last, I thought, I'd found the one part I could play for the rest of my life—the part of family man.

But then I took the DNA test, and it revealed what it revealed, and it presented me with an incredible new adventure that was mine for the taking—the journey to discover the real me. And that proved too alluring, too exciting, for me to resist. So I plunged in, once again not fully considering the downside.

Of course, I didn't know then what I know now.

I didn't know that the white picket fence could end up being a hard brick wall.

About a year after the divorce, I went on a date with a woman who was introduced to me by a mutual friend. Her name was Kate. Now, I am someone who really craves companionship. I want to share my journeys with someone, and I don't really like being alone. Even so, I hadn't been actively looking for anyone when I agreed to go on the date. I just did it on a whim.

The date went better than I'd expected. Kate and I started talking about music, and I brought up the name Geddy Lee, the bassist and vocalist for Rush, my favorite band. Kate knew all about Geddy, and wound up being fully conversant on the subject of progressive rock music. She knew Chris Squire, the bass player from Yes and one of my idols, and she said her favorite bass guitars were Rickenbackers, the kind I played. We talked about music for most of the night, and after that we began seeing each other.

Before long, we were a couple. We got along really well, and the time we spent together was effortless. When we met, I owned an 883 Iron Harley-Davidson, a single passenger motorcycle. I traded up for a two-seat Harley Electra Glide Classic so Kate and I could ride together. Early on Saturday mornings, we'd cruise down Las Vegas

Boulevard, heading south on the old highway and blasting Rush or Jethro Tull. Those mornings seemed perfect to me.

One weekend, we rode out to Nevada's Valley of Fire, taking in the beautiful, swirling red sandstone formations as we roared down two-lane Fire Highway. It was about 120 degrees that day, and the sun was blazing. Unfortunately, Kate wore closed-toe sandals that left the tops of her feet exposed, and by the time we got to the Valley, her skin was blistering. I gave her my fingerless riding gloves, and she pulled them snugly past her toes to cover the exposed part of her foot. We both laughed at how silly it looked, but it was kind of symbolic of how our relationship was going. Everything just seemed to fit. I bought Kate her own motorcycle helmet, and she bought me a brown leather Harley jacket. We had become a team.

I waited a few months before telling Kate my story, but by then, she already knew about it. Google, of course. At first, she was intrigued by it, and also interested in my ongoing search for the real Paul and Jill. She became my partner in the journey, the one I called with new developments, and she was incredibly supportive.

But over time, her interest began to wane. A familiar dynamic was playing out—the more time I spent on the search, the less time I had for her. On top of that, Michelle and I had made a commitment to put our daughter Emma before anything else in our lives, and to be the best, most involved co-parents we could be. So my time with Emma was sacred to me, and I tried very hard to keep to our set schedule of visits at all costs. But that also cut into my time with Kate, who had her own obligations and her own schedule to deal with.

In the third year of our relationship, the cracks began to show. Kate didn't enjoy plane travel, so she never went with me on my frequent trips to Atlantic City or elsewhere. She never once told me not to travel, but I could tell she was unhappy whenever I left on a trip or had to spend a day working on the search. The same was true on the weekends I had Emma. Kate began to feel like she wasn't a priority for me.

This anxiety about our relationship was hard for both of us to handle. For me, I often felt like Kate was jealous of the time I spent with Emma, as if I was choosing someone else over her. Sometimes if I simply called Emma when I was with Kate, I would sense that Kate was upset. One day when we were together, I noticed Emma calling on my cell, and for the first time I debated whether or not to answer her. That was when I realized Kate and I had a real problem we might not be able to solve.

Nevertheless, I bought a ring and proposed to Kate, and she said yes. I knew we had issues, but I truly thought we could overcome them and be together for the long haul. Then, one week, I had to fly to Chicago for a search-related project, and I was away from Kate for several days. When I returned, she picked me up at the airport, and things seemed fine. We were both really happy to see each other. Back at my apartment, I told Kate all I needed to do was swing by Michelle's house and spend an hour or so with Emma, who I hadn't seen in more than a week, and then Kate and I would have the next two days all to ourselves.

That was the breaking point. Kate took off the engagement ring, put it on the kitchen counter, and told me I was free to spend all the time I wanted with "my real family." She was done, she said, finished with me after five years together. Then she just walked out. It was a horrible, heartbreaking moment for us both. I held out hope that I might be able to fix things between us and salvage the relationship, but Kate was adamant, and after that night, she never really looked back.

Kate never once blamed me for the break-up. She accepted that she had her own issues, and all she ever said was that it wasn't going to work out between us. In the aftermath of another wrecked relationship, I had to confront yet again the toll my search had taken on my life. I wondered if, had I not devoted so many days and hours to the search, would Kate not have minded my time with Emma as much? Would I have been more present, more attentive, less divided in my focus? Would I have been a better man, a better partner, to be with?

Was I the real problem all along?

The answers to such questions are never simple. Relationships are complex, and so are emotions, and it's pointless to pretend there was ever one reason, one fault line, which caused everything to collapse. We are complicated creatures. Still, my devotion to the search for the real Paul, and for Jill, was, I had to accept, causing a lot of sadness and destruction in my life, and in the lives of other people.

As always, I had to ask myself a central, essential question—were the searches worth all that pain?

I answered that question with my actions: I continued the search. I simply couldn't fathom giving up when I knew that my twin sister Jill could be out there somewhere. I felt I had no choice but to keep moving forward. Would there come a time when, in a flash of realization, I would accept that it was time to finally move on, regardless of what mysteries remained? Perhaps. But all I knew for sure was that that time had yet to come.

And as for the costs? The repercussions of my obsession?

I would just have to bear them, I decided, and try my hardest to minimize the damage they caused to the people I loved most in the world.

And when the search itself hit a standstill, and I wasn't getting anywhere with finding Jill, and Covid was preventing my mother from reconnecting with her biological son, and Kevin didn't seem all that interested in ever meeting his mother, and weeks would pass without any kind of break or even good news in the case—that was when the sacrifices I was making didn't seem worth making. That was when I would question if the time might not be drawing near.

But as it always seemed to happen in this bizarre journey of mine, that was also when something unexpected and remarkable did occur.

One day, out of the blue, Kevin, the real Paul, picked up his phone and called my mother, and *his* mother, Dora Fronczak.

CHAPTER 19

A year had passed since we discovered the real Paul was still alive, and in that time, Kevin had not tried to reach out to his biological mother, Dora. The last news I heard from the Tipster was that Kevin's health was improving, and he was thinking about connecting with Dora sometime soon. But after that, several more weeks passed without anything happening.

Then Dora went into the hospital to have shoulder surgery. The operation went well, and Dora spent the next three weeks in a rehabilitation clinic. My brother Dave came down from Colorado to be with her, and I called her on the phone as often as I could. When she finally got back home, she called me to tell me that she found a message on her answering machine.

She'd received a call from Kevin.

When I heard that, I was elated. I wanted so desperately for Dora and Kevin to connect. And now, it seemed, it was finally going to happen. Nearly fifty-seven years after having her baby taken from her arms, Dora was finally going to be able to hear her son's voice again.

Dora had an old answering machine that didn't save Kevin's phone number but did give her the option of returning the call. She tried to do that, but for some reason the call wouldn't go through. All she could really do was wait for Kevin to call again, which, in his message, he had promised to do. Every day, I asked Dora if she'd heard from Kevin, only to learn he hadn't yet called.

The week before Christmas, I flew to Chicago with my daughter, Emma, to see Dora. She loved having her granddaughter around, and the feeling was mutual. The three of us were hanging out together in Dora's living room one afternoon when the telephone rang. My mother picked it up and answered.

"Oh, Kevin!" she said. "How are you?"

My heart jumped. I took Emma and gestured to Dora that we were going to another room, to give her privacy for her call. Emma and I went into Dora's bedroom, but I could not bring myself to close the door behind us. I left it slightly open, so I could hear Dora's end of the phone call.

She and Kevin had a warm, unhurried talk that lasted ten minutes. "We knew you were going through a lot of treatments, so we thought it would be good to wait until you were ready to talk, because I am quite sure all of this has been very shocking to you," Dora told him in her calm, motherly voice. "I know this must have been a terribly long, hard year for you between your health problems and then to learn something like this, but I guess that's the way it was meant to happen. It's been many years that it took to get some answers, and now that we know, I think it is a good thing, Kevin."

It seemed that Kevin agreed with her.

They never spoke about the past, or even about the intervening years of their lives. They simply expressed how happy they were to finally be speaking. "I'm fortunate that I'm still here," Dora told him. "We lost your father Chet about two and a half years ago, but I know he would have been more than elated to have this good news also." Dora asked Kevin about his health, and if he was able to get around. Then she mentioned that Emma and I were there on a visit, and she asked Kevin if he wanted to speak with me. Kevin said no.

He told Dora he was wary of all the publicity surrounding the case. By then, several local newspapers knew about him and had tried to contact him, and he had rebuffed them all. "That is what I do, Kevin," Dora said. "I knew that if anything ever came out about this case, there would be a lot of publicity, and that's what I've always tried to avoid. We didn't want that. The media still calls me from time to time, and I just never talk to them."

As I heard her say this, I thought back to how angry she'd been with me when I first went public with the case back in 2012. I had been the one to summon the media and cause them to become such an unwelcome presence in Dora's life. And though I hadn't gone public with the news about Kevin, someone else had, and now the media was a problem in his life too. No matter how hard I tried to protect the dignity and privacy of those I approached throughout my search, it was, in fact, already too late for that. The story of Paul Fronczak did not belong solely to me anymore, or to Dora, or to Kevin. By going public, I ceded the story to the world.

The conversation between Dora and Kevin never seemed forced or awkward, though I'm sure they were both a little guarded going in. At one point, Kevin wished Dora a Merry Christmas. "Oh, Merry Christmas to you too, Kevin," she said. "This is the best Christmas I've had in many years, just knowing that all of this has come together, and that we both have a good outlook about it." Kevin suggested a time in the future when he might be able to travel to Chicago to meet Dora in person. "That would be wonderful, Kevin," Dora said. "If you want to do that, that might work out really well. I'll be looking forward to it."

And then the call was over.

When Dora last held her tiny son in her arms on April 27, 1964, and marveled at the perfection of his tiny features, and listened to the tiny gurgling sounds he made, and thanked God for the blessing of being this precious infant's mother, she could never have dreamed, not in her very worst nightmare, that she would not hear his voice again for nearly six decades—an entire lifetime. Such a possibility was simply not conceivable back on that spring day in 1964, when Baby Paul's future seemed limitless in its promise, and the sheer bliss of a young family could not be measured by any metric known to man. The child's presence in this world could only have been interpreted as a portent of good things, of pure and wonderful things, of the joy of life itself, with all its marvels and mysteries still to be revealed.

And then, after it all went wrong, after something worse than the very worst happened, after the nightmare began, how often did Dora think about the day she would finally hear her son again, if she even believed such a day would ever come?

Then the moment did come, and they got to speak to each other, a mother and her son. Connected in unbreakable ways, yet essentially strangers. Was it what my mother imagined it would be? Was it what I thought it would be? Had something of value been accomplished—something that might even be called a gift? Or was it all something less than that?

I didn't know. I wasn't sure how I felt about the phone call I'd tried so hard to make happen for the last eight years. It was, like so many moments in my journey, complicated and not easily summarized. After the call, I asked my mother how she felt about finally speaking with Kevin. She said she was happy. She said it felt good. She believed it was a good thing that it had finally happened—that the mystery of the real Paul had been solved. I agreed with her—I thought it was a good thing too.

Emma and I spent the rest of the weekend with Dora, and the subject of the phone call did not come up again. Dora seemed very content to focus on Emma, and on me. And I was glad that she did. I wanted to focus on us too. I wanted to appreciate what I had, at least as enthusiastically as I anticipated whatever it was I didn't have, and seemed so hell-bent on having.

"I love you, Mom," I said to Dora just before Emma and I got in the taxi that took us to the airport.

"I love you, Paul," Dora said back.

Then we hugged, and Emma kissed Dora, and so did I, and my daughter and I got in the taxi and headed home.

CHAPTER 20

The search for my twin sister, Jill, had a secondary search attached to it—a mission to find a photograph of the twins.

Even though Jill and I had spent only two years with our biological parents, I felt reasonably sure that photos of us did or had existed at some point. Who doesn't take pictures of twins? I also knew that my father Gilbert's mother, Bertha, kept a baby keepsake book of sorts, in which she had photos of her grandchildren. But, I learned, several pages had been ripped out of the book—the pages that would have featured photos of the twins.

But what about the photos taken by other relatives? Not long after my DNA connected me to Lenny Rocco, the former doo-wop singer in New Jersey, I made a trip to visit Lenny's sister Sandy in her home in south Philadelphia. Sandy, I was told, was the one with all the pictures; surely, she would have a photo of the twins. In fact, Sandy even recalled having seen a specific photo of us and felt pretty sure she had it somewhere.

Sandy and I spent a really pleasant evening sitting on her suede sectional sofa and poring through dusty old photo albums and emptying manila envelopes stuffed with snapshots. But after several hours, we hadn't found a single image of either Jill or me. When we closed the last photo album, my heart sank. How could the twins have been so thoroughly erased from the Rosenthal history? Even if you try to eliminate every trace of someone, surely you're going to overlook something. But no—Jill and I were totally absent from the photographic history of the Rosenthals.

"Wait," Sandy said after we finished. "There's more."

She remembered a couple of big plastic bins crammed in the back of a bedroom storage closet. I went in and made my way through years and years of clothes, shoes, boxes, and board games until I found two bins all the way in the back, hidden by clothing storage bags. They were heavy, which I took as a good sign—lots of photos. I hauled them out into the living room, and Sandy and I got back to work.

Many of the photos we found were fascinating to me—my great-grandfather, the boxer Thomas Rosenthal, square and sturdy, the picture of a patriarch. Lenny and Sandy as children, carefree and watched over by a stern Bertha. Layers and layers of family history, captured in hundreds of random moments—life playing out in all its sweetly mundane glory.

But—not a single photograph of the twins.

Sandy had one last hope for where the photo might be. She had an old tin shed on her property that was stuffed with storage, and she thought there might be another bin of photos in there somewhere. The shed, I was told, would not be as easily excavated as the bedroom closet, which hadn't yielded its treasures without a pretty good struggle. The shed might take hours to comb through.

It was late, and I had a flight to catch the following morning, so I had to pass on digging through the shed myself. Believe me, I wanted to. I wanted to have that moment of discovery—of first laying eyes on an image of my sister Jill. I wanted to feel the emotions of that. Still, we left it for Sandy's young son to do, and I flew home with at least a shred of hope that a photo of the twins, the holy grail, might be in that shed.

But there was no bin of photos in the shed.

I was baffled. It just didn't seem plausible that not even one picture of the twins had survived. The closest thing I had to a photo of us was a picture of my mother Marie, holding on to one of my older sisters on a carousel horse. In the photo, which was taken in

April of 1963, Marie was just starting to show her pregnancy. Jill and I were born that October.

So, yes, technically the twins are part of that photo. Yet they are invisible, not quite a reality, not yet tangible. Symbolically, I guess, that was fitting.

The search for a photo of Jill went on for five years. I was desperate to find one, if only to sharpen the mental picture I had of Jill in my mind. Without any evidence of her existence, beyond a copy of a birth certificate, I was finding it harder and harder to summon Jill in my thoughts. Was she still a child? Was she a grown-up Jill? There was no form, no shape, no dimension to her that I could hold onto, and that absence began to turn her into a specter—a ghost. There, but somehow not there too.

In the end, there was only one solution to the problem.

If I didn't have a photo of Jill, then I was going to have to create one.

I did some research on forensic artists and found one I liked in central Texas. Forensic artists are the people who create composite images, age progression likenesses, and reconstructions from skeletal remains, all in the service of law enforcement. We all know some of the more famous police sketches—the hooded Unabomber, the sunglasses-wearing D. B. Cooper—and they are a staple of TV crime dramas and movies. The artist I found, a really smart, friendly woman named Natalie Murray, was one of the top forensic artists in the field.

Natalie's background was in law enforcement; she'd been a police officer in Washington State. When her sergeant asked her to take a training class in composite sketches (he knew she liked to draw), Natalie jumped at the chance and never really looked back. She has worked on hundreds of criminal cases, including the well-known "Rebel Ray" cold case in Texas. One of her strengths, I would learn, was questioning victims and witnesses and getting them to provide vivid descriptions of facial features.

Or as the straightforward Natalie herself phrased it, "I sit down with a witness and draw a bad guy."

When I emailed her, though, I was asking her to do something altogether new and different—not draw a bad guy, or even a dead guy, but to create an age progression drawing of a missing person *without a single photo of her at any time in her life.*

Natalie didn't hesitate. She listened to my story and wanted to help. I collected and sent her every bit of evidence I thought might be helpful—photos of me when I was two years old; photos of our parents, Gilbert and Marie Rosenthal; the photo of my biological sister Linda that I took when I first met her in Atlantic City; and the photo my brother Fred sent me of himself. I also sent her the description of Jill provided by Susan Wolhert, the woman who babysat us just before we vanished.

"Did Jill look like me?" I asked Susan, desperate for any hint or clue about my sister's physical appearance.

"Jack, she looked *so much* like you," Susan said. "I know boy and girl twins can't be identical, but that's what it looked like with you two. She was just a little more feminine version of you. It was an amazing thing to see."

Thankfully, Natalie believed she could create an age progression likeness of Jill—an image of what she would look like today—based on the few meager bits of evidence I gave her. It seemed like a whole lot to ask of someone—create a likeness of a person who, for all practical purposes, had never existed—but I will be eternally grateful to Natalie for her willingness to take on the task. Because I was interested in the details of her work, Natalie agreed to take me through the process with her.

She explained she had a good starting point—the Rosenthal chin. My mother and father both had prominent chins, and "it looks like all of the kids inherited it, so that's a good bet," Natalie said. Men, she further explained, tend to have larger mandibles and wider chins than women, so she kept that in mind while fashioning her sketch. The nose, however, was trickier, since neither my sister Linda nor my brother Fred shared the length of my nose. They had more of what Natalie called "little button noses."

Similarly, the eyes and mouth were different for all the siblings. Natalie chose to focus on the eyebrows and lips. "I like the shape of Linda's brows, and her mother has them as well," Natalie told me. "I think that could be something in the maternal side, so I'll give Jill some angle to her brows." No one in the family, she added, "has particularly full lips. I like your facial lines, Paul, the slight dimple, the vertical mid-face from the zygomatic. It shows the muscle structure of the face. I'm keeping it in."

It took her only two weeks to complete the drawing. At one point, she considered having me on the phone with her while she worked on it, "as a way to sort of channel Jill," she said, but she opted against it. She made sure to warn me that forensic artists "go with what is most likely in our opinion. There's always a chance you'll get something unexpected for one feature, but this should be right for the majority of features."

Natalie sent me a PDF of the image in an email. I took a long pause before downloading and opening it. I had no idea what to expect, nor did I know how I might react to it. I had no better idea what Jill might look like today than anyone else, so would the image resonate with me in some special way? Would it touch something deep inside me—some distant memory?

Finally, I opened the PDF, and there she was—Jill Rosenthal. My twin sister, Jill. Natalie had aged her to my age at the time, which was fifty-six. She sent four images altogether, two of her smiling and two of her not smiling, as both a brunette and a blond. The images were warm and lifelike, and the eyes looked off to the side instead of directly at you. They gave the impression of having captured a casual, relaxed moment.

When I first looked at them, I felt almost giddy. Not because I recognized the face in the sketches, or because they triggered any memory or anything, but because, at last, I had a picture of my sister. I had something to tell me what she might look like, instead of having nothing at all. The sketches were objects of value to me, not evidentiary value, but real, meaningful value nonetheless. I could share them with people. I could post the images online. I could send them to the detective working on finding Jill in Atlantic City. I could try to circulate them nationwide. *This* is who I am looking for, I could now say—this person right here. *This* is what she probably looks like today.

The drawings made Jill far less of an abstraction or a specter, and much more of an actual human being we had to somehow find. And that made me feel closer to Jill than ever. In a very significant way, Natalie's drawings brought Jill to life for me. And it wasn't long before I convinced myself that Natalie's drawings would also, one day, lead me straight to Jill.

Meanwhile, the official police investigation into my missing persons report for Jill was at a dead standstill, if it had ever really started at all. For months after traveling to Atlantic City to personally file the report with Det. Jenkins of the local police department, I had neither received any updates about the case nor been able to reach Det. Jenkins on the phone.

Again, I well understood that the investigation would not be a priority for the ACPD, or anyone else, for that matter. The case was colder than most cold cases—a full fifty years cold—and there were obviously many more pressing matters the police had to handle. I didn't expect a full-time investigation, or even a part-time one—all I hoped was that Det. Jenkins would deliver the official case number to two national organizations, and that, if he ever found himself with a spare hour, he might interview my sister Linda about what she knew of our disappearance.

Ten months passed, and neither of those things happened. For some reason, Det. Jenkins had yet to make the phone calls to NCMEC and NamUs, the two national resources for missing persons cases. All he had to do was give them the eight-digit case file number, without which they could not open their own investigations into Jill. The calls would literally have taken him just a few minutes. But he didn't make them. NCMEC and NamUs felt bad about the situation, and even tried, without success, to reach Det. Jenkins themselves, but without the number, there was nothing they could do.

I couldn't understand it. What possible reason was there for Det. Jenkins not to make those calls? Had I not left him several messages asking him to do it, I might have accepted that he'd simply forgotten. But unless he'd deleted all my messages without listening to them, there was no way it could have slipped his mind. And why couldn't I reach him for a five-minute phone call in the ten months he'd had the case? I deliberately waited months before calling him the first time for an update, because I did not want to be a nuisance. But not one single update or phone call in ten months? I couldn't make sense of it.

Finally, I asked Nino Perrotta, the private investigator, what I should do. Nino had a very good contact at NCMEC, and he had facilitated my first in-person meeting with officials there. He also had a lot of contacts in local law enforcement. I wanted to know if he'd ever run into a detective who inexplicably dropped a case, and what could be done about it. Nino agreed to look into the matter. At the same time, in one of my conversations with Susan Wolhert, the babysitter, I learned she was friendly with a detective at the Atlantic City Police Department. That gave her access to people in the department, and Susan volunteered to ask around about Det. Jenkins and the missing persons case.

When Susan got back to me, the news was good. "I spoke to a detective there," she said, "and the detective said he will personally go question your siblings Linda and Fred, and if they don't want to talk, he will subpoena them. He apologized for the delay, but they will question them soon and give us an update."

I allowed myself a little cautious optimism. But then several more weeks passed without any word from Det. Jenkins or anyone else. Susan tried again and actually spoke with Det. Jenkins, but all he told her was that he had definitely referred the case to NCMEC already. He didn't say why it had taken him so long, or why he'd declined to return any of my calls.

I checked back with my contact at NCMEC, and quickly received an email with a response. "Unless the case was called in with a different name than Jill Rosenthal, we have not received it yet." The intake process for Jill, he explained, had not yet begun.

Now I was angry. I felt like I was getting the runaround. By then, Nino had gone through his own contacts and spoken with Det. Jenkins's direct superior in the ACPD—who, incredibly, happened to be at a convention in the same state where Nino was vacationing with his family. In their talk, the captain assured Nino he would deal with the matter.

That was progress, but Nino wasn't done. He was frustrated that his efforts to reach Det. Jenkins had so far failed to get a return phone call, and he was determined to speak to the detective one way or another. I was on the phone with Nino when, at 2:00 a.m. East Coast time, he called Jenkins, who was working the late shift at the precinct. I stayed quiet on my end, and was surprised when Jenkins actually answered. Both Nino and I listened patiently while the detective explained why everything was moving so slowly—the case was too cold, it wasn't a priority, Covid had cut into work hours. These were legitimate excuses, to be sure, but still, they were excuses. Nino asked Jenkins why he hadn't spoken with me to give me an update. Jenkins had no good answer for that.

"That's okay," I heard Nino say, "because I have Paul on the phone with us right now." Nino patched me in, and I got to speak with Jenkins for the first time in nearly a year. To say the least, he was surprised to be talking to me. Even so, he didn't tell me anything important, or apologize, or explain why he hadn't returned my calls. Instead, he seemed distracted and disinterested. The message he tried to convey was that there was only so much he could do on a case this cold. Never mind that I had given him contact information for three key living witnesses to the disappearance of the twins and its aftermath, all of whom he could have easily spoken to. Jenkins stuck to his assessment: *Hey, don't expect miracles with a case that's been unsolved for fifty years.*

I didn't argue with him. At least we had his assurance that he would make sure both NCMEC and NamUs had the case file number they needed, and that was hugely important. I waited a week or so before checking with NCMEC again, confident this time that Det. Jenkins had followed through on his promise.

But—

"Unfortunately, nothing has gone through our intake process yet," my contact at the center replied. "Unless law enforcement intakes the case with NCMEC, we're unable to provide assistance or resources on this case."

Now I was good and mad. Yes, my twin sister had been missing for a long time, but she was still a human being, and she was still missing, and didn't she at least deserve five minutes of a detective's time? Nino reached out to Det. Jenkins again, every bit as angry as I was. Jenkins responded with an email.

"I have just emailed NamUs, and I am momentarily contacting NCMEC," he wrote. He also referred to the nearly yearlong delay in making the call as "confusion" that had somehow come to surround Case No. 2003-0214.

Now we had another direct statement from Jenkins that he was finally going to make the calls. When I checked in with NamUs about a week later, I learned that Jenkins had indeed made contact. In his email to an official there, he provided an update about the case. "At this point in time I am at a standstill in the investigation," he wrote. "Due to the amount of time that has passed, unfortunately this case could not take priority over active cases I receive daily. At this point, I have no additional evidence. A sister was attempted to be contacted, however I have not received calls returning my voicemails."

I was disappointed by his explanation. In one year's time, all he'd been able to do was make a couple of phone calls to Linda? Then again, I could not expect Det. Jenkins to approach the case with anywhere near the same focus and intensity as me. I could not apply my own mindset to his. Instead, I had to accept that anything he did to help me was better than nothing at all. At least he had finally made the call to NamUs and, he assured us, to NCMEC as well.

Not much later, I emailed my contact at NCMEC to verify that they were now officially on the case. Though I'd learned not to be shocked by anything that occurred during my search, I was, yet again, floored by what happened next.

"At this moment," my contact explained, "the case has not yet come through our intake process."

Okay, I told myself—stay calm. Paperwork takes time. I let another week pass before I checked back with my contact, who had said he would reach out to Det. Jenkins himself. This time, his reply was even more inexplicable.

"After speaking with a number of people at the Atlantic City PD, there does not seem to be any missing persons report or case under the name Jill Rosenthal in their system. A sergeant I spoke with today indicated that the case file number 2003–0214 is blank in the computer system. From the best I can determine, there simply is no missing persons case for Jill on file."

No missing persons case for Jill on file??

How could this be? How could there be no open case for Jill? How could the case file number I'd been given come up blank in the computer system? What the hell was going on?

I sat there and thought about these questions for a long while. Only two possibilities made sense. Assuming there hadn't been some misunderstanding about the case file name or number—and I triple-checked that there hadn't been—either Det. Jenkins had never opened the case at all, or he'd closed it somewhere along the way.

I felt a deep swirl of dread and dismay in my gut. A possibility that I had long refused to entertain suddenly made a lot more sense.

What if it hadn't been just incompetence, or inefficiency, or a stifling workload that had prevented Det. Jenkins from making two simple phone calls regarding Jill?

What if he'd never even opened the case, because someone had told him not to?

CHAPTER 21

It was never my primary goal to "solve" the kidnapping of Baby Fronczak. I wanted to find the real Paul, that's for sure, and I wanted to reunite him with his biological mother. But solving the actual crime? Figuring out the identity of the phony nurse, and the motive behind the abduction, and the whole question of accountability? I always thought that would be handled by the FBI. Obviously, they have an enormous reach and access to resources I could never hope to have, on top of the power to compel people to talk. I couldn't compel anyone to do anything.

But as time went by, I came to the conclusion that the FBI wasn't all that interested in solving the crime.

Again, the FBI has a million more pressing cases they need to focus on, and tying up the loose ends of a fifty-year-old crime was clearly never going to be a priority. I really did understand that. At the same time, they had bothered to reopen the case after I took my DNA test, and they had at least two agents assigned to work it. I knew that FBI Special Agents were in touch with both my mother and with Kevin, the real Paul, as well as with Kevin's daughters. They were making calls and conducting interviews, evidence of an active investigation. But were they committed to digging into the circumstances of the kidnapping in 1964? I had no way of knowing. All the FBI would ever tell me when I checked in with them was that they were prohibited from discussing an open criminal case with me.

Mainly, it seemed to me the FBI was more interested in keeping the case under wraps than in solving it.

So, the question for me became—is it important to know the identity of the kidnapper, and the motives behind the crime? Is that important for my mother, Dora, or my brother, David? Do we all need the closure that would come with a conclusive parceling of blame and judgment?

What did we *need* to know?

I started with my mother and brother, who after all were the only ones that really mattered. The crime had been committed against Dora and her husband, who were deprived of a child, and against my brother Dave, who had his brother stolen away. Did they need to know all the details?

I knew without even asking my mother that she didn't. She was not interested in knowing who exactly took her son, or why. She had dealt with the kidnapping in her own way, and she was long past the point of feeling anger or wanting accountability. The gift of getting to speak with Kevin was enough for her. Besides getting to meet him in person, there was no other endgame.

My brother Dave was another matter. Getting inside my brother's head has never been easy. We've always been on different wavelengths. I was like Seth Gecko in *From Dusk Till Dawn*, trying to understand the brother I could never figure out. For instance, though I would only learn this later, Dave knew about the real Paul before I did. He was the one who matched with Kevin's daughter on a DNA site, and so Kevin's daughters contacted him. For reasons I still haven't asked about or don't understand, Dave decided not to tell me anything about the discovery. He knew I'd been searching for the real Paul for nearly a decade, and he shut me out of his life for undertaking the search in the first place, yet when he got the startling news, he kept it to himself. Perhaps he felt it was now his turn to be the detective in the family. I just don't know; as I am writing these words, I have yet to have that conversation with Dave.

I would also learn that Dave harbored a pretty intense anger about the kidnapping. Unlike me, who had been rebuffed in my attempts to talk to Kevin's daughter, Dave had access to them—at least until it became apparent that Dave's main goal was not reunifying Kevin with our mother, but rather getting to the bottom of the who and why of the kidnapping.

Dave felt it was essential to hold someone accountable for the crime. Even if that person were long gone, Dave wanted to know their name and affirm their guilt—he was out for justice, for Dora and for himself. When he ran into walls in his investigations, it only made him more hell-bent on digging up information about the woman who raised Kevin. "Literally nobody is helping my family understand who this woman was," Dave wrote in one online post. Though the woman was dead, Dave added, her relatives "have no remorse for her actions, or understanding for the agony my parents suffered over fifty years."

Dave even reported that someone in Kevin's family had told him, "Stop bothering us; she is dead; the story is over." Dave responded in his online post: "I'd like anyone reading this to imagine the family of a felon saying that to you, simply because the woman who committed the crime was dead. As if the crime never happened or impacted anyone."

I could certainly understand Dave's anger and frustration. Lord knows I'd been shut down by plenty of people who could have provided me with crucial information. And while I didn't have the same burning desire as Dave to hold someone accountable for the kidnapping, I *did* want to know who the kidnapper was, and why they stole Baby Fronczak. It *was* important for me to know these things.

Why? I'm not sure I know. If I had to say, I'd say it was out of a sense of duty to my mother. She was the victim of a horrific deed, a crime of nearly incomprehensible scale—the taking of her one-day-old infant *from her very arms.* The consequences of that had been monumental, and continued to resonate after fifty years. To me, it did not seem like an exaggeration to say that the person my mother had been died the day her son was abducted. Could such an atrocity really be written off as "old history"? Should its victims simply have to accept that the kidnapper is dead and the story is over?

And if pursuing justice and accountability disrupted the lives of people who had nothing to do with the crime, was that okay? Was that just the cost of justice?

These were not easy questions to answer, at least for me. A detective could approach the case neutrally, and devote himself to the pursuit of justice at any cost—after all, that was his job. But I had to ask myself if Dave or I had the right to get the information we wanted at literally any price. I had to decide if the family of a suspect had the right to stonewall the investigation to protect the memory of a deceased relative. Put simply, I had to decide if I would dig deeper into the matter of the identity of the kidnapper, or if I would accept that the story was over, and just let it go.

Once again, I ask you—what would you have done?

In a way, I didn't have to answer all these questions, because, as it turned out, information began to come to me.

I'd already found several people who knew Kevin, and they'd told me a little bit about his life. My hope had always been to meet Kevin personally; he was, after all, the man whose name I took and whose life I wound up living. I thought we could find certain common emotions related to our parallel experiences, and maybe even help each other heal. But Covid and Kevin's illness put that plan on hold, and all I could do was learn a few things about who he was and the life he led.

One of the people I spoke to about Kevin led me to another source of information. I will call this source the old man, to honor their wish that their identity be protected. The old man was someone who was not part of Kevin's family, but who was very close to Lorraine, the woman who raised Kevin. I was told before I reached out to the old man that he would likely never agree to talk to me. He had no interest in revisiting events that happened fifty years earlier. Nor was there any guarantee he knew anything to begin with. All I was told was that he'd been close with Lorraine, and that if anyone would know something about the kidnapping, it would probably be him.

That was good enough for me.

I dug around for the old man's phone number, and when I found it, I called him early one evening. No one picked up. The same was true of my next three calls. But on the fifth try, someone finally answered. It was the old man. I explained who I was, and I expressed my hope that we might be able to talk a little about Lorraine. I was expecting an immediate hang up, but the old man stayed on the line.

"Go on then," he said in a raspy but steady voice. "Ask me what you gotta."

I began with an innocuous question about Lorraine's background: Where did she come from? The old man told me a story about Lorraine's parents arriving in America, her mother on a schooner from Ireland "with one kid and another in the belly," and her father from Russia, where "he'd broken horses for the Russian Army just before the Bolshevik revolution." They both came through Ellis Island and met and married in Chicago, but tragedy soon befell them. "The mother had three boys, and two of 'em died in Chicago," the old man explained. "She blamed city living, and they got away from Chicago and moved north."

Lorraine, apparently, was raised in Michigan. I already knew from my research that Lorraine had been married several times, but I wasn't interested in sorting through her marital history. I was interested in the part of her story that included Kevin. I asked the old man how and when he first met Kevin.

"I met him when he was this little doe-headed kid running around," he said. "I asked Lorraine if he was someone's grandkid, and she said no, that's my son."

I asked the old man if he pursued the issue of how Lorraine ended up with Kevin. I learned that no one in the family was ever told that Lorraine, who was living in Chicago, was pregnant. Instead, she just showed up in Michigan one day with a boy who was already four or five years old. This was an astounding detail to me. It meant that if Lorraine was the actual kidnapper, she had kept Kevin with her in Chicago, or somewhere else, for several years after the abduction, before returning to Michigan, where much of her family lived.

I'd always assumed that whoever took Baby Fronczak got out of town as fast as possible, to avoid the largest manhunt in the history of Chicago law enforcement. But it was possible that, if Lorraine was the kidnapper, she had stayed right there in the city—right under the noses of the hundreds of police officers and FBI agents desperately searching for her. If that was true, it would certainly tell me something about who she was—and about how brazen her crime had actually been.

As I narrowed the focus of my talk with the old man, bringing it closer and closer to the kidnapping, the conversation changed. "Look," he said, "on that day back then, and still to this day, business is business, and people's business is their own business. Besides, that woman is dead and gone now. She's not in heaven, but she ain't in hell either. She's in the grave until Christ comes back, and then you decide which way to go."

It was the first of many admonishments to me to simply drop the matter—to "let that sleeping dog lie." I tried my best to explain my interest in finding out more, so that I could finally bring peace to my own mother, who had to live her whole life not knowing who stole her son. The old man softened a bit, and for the first time volunteered something about the crime.

"I do not believe Lorraine kidnapped that baby," he said. "She was a loving woman, and to put it simple, if it hadn't been for her, there's no telling where Kevin would be today. Leave it at that. Leave it at, she saved him from something worse."

I pushed my luck and asked the old man to explain what he meant by that. What he meant by "something worse."

"When it all went down, and everything was said and done, there was a mother with a loving heart, and she got him, and she said,

'Alright, give him to me,'" the old man said. "She helped out, and she did it out of the love in her heart, and she was helped financially to take care of Kevin."

Helped out financially? "By who?" I asked the old man.

"People," he replied.

When I pushed further, the old man shut me down.

"You will never get me to tell you what I know," he said. "It's all dead and buried now. Whoever it was took that boy, they are good and gone now. But let me tell you this. Lorraine was a loving mother. She knew right from wrong. She wasn't the monster in this. And people who make monsters up are usually people who have monsters in their own backwoods."

That was it for our first call. It lasted about thirty minutes, much longer than I could have hoped. After we hung up, I tried to make sense of everything I'd heard. There were, obviously, a lot of unanswered questions. Who did the old man mean by people? Why was Lorraine in a position to take Kevin as her own son? And if she hadn't kidnapped Kevin, who had?

I had one other question I needed to answer, and it was the most important question of all.

Could I trust anything the old man told me?

It was obvious to me the old man was very fond of Lorraine, and had maybe even loved her. He was insistent she was not the kidnapper, but rather just the loving mother who wound up with the stolen baby, presumably after he hadn't found another home. But what was Lorraine's connection to the person who gave her Kevin? Were they both part of the same child-kidnapping ring? Were they just friends, or relatives? Were they both complicit? More importantly, did this other person—the "real" kidnapper—even exist? Or did the old man create the person as a way to deflect all the attention focused on Lorraine?

I had to decide his motives for myself, which meant that, basically, it would be a gut decision. Maybe some of the information he was giving me was true, and some wasn't. Maybe all of it was a lie, or all of it was true. I decided I would get all the details I could from the old man, then do my best to corroborate them through other sources and records. Certainly, I didn't think I could take anything he told me at face value.

There was another factor that made me want to keep talking to the old man, even though I didn't know if I could trust him. I found that, during the course of our talk, I liked him. He was blunt and he was funny, and he had opinions about the world that were shaped by his own varied experiences, and those opinions were, I felt, rich with a unique kind of wisdom. He was a pretty fascinating guy to have a conversation with, and I hoped we'd get the chance to have a few more.

I waited a week before trying him again, and this time he picked up the phone right away. Our second talk was relaxed and friendly, just like the first. I got the impression that, though I'd been told the old man didn't want to talk about past events, he was actually enjoying looking backwards and, in his way, closing the door on certain events he felt were no longer worth his time. Or maybe it was just that he liked talking with someone. Maybe he was, like me, a person who'd found a way to get through his life and move past disappointments and character flaws, even if it meant being alone or lonely some of the time.

Whatever it was, we seemed to get along. I asked him about his life, and he asked me about mine. Eventually, I crept up on the subject of Lorraine. I really wanted the old man to tell me who he meant by "people"—the people who gave Lorraine money for Kevin's care. I figured if I could get a name from him, I could then do research on my own that might uncover the truth about the kidnapping. But the old man had his usual warnings for me.

"Why do you even care?" he asked. "The FBI don't care. It's all put to bed as far as they're concerned. Kevin don't care. Lorraine was his mother, that's all he knew, and he more than worshipped the ground she walked on, believe me. They settled down in Michigan, and it all worked out okay. They were happy with what they had, and they still are; they don't need you poking around. I'm sorry you got all wrapped up in this, but you ain't nothing to them. Nobody cares no more."

I asked him if he believed in the idea of justice in the world. "Justice?" he said. "Listen, this ain't God's world. This is Satan's world. Satan owns this world. God is the one who doesn't let nothing happen to you that you can't bear. He did it for me, and he can do it for you. But don't think God is running things."

I kept going. What did he mean when he said Lorraine took Kevin only because someone had to? Why hadn't the kidnapper kept him?

"Okay, look," the old man said. "Nobody wanted him. Kevin was shuffled, shuffled, shuffled around three times. Three times, and nobody wanted him, until finally Lorraine said, 'Give the kid to me.' If she hadn't said that, he might not have even lived."

Every answer led to another question. How could no one want a child who was deliberately taken from his mother? Why had they stolen him if they didn't want him? And who was doing all the shuffling? I needed the old man to be more specific. Despite his warnings to let it go, I kept pushing him to give me a name. If Lorraine wasn't the kidnapper, I needed to know who was behind such a hideous crime. I needed a name.

The more I pushed, the more upset the old man got. I still expected him to hang up on me, but he never did. He just kept trying to dissuade me from asking the kind of questions I was asking, and he kept warning me he'd never tell me the truth at the bottom of it all. And yet, he kept talking, kept giving me little kernels, little details, a bit more every time. I felt like I was on my favorite TV show, *The X-Files,* which always preached, "The truth is out there." I was Fox Mulder, asking the tough questions, unraveling the mystery, teasing out the truth.

"Who were these people?" I asked the old man. "Just give me a name. That's all I want. Give me a name."

"You want a name?" the old man said, anger rising in his voice. "Okay then, I'll give you a name."

I waited through a pause with my breath held.
And then the old man gave me a name.
"Al Capone."

CHAPTER 22

Alphonse Capone. The infamous 1920s gangster better known to many as Scarface, a nickname earned by getting slashed with a knife while working as a bouncer in a Coney Island saloon. The old man was toying with me when he dropped the name Al Capone. He was basically saying, "I can give you a million names, but none of them mean a thing." I figured it was his way of getting me to drop the subject.

Except that it wasn't.

The old man was dead serious.

He had to go back in his story to explain what he meant, all the way back to when Kevin's mother Lorraine was a young woman living in Chicago.

Back then, the old man told me, Lorraine "was like a movie star. More than beautiful. She would make Marilyn Monroe have to put on more make-up. When she was young, there is no word for glamour that would cover her. She was a little tiny thing, just five foot tall, and she was 52 inches in the bust with a 24-inch waist. Looked like Dolly Parton."

Lorraine's looks, apparently, drew the attention of some of the local gangsters in Chicago. She became, according to the old man, a high-priced escort for well-connected wise guys. "She was the mink coat on the guy's arm, the decoration for the boys," the old man said. "And she had the diamonds, and the minks, and she was always dolled up and ready for the show. She worked for the mob, and the mob wanted her around town because she would keep the guys happy."

Lorraine was not, however, a typical prostitute. "She was about the money, and she wasn't the broad you'd put up in a cheap motel," the old man insisted. "She would only get rooms at the highest-class places in Chicago. Lorraine once told me, 'Honey, I never lie; I was a hooker. But nobody ever touched me for less than five thousand dollars.'" Nor was Lorraine part of anyone's stable. "She didn't have other girls under her; she was her own woman. That's just the way she was. Her nickname was Penny—Penny for luck. She would be some fancy guy's good luck charm."

Lorraine would not have interacted with Al Capone; he was out of the picture by 1931, when he was convicted of income tax evasion. But in his day, Capone was the most influential gangster in the country. He basically cofounded the mob in Chicago, where his crime syndicate became known as the Outfit. The Outfit thrived during the Prohibition Era in the 1920s, and branched out into just about every illicit activity: gambling, loan-sharking, extortion, and prostitution, all policed by one of the most murderous crews in mafia history. Capone was behind the St. Valentine's Day Massacre, in which seven rival gangsters were executed in a hail of bullets in a garage on Chicago's North Clark Street, still one of the bloodiest mob hits ever.

After Capone was arrested, the Outfit only grew in scale and reach, with plenty of politicians and police officers on the payroll. The Outfit was particularly powerful in the 1960s, under the leadership of the legendary mobster Sam Giancana. As the story goes, Giancana rigged the 1960 U.S. presidential election to guarantee a win for John Kennedy, was hired by the government to help with the Bay of Pigs invasion of Cuba, and masterminded the assassination of President Kennedy in 1963.

Now, incredibly, the old man was telling me that, just one year after playing a part in the killing of President Kennedy, Sam Giancana, boss of the Chicago Outfit, had somehow also been involved in the 1964 kidnapping of Paul Joseph Fronczak.

My first thought was—the old man is nuts.

Even so, I didn't want to cut him off. He was really good at telling stories. Like I said, I didn't know if I could believe a single word that came out of his mouth. But what was the harm in listening to his stories, and filing them away, on the chance that maybe, just maybe, some of them were true?

I tried to steer the old man closer to the specifics of the kidnapping. He explained that there were two mob families involved in a child kidnapping ring in Chicago in the 1960s—"running kids" is what they called it. Lorraine, according to the old man, had some connection to these families, and played a role in the kidnappings. "Before Kevin, there had been a couple of other children she took care of for two weeks or a month, whatever, some short span, until they got to where they were gonna go," he said. In other words, Lorraine was not the kidnapper; she was the woman who cared for the kidnapped children until they could be sold off to a family.

"So what happened with Kevin?" I asked. "How did he end up with Lorraine?"

"When it came to Kevin, the mob had him placed with a family, but the heat got hot, things got smoking, and they looked like they were gonna get caught," the old man said. "So they ditched him. They gave him back. He was taken by the mob, placed by the mob, and then given back. He'd been lined up to be somewhere, and then things went awry. Lorraine never knew how or why that happened."

The old man said the mob tried to give Kevin to three different families. "The first one was a bought and paid-for deal, and when the deal went down, it went sour, and then it got even sourer with the second family, and then with the third, and so how do you explain this kid that you have that you can't give away? They could have just killed him. They could have dumped him in an alley. But they didn't want to do that."

It didn't escape my mind that while the old man was referring to Kevin as a "child" or a "kid," Baby Paul was actually only thirty-six hours old when he was taken. Not thirty-six days—thirty-six *hours.* He was just a tiny, fragile infant with a milk allergy, and here he was getting passed around to different families, none of which wanted to keep him. It was a truly sickening thought, and it showed a level of cruelty and indifference to human suffering that I could barely fathom. How heartless would a person have to be to do something like this to a tiny infant? And yet the people behind it seemed to handle it like they'd handle any other routine business. Apparently, there was no room for empathy, or even basic human decency, in the Chicago Outfit.

In the end, the old man said, it was Lorraine who stepped up and offered to care for the child. "She said, 'Well, fellas, I been here, been there, done this, done that, so I will raise him myself.' Now, Lorraine didn't have to take Kevin. But she loved kids, she missed raising her own boys, so when the deal came with Kevin—no family, no love—she said I'll take him. That took a strong person to do that. And she did it out of love."

According to the old man, Lorraine officially took possession of Kevin when he was three months old. With help from the Outfit, she arranged to get a fake birth certificate for him in a southern state. Lorraine raised Kevin as her son in Chicago for five or so years before finally fleeing the city and settling in northern Michigan, in the small town where Kevin essentially spent his whole life.

And that was the story of how Lorraine wound up with Kevin, and kept his identity from him for more than fifty years.

I didn't know what to make of the old man's tale. I had to admit that, at the very least, it was plausible. I did some research into the Outfit's history of child abduction in Chicago in the 1960s, and I wasn't able to find anything about a specific kidnapping ring. But that doesn't mean there wasn't one. Certainly, the Outfit had been involved in many kidnappings, both of children and adults, in the decades since its inception around the turn of the century. To think it was behind the kidnapping of Baby Fronczak was not all that far-fetched.

In some ways, it was almost too obvious. I could not believe that it had never occurred to me to even consider the possibility of the mob's involvement in the crime. After all, Chicago was famous for its mobsters, and the Outfit was fully functional, and indeed flourishing, at the time of the abduction. In fact, the idea that someone was kidnapping babies without the Outfit's knowledge or consent seemed unlikely.

Yet I had never considered the possibility. I had always assumed it was a woman working on her own who kidnapped Baby Paul, so she could raise him as her son. That's just the way the story played in my head. It was such an intimate crime—a nurse literally taking an infant gently from his mother's arms—that I just didn't associate it with typical mob criminality. And neither, apparently, did the FBI, or any of the many newspapers that covered the kidnapping back in 1964—in all the police files and investigative reports I'd read, the Outfit never came up.

But now that the old man had told me his story, it all made sense, at least theoretically. The original witness descriptions of the kidnapper—including testimony from my mother, Dora—painted a picture of a woman who was at least five feet, four inches tall, with an unexceptional build.

But the old man described Lorraine as being barely five feet tall and having—how do I put this—a more than ample bosom. Surely witnesses would have mentioned such a prominent detail to investigators. But they didn't, which gave credence to the old man's story that Lorraine was not the actual kidnapper—unless, of course, he was lying about her appearance. Later on, as I began to gather photographs of Lorraine, I could see that she did indeed fit the old man's description.

So then—if Lorraine wasn't the mysterious fake nurse who abducted Baby Paul, who was?

I asked the old man this question. Right away, it was clear he was not interested in giving me a name.

"The nurse who took him was affiliated with the mob, and she was a real nurse," he said.

That was basically all he was willing to tell me.

"There are mobsters still around who know about this," he warned. "Bad guys. And after it happened, the FBI dropped it, and the baby's family dropped it, and everyone dropped it, and that was just the way it played out. Crap happened, you know?"

I asked the old man if he understood that I couldn't just drop the matter and file it all away as "crap happened."

"Even if you find every shred of truth to it, it ain't gonna change a thing," he said. "They're all dead. All the people are dead. When it's all said and done, it's old history. All we're doing here is just talk. And talk is cheap, takes money to buy whiskey. So it ain't really worth talking about."

"Son," he concluded, wrapping up our long call, "you just gonna have to find a way to live with it."

CHAPTER 23

My talks with the old man led me to do a lot of thinking about the reasons I was on my mission of discovery. In his estimation, the mission itself was pointless. It would not lead me anywhere. No matter how hard and how deep I dug into the past, in the end, the old man said, "It ain't gonna change a thing."

Was he right?

When I decided to name this book *True Identity*, I could have put a question mark at the end of that phrase, and maybe that would have more accurately described what you're reading. Because, really, is there any such thing as our true identity? And is the act of trying to definitively pin down such an identity ultimately a foolish and maybe even destructive exercise?

In my reading, I came across this quote by a spiritual writer named Robert Colacurcio: "An inherent, essential nature whose identity is permanent gives rise to suffering, because this view of self is in radical opposition to the way things really are." In other words, those who try to define their identity as any one set thing are bound to run into trouble, because our identities are not fixed, but rather always changing. So many things influence our identity—influence *who we are*—that trying to wrestle some fixed meaning from this constant flow of influences isn't really worth the effort. Our identities will always be ever changing, all the way to the very end.

So maybe the best we can do is come up with a more general set of values that, we believe, represents who we are. Some collection of our relationships and memories and experiences that together make up an identity.

Or—maybe the smartest thing to do is to stop spending so much time defining your identity and just live your damn life.

That's certainly the advice I got from a whole lot of people. Move on, forget about it, it's history. "Learn to live with it," as the old man put it. But, as I've mentioned in this book before, that was something I just couldn't do—not while my twin sister, Jill, was still out there. Instead, I *did* spend a lot of time thinking about the meaning of identity and, in a way, searching for mine. I will admit, however, that there were times when I thought the old man might be right: even if I did learn everything I wanted to know, it might not make any difference.

But to me, that didn't mean the search wasn't worthwhile. The search was something I *had* to go through, because before I went through it, I had no real sense of identity *at all*. This was my attempt to discover more truths about myself, so that I could be a better man, a better husband, a better father. This was my mythical trip through the forest, so that I could wage battles and win victories that would allow me to emerge from the darkness a wiser, more capable person. The decision I made was to be open to everything and anything along the way, so as not to miss any opportunity to learn and grow. I'm proud that I stuck to that philosophy all the way through—I took my lessons where I found them. I learned from everyone I could.

That's how I wound up having a conversation about identity with a young man who knew a few things about it.

His name, coincidentally, is Jack, and we are family.

A friend of mine was going through some posts on the social media app TikTok when he came across a short video about my story. It was narrated by a man who said he had a connection to the Rosenthal family. When I did some research, I discovered that the man, Jack, was the son of Alan Fisch—my second cousin, and the very first close relative I was linked to by DNA. Alan, as I mentioned earlier, was a remarkable guy who lived in upstate Beacon, New York, and who I was all set to meet when tragedy struck. One day before our planned get together, Alan died of a heart attack.

He left behind a wife and three children.

Now, his son Jack was trying to sift through the trauma of his father's death, as well as Alan's recent discoveries about who his biological relatives might be. The short video he made about his father's role in my case was a compact, funny, entertaining recap of the whole amazing journey, told by someone with a personal investment in the story. It wound up getting more than a million views.

I called Jack so we could talk about his video and his father and his life. Technically, Jack and I are cousins, and when we spoke, we got along really well. Jack was very forthcoming about the challenging personal journey he himself was on: he'd been born female and had transitioned to a male.

"There were a lot of indications when I was six or seven that this was going to be my journey," he told me. "I cut my long hair short. I played boy games. I responded to certain androgynous stuff in the media. I did a lot of girl things, too, like painting our nails with my mother. But it was always there."

Jack was in his teens when he came out to his parents as a lesbian. I asked him how they took it.

"My parents were both conservative, but they didn't raise us with any gender holdbacks," he said. "They were always just really supportive. The day I sat down with them and came out as a lesbian, they both said, 'Yeah, we know,' and that was it."

Nor were Alan or Randi taken aback when Jack told them he planned to transition to a man. "I mean, it was hard for my mother, because when we finally talked, she said she was afraid of losing things like us doing our nails together," Jack said. "I said, 'Mom, I am not changing. What's changing is how I look.' After that, we used to just joke about it. My mom would say, 'Jack, if you don't wake up, I'm gonna sprinkle holy water on you.'"

His father, Alan, was equally kind and supportive. "By my teens I had just started wearing men's clothes, and my father took me to shop in L.L.Bean," Jack said. "The sales guy came up and said, 'Oh, the little girl's section is over there.' And my dad just looked at him and said, 'No. We're looking for the *men's* department.' It was one of the coolest moments of my life."

When he was eighteen, Jack enlisted with the U.S. Marine Corps. His maternal grandfather had been a Marine, and he always wanted to be one himself. "I hadn't started taking testosterone yet, so I was just this skinny little thing, and I was concerned about how they would take me, because they'd never had a transgender person in the unit," Jack explained. "But the military was like, 'We don't care, if you can shoot and take orders, we want you.' My whole generation was so tolerant of a lot of issues, and they fought for a lot of people's identities."

Jack trained hard for a full year to pass the initial strength-training test and scored the numbers he needed: a certain amount of chin ups and crunches, running 1.5 miles in under 13 minutes and 9 seconds. But just before he was set to ship out to Parris Island, an executive order by President Trump banned transgender individuals from serving in the military. "That was rough, very rough," Jack said. "That was the end of my military ambitions. But everything happens for a reason."

Not much later, Jack started working at a school facility for people with developmental disabilities, a job he still holds today. In his free time, he is also a very successful internet personality and a well-known performer in the thriving cosplay community, the arena for those who enjoy dressing up as characters from movies, books, and video games. "Because of my background, a lot of kids on the internet come up to me and tell me their stories, their struggles being gay, dealing with family members, all of that, and I dish out a lot of social service advice. I see my role as, I am the shoulder."

I was amazed that someone so relatively young who had gone through so much, including the unexpected death of his father and, just recently, the passing of his mother as well, could be so self-assured in his identity—confident enough to dole out advice to others struggling with their identities. Jack explained that it had been a process, both for himself and for those who were unsure of how to talk to him.

"People still approach me like I'm a wild animal," he says with a laugh. "I always say, 'Don't worry, don't be intimidated, just let's talk, be cool.' To me, comedy and laughter is the best icebreaker into any kind of real, meaningful discussion."

We talked about my struggles to understand my own identity, and how they related to his. Here was someone who, at age eighteen, several inches smaller and many pounds lighter than nearly all the other male recruits, stepped up and declared he wanted to be a U.S. Marine. To me, that seemed like an incredibly brave and gutsy thing to do. I asked him how he could have been so sure of himself and his identity, even while he was transitioning from a female to a male.

"The thing is," he corrected me, "I regard myself as non-gender. No box. I kept some traditional feminine aspects of my personality, but I also fix cars, build pools, do all that stuff. I'm very motherly, and I helped raise my two nieces and nephews, and my niece and I always talk about fashion together. So I feel like I can encompass everything in who I am. Why limit yourself?"

It occurred to me that by trying to define myself as a Rosenthal or a Fronczak, I might have been trying to force a change in my identity, when there wasn't any need for me to do so. "For me, I didn't change, I grew," Jack said. "I just feel like more of who I wanted to be. I always wanted to be the person I looked up to as a kid—a nice person who other people could trust and come up to and talk to. Someone loving."

I was amazed by how Jack, who is only thirty-one, made it sound so simple. And I admired, and was maybe even envious of, his genuine understanding of the person he was at his core. Throughout his life, he'd faced questions about his identity—was he a girl or a boy? Straight or gay?—but in the end he felt no pressure to answer those questions definitively, because, in fact, he believed there *were* no definitive answers to them.

"You don't fit into a box anywhere, so don't try to put yourself in one," he said. "Gender doesn't matter. We are all unique. We are all a lot of different boxes."

I thanked Jack for sharing his wisdom with me, and I made a promise to meet up with him as soon as the Covid pandemic passed. His thoughts about the nature of identity struck right at the core of my own journey, and the clarity of his insights really stayed with me, and probably will forever. He made me think anew about the reasons behind my mission of self-discovery, and made me question whether I might have been placing too much emphasis on the matter of my identity. Maybe our identities aren't meant to be pinned down or easily defined. Maybe they are perfectly fluid, always adapting, always growing, not ours to fully comprehend as much as they are ours to live.

Perhaps the only answer to the question, "Who am I?" is a simple, "Let's wait and see."

CHAPTER 24

After my mother's first phone call with Kevin, her biological son, the lines of communication between them shut down again. Several weeks passed without a follow-up call from Kevin. Their talk had gone well, and I think we all expected, or at least hoped, that it would be the first of many calls, eventually leading to an in-person meeting. But that was not the case.

I spoke with Dora about it, and she said she didn't feel comfortable being the one to make the call. "It is hard for me to talk with Kevin," she explained. "What am I going to say? After what that poor guy has been going through with the chemo? I just ask him how he is feeling. And he doesn't talk much either. It is going to be a little hard for me to call him, because I don't know how I'm going to strike up a conversation with him."

That was understandable. As I said, they were essentially strangers. And they both bore the burden of the terrible tragedy that united them, a burden so complex and extraordinary in scope that neither of them could have known how to process it. What's more, Kevin and Dora weren't exactly chatterboxes. Dora had never been interested in delving into what happened in 1964, and from what I could tell, Kevin wasn't much interested in it either. It wasn't a subject they were likely to unpack on their first call, or even their second or third. Perhaps it was something they would never talk about at all. So, what was left for them to discuss? My mother wasn't much for small talk, and clearly neither was Kevin.

In the weeks after that first phone call, news about Kevin's true identity began to leak in the local press. That presented an opportunity for scammers. My mother received a few calls from men claiming to be her "grandson" and asking for money. That made Dora so suspicious she began to dread a phone call from Kevin, since she didn't feel sure she'd be able to tell if it was actually Kevin or a scammer on the line.

Nor did Dora receive any calls from Kevin's daughters, who had been extremely friendly to her and seemed to want to get to know her. When my mother spent a month in a rehab clinic following shoulder surgery, she expected one of his daughters, the one who lived not too far from her in Chicago, to call or stop by for a visit, but she never did.

"I just didn't know what was going on," Dora said. "I didn't know if they wanted to get to know me or not."

It was, to say the least, a complicated situation. Kevin's daughters had a falling out with my brother Dave, who was determined to find out more about the kidnapping, and that probably made the daughters more hesitant to reach out to Dora. Meanwhile, Kevin was dealing with a potentially terminal illness *and* coping with the news that his whole life had been a lie. On top of that, a global pandemic had basically shut down the world. Nothing seemed stable; everything seemed scary and uncertain. Who could blame Dora and Kevin for having trouble connecting?

Eventually, Kevin did call my mother again, and they spoke a second time. I didn't ask her too much about the call, other than if it went okay. I wanted her to have the privacy she needed to feel comfortable talking with Kevin. Dora did say they talked about meeting in person, though no plans were made.

It was around then that I got an email from the Tipster, the person who had alerted me to Kevin's real identity more than a year earlier. They did not have good news.

"Kevin took another fall and is now back in the hospital," the Tipster wrote. "They also found two spots on his brain, and it is not looking good."

I was devastated to hear this. Kevin had been improving, and of course I was hoping for a complete recovery, which would pave the way for him to have some kind of relationship with his biological mother. I decided not to tell my mother about the setback just yet, but it turned out Kevin soon called her and told her himself. He was going back on chemotherapy, and their face-to-face meeting would have to be delayed again.

This was a really rotten time for us all. I hadn't had the chance to meet Kevin or even talk to him, but I still felt profoundly bound to him, and it hurt that there seemed no path for us to connect. It left me with a sad, empty feeling I couldn't shake. Why did he have to get cancer now? Why did Covid have to happen now? It all seemed so impossibly unfair, and sometimes it made me want to punch a wall. Still, there wasn't anything any of us could do except wait.

A few weeks later, we learned Kevin was being sent home from the hospital with hospice care. The cancer had spread, and Kevin decided he wanted to die at home.

This time, I called my mother and told her how sick Kevin was. Dora called one of his daughters, and said she wanted to travel to Michigan so that she could finally sit with Kevin face-to-face. The daughter told her she would ask Kevin about it and call her right back. Meanwhile, I booked a flight to Chicago, so I could pick up my mother and drive her up to Michigan to see Kevin.

My mother waited for Kevin's daughter to call her back, but two days passed without hearing from her. On the third day, Dora called the daughter and left a message. She also sent her two emails. More time passed without any word from Kevin's daughter. It felt to all of us like we were racing against the clock.

Another full day passed, and my mother still didn't know if Kevin was willing to see her. That's when she picked up the phone and called me. It was a sad and heavy call. My mother told me she no longer wanted to go to Michigan to see Kevin. She said she did not want to have to beg him to see her. A year and a half had passed since the discovery of his identity, and my mother felt Kevin had had plenty of opportunities to make a meeting happen, even with his illness and Covid. To know that Kevin was now seriously ill, and he and his family *still* didn't seem to want to make the meeting happen, was crushing to Dora. She felt deliberately shut out and deprived of the chance to see her son.

I hated to hear her say those things, but I understood why she'd come to that decision. I also understood why Kevin and his family might not want the meeting to happen, though sometimes all I could feel for them was anger. Why didn't they care as much as I did about reuniting a mother with her son? Didn't they see it was something that *had* to happen? That fate had ordained it by revealing the truth after so many years of silence and lies? Of course, I was projecting my own passion and perspective on them. They were entitled to see things differently, and they did.

I didn't try to talk my mother out of her decision. Even I understood that forcing a meeting to happen wouldn't do anyone any good. I apologized to her for failing to arrange the meeting earlier. She told me there was nothing to apologize for.

"I only have two sons," Dora said. "You and Dave."

I cried when I heard her say that, and I didn't know why or for whom I was crying. Maybe it was for all of us. Maybe it was just because life is so full of pain and loss.

On April 24, 2020, my mother got a call from one of Kevin's daughters. The daughter told her Kevin was dying and wanted to speak to his mother one last time. She passed the phone to Kevin, but by then Kevin couldn't speak. He was too ill. So, my mother did all the talking, assuring her son that she loved him, and that everything was going to be okay.

One day later, on April 25, 2020—seven years to the day that I first went public with my story in 2013—Kevin passed away.

He died with his family gathered around him, two days shy of fifty-six years from the day he was taken from his mother.

Not the best photo, but I believe this is Lorraine with the real Paul Fronczak a few years after his kidnapping. This photo gives me chills.

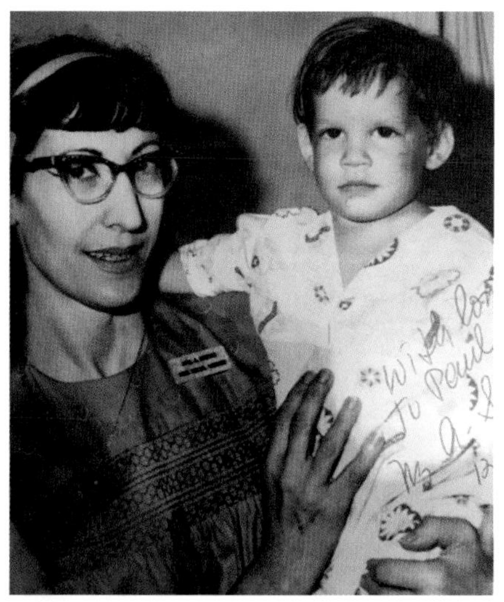

Me with a social worker not long after I was abandoned in 1965. Notice my black eye.

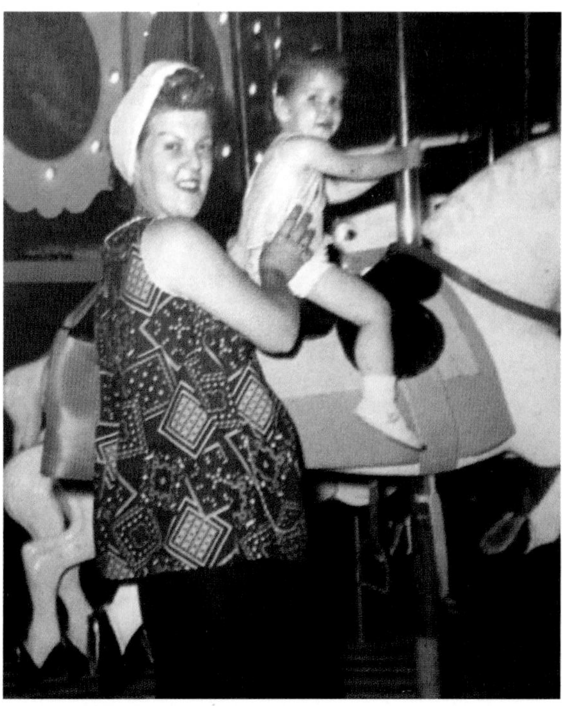

Paul's mother.

An old photo of Lorraine Fountain and her husband. She was the one who raised the real Paul Fronczak in Michigan.

Me with my father Chester Fronczak and my brother Dave. This photo always gets me, because I look like the odd man out.

Teaming up with my friend, the great private investigator Nino Perrotta, in Atlantic City. Without him, I'd be nowhere.

My buddy Alex Tresniowski and me in Angelo's in Atlantic City. He's been with me on my search since 2013.

At the police station in Atlantic City. It's not every day someone reports a sibling who's been missing for half a century.

STATEMENT FORM

CITY OF ATLANTIC CITY
DEPARTMENT OF POLICE
2715 Atlantic Avenue
Atlantic City, New Jersey 08401

** * PLEASE PRINT ALL INFORMATION CLEARLY * ***

DATE: 3/6/2020 CASE NUMBER:
THE FOLLOW... PAUL J... FRONCZAK
ADDRESS: ZIP: 89052
CITY/STA... HENDERSON, NEVADA
SSN#: DOB: 10/27/63 AGE:
HOME PHONE: — WORK: — CELL:

I, PAUL FRONCZAK, swear and/or affirm that the information contained in this statement is true. I understand that it is unlawful to provide information in this matter which I do not believe is truthful. In addition, upon signing this statement I acknowledge that I am aware that if I willingly provide false information in this matter, that I am subject to criminal prosecution for same. I further acknowledge that I have re-read this statement before signing it.

Please tell us the name and address of the nearest friend or relative that will always be in contact with you:

Please describe what happened.

IN 1965, I WAS FOUND ABANDONNED OUTSIDE A DEPARTMENT STORE IN NEWARK, NJ. THE NEWARK P.D. AND F.B.I. MISTOOK ME FOR PAUL FRONCZAK, A BABY KIDNAPPED FROM A CHICAGO HOSPITAL IN 1964. I GREW UP AS PAUL FRONCZAK, BUT IN 2015 I TOOK A DNA TEST AND DISCOVERED MY TRUE IDENTITY — JACK THOMAS ROSENTHAL. I WAS BORN TO GILBERT AND MARIE ROSENTHAL

JILL ROSENTHAL

SIGNATURE: DATE: 3/6/20 TIME: 12 Pm

TAKEN BY: PAGE ___ OF ___ PAGES

The summary I provided to an Atlantic City detective when I finally declared my sister Jill a missing person in 2020.

This is me in Atlantic City, just about to meet my biological sister Linda for the first time (in fifty years, anyway).

Digging a hole in the empty lot where my grandmother's house used to be in Atlantic City. We came up empty that day.

My first visit to the New Jersey cemetery where my biological parents are buried side by side.

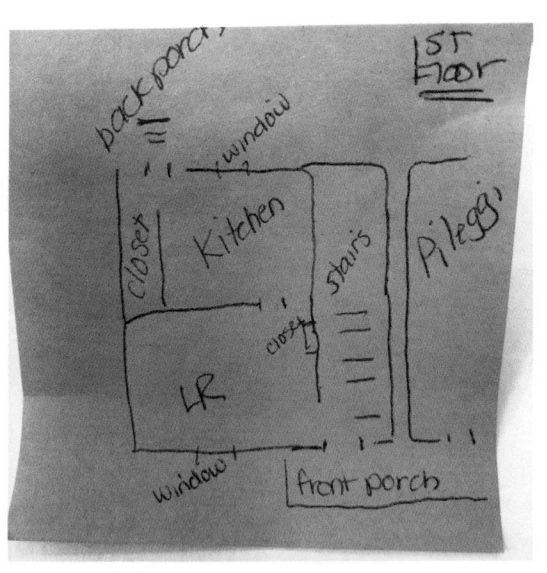

My former babysitter Susan Wohlert sketched out the layout of the house where I grew up, and was kept locked away, in Atlantic City.

Me and Susan Wolhert, who remembered babysitting me and my sister Jill way back in 1965. She changed how I view my story.

My mother Dora Fronczak and me in her Chicago home. In the last three years we've become closer than ever.

Meeting some of my Rocco-line relatives for the first time in 2015. I was nervous but they embraced me like family.

Visiting Elizabeth Stewart and her husband in their New Jersey home; Elizabeth's father, Newark detective Joseph F. Farrell, linked me to the Fronczak case in 1965.

My closest new relative, Lenny Rocco, and me outside his home near Philadelphia. Even the way we're standing seems similar to me.

Lenny Rocco and me jamming in his garage studio. He was the first relative I met who shared my passion for music.

Reuniting with some former Band X mates in 2020 (from left to right: Dice, Dan, Rick, and Henry).

Emma and me a few years ago. She calls me Jack Cheddar. I call her Soup (because she loves soup).

Emma once said I was a really cool dad. After all my searching, she finally showed me who I really am.

My precious daughter Emma and me in Las Vegas. We do a lot of activities together and she wears me out but I love her dearly.

Me and Emma. It's amazing to see so much of myself in her—that genetic kinship is something I never felt growing up.

CHAPTER 25

The first online obituary for Kevin made no mention of him being the real Paul Fronczak, sticking instead to his assumed name, date of birth, and parents. The obituary said that Kevin "enjoyed spending time outdoors and in his garage and garden. He also enjoyed time spent with close friends and family." When he passed, Kevin left behind three children and four grandchildren. "Cremation has taken place," the obit said, "and no services will be held at this time."

Kevin never got to meet his biological mother. They spoke on the phone three times, but that was it. For some reason—perhaps because I saw a certain fateful symmetry to it—I really believed the last-minute trip to Michigan was going to work, and that Dora, who last held her son on the day of his birth, would now get to hold him again as he neared his death. But then, maybe that was just my often-delusional optimism.

"I know this picture looked very different in your mind when you first found out Kevin was alive," the Tipster wrote to me around that time. "I keep trying to blame someone for why it all ended like this, but the reality of the situation is that we cannot predict how people will react to things they feel are bigger than them."

Of course, the Tipster was right. The decision for Dora and Kevin to meet was never mine to make, nor was it either Dora or Kevin's decision alone. So many factors were at play: long-buried emotions, fear and apprehension, suspicion and distrust, confusion, sadness, even despair. Maybe I should never have inserted myself in the middle of it all. Maybe if I hadn't gone public with the story and written a book, Kevin might have felt freer to reach out and seek a relationship with Dora. And what if my brother Dave hadn't been so forceful about wanting to solve the kidnapping? Would that have relieved some of the pressure Kevin and his family must have felt? Of course, looking for someone or something to blame for what happened was pointless. You could go all the way back to—what if Kevin hadn't been kidnapped in the first place? What then?

I didn't talk to my mother all that much about Kevin's passing. My emotions were pretty complicated, and I figured hers were too. I let her know that if she needed to talk, I was always there for her, around the clock. But I knew my mother. I knew she could handle bad news and surprising events. When the FBI first called her after they learned of Kevin's identity, they told her they could refer her to a very good therapist to talk with, if she needed that.

"I've survived this long," Dora replied. "I don't need a therapist now."

I didn't talk to my brother Dave about Kevin's passing either. Dave and I were still not on the friendliest of terms. But I did notice he made an online donation to a memorial site just a day or two after Kevin's passing. "Three Memorial Trees were ordered in memory of Kevin," Dave wrote on the site. "We wish we had the chance to meet you. Rest in peace. From your brothers and your mom, Paul, David and Dora Fronczak."

Local newspapers picked up on Kevin's passing and ran stories that identified him as the real Paul Fronczak. But once again, the story did not break nationally. I was glad it didn't. I knew the media would descend on Kevin's small hometown and dig around for quotes about him, and I didn't want his family to have to deal with an onslaught of reporters. It's true that I made my own share of calls digging around for information about Kevin before his passing, but I never set foot in his town or pressured his family after they told me to stay away. I have still never spoken to any of his daughters on the phone.

As was my habit, I followed certain online chat-room discussions about my case, and in the days after Kevin's passing, there was a debate about who was at fault for a meeting not happening between Dora and Kevin. Both sides were passionate about their beliefs. One poster fiercely defended Kevin's family and felt his daughters had no obligation to help Dave or me in our search for answers about the kidnapping.

"Why should the family feel remorse?" they wrote. "They are likely victims of this woman, too, or are at the very least traumatized by finding out 55 years later that their loving grandma was actually a kidnapper. But they had no hand in what grandma did, so why paint them as bad guys? The only person responsible for this crime is dead."

Another poster disagreed. "The Fronczaks want to know about their son and brother, and I feel the family could give that to them. They want to know about the woman who ripped their baby away from them and never thought twice about it. And even if all Kevin's family told them was, 'She was a great woman; we loved her; she loved Kevin so much; he had a great childhood,' that would probably mean the world to the Fronczaks. But what I see is the family of a felon being off-putting and selfish—too selfish to risk tarnishing their precious memories of this woman."

Others felt there was nothing Kevin's family could do for us. "What do they want to know? Kevin's family likely doesn't have any answers for them. And how would traumatizing Kevin's family help the Fronczaks? As for Kevin, he probably didn't want to meet his real mother because he felt it would be a betrayal of the woman he always believed was his mother. These people need to accept that this woman committed a crime nearly six decades ago, and the only person responsible for it was her. What insight could Kevin's daughters have into a crime that was committed before they were born and kept hidden from them their whole lives? If a bunch of strangers were trying to hold me accountable or demanding answers about something I knew nothing about, I'd probably want to be left the hell alone too."

Obviously, I was biased, but I could see both sides of the debate. Neither, I felt, was completely wrong. But I believed then, and still believe, that my family is entitled to look for answers about a crime that tore them apart and continues to cause them damage to this day. I am not saying that anyone has an obligation to cooperate with us, but we certainly can't be faulted for wanting to know the identity of the kidnapper. The idea that the crime happened "long ago" and is thus no longer important just doesn't make sense to me. Who is anyone to tell my mother how long she is allowed to grieve her kidnapped son, or want to find the monster who stole him from her arms? Or to tell Dave and I to back off from helping our mother do it?

You can bury the past if you want to. But there are no guarantees the past will stay buried.

I called the old man to talk to him about Kevin's passing. He took my call, like he always did now, and we spoke about Kevin in general. I was aware the old man had known Kevin well, and had spoken to him after Kevin learned his real identity. "He called me saying he was scared and asking me, 'What do I do?'" the old man said. "It scared the crap out of him when the FBI reached out to him. He didn't want nothing to do with any of that. He was ready to pack his bags and leave town. I told him, 'There's nothing to worry about, it's all a done, dead deal.'"

I asked the old man if he knew whether Kevin had truly wanted to meet his biological mother, or if he'd never really been that keen on the idea. "Look, Kevin was happy with the life that he had," he said. "When he found out, he was sorry for what happened to this lady, but he didn't feel the need to meet her and become friends. Kevin didn't want to hurt anybody."

Then I asked if he and Kevin had ever discussed the possibility that the woman Kevin knew as his mother was actually his abductor. "Kevin knew it wasn't his mom who did this," he said. "I told Kevin it wasn't her, so he knew the whole situation. As far as he was concerned, it was a dead subject."

The old man tried to impress upon me how insulated Kevin's life had been in upper Michigan, and how that affected his willingness to, in effect, welcome a new family into his life. "People don't realize what it was like up there," he said. "It's the backwoods. It's two sides of the tracks. The kind of place where sometimes you gotta whip a guy in a bar, you know, wrap a pool cue around his neck. That's just the way it is. Lorraine was happy with Kevin, and she took care of him and loved him, and they were happy. They didn't need any new people in their life."

We wound down our talk, and I told the old man I'd like to come up and see him in person some time. He said that would be fine with him. He'd never wavered from his statement that he wasn't going to tell me the whole truth about what happened in 1964, no matter how many times we spoke. It was something he was going to take to the grave with him, he said. So, it wasn't like I thought he'd be more likely to open up to me if we were sitting across from each other over a beer. But like I said, I liked him, and something was drawing me to see him.

After that call, I sat down and shared a beer with myself. I wanted to sift through my feelings about Kevin's passing. I thought back to the day when I sat at my desk at work and got a call from someone at Identigene with the results of my DNA test, about when I first knew for sure that I wasn't Paul Fronczak, and that the real Paul might be out there somewhere. The length of time that passed between that day and the day Kevin died was just about eight years—a pretty good chunk of my life. So much had happened in that time, but so much remained undone as well. Incredibly enough, I'd found the real Paul, alive and living only four hours from where he was kidnapped. But I'd failed in what was my primary goal—to reunite my mother Dora with her long-lost son.

So then—what did it all mean in the end? Had something worthwhile been accomplished, or not?

I just didn't have the answer, and I suspected it would take a lot more than one beer's time to figure it out.

One of the people I'd spoken to about Kevin was someone who had a relationship with him many, many years earlier. I reached out to her again, and we spoke about Kevin's passing, and the fact that he never got to meet his mother.

"I'm not surprised it didn't happen," she told me. "Kevin was always stubborn on change."

She believed one of the reasons Kevin drank so much and felt so much rage was because of not having a father. "He was always angry, and I think it was because of how he was raised," she told me. "I know he was angry because supposedly his father didn't want anything to do with him. He always said he'd never not want to be with his kids. So that really hurt him."

Of course, that wasn't true—Kevin's biological father would have raised him as lovingly as he raised his other sons had the kidnapping not happened. I was saddened to hear that was the trauma behind Kevin's anger, because it was based on a lie. And now I could see how hurtful that lie had been for him, and how his misguided animosity towards his missing father had, in a way, ruined his life. Imagine believing your father wants nothing to do with you, when the truth was that his father would have done *anything* to get him back. Letting Kevin continue to believe his father rejected him—letting the lie live on—was, in its own way, as sick and destructive a crime as the kidnapping itself.

The woman told me she did not try to talk to Kevin after learning he had cancer, because her feelings about him were still too raw. "Evidently, I have forgiven him without even knowing it, because when I heard he had cancer I actually felt sorry for him," she said. "But not sorry enough to hear that voice. He will have to ask God for forgiveness now." When Kevin had to go back on chemotherapy, word got back to her that he wanted to talk to her. But she still couldn't bring herself to call him.

Nevertheless, she says she feels sadness for him when she looks back on his life. "When I found out he was the boy who got kidnapped, I started to feel sorry for him then because I knew he would never know the full truth of anything. He had a right to know it, but the truth went to the grave with Lorraine."

I wondered if knowing the truth about his mother would have changed the way Kevin lived, just as I wondered if knowing the truth about the kidnapping would make any difference in my life. As always, these were unknowable things. We only get one life, and when bad things happen, usually they can't be undone or even explained. The only direction we can go is forward, away from the past, not towards it.

Yet there I was, in my eighth year of looking backwards, of trying to change the past—of *living* in the past, like the Jethro Tull song says. Even my effort to reunite my mother with her son was an attempt to fix something that had gone wrong fifty-six years earlier—a future event that could somehow influence or change a past event. Theoretically possible? Maybe when you're dealing with photons and laser beams. But with people? With human emotions and psyches? Kevin's tragic, untimely death showed me that the past, with all its twists and mysteries, can never really be undone.

Mostly, Kevin's passing just made me feel sad. I reread a letter I sent him not long after confirming he was the real Paul. There was such a hopefulness to it, a real expectation that something good was going to come from all the madness. "From the day I started looking for you, I always had the feeling that you were out there somewhere, and I always thought that the real Paul might be the only person in the world who could really understand what I've been through, and how hard it's all been," I wrote. "And I always, always told myself that when I found the real Paul, all I would want to do is sit down with him in a bar and have a couple of beers, and just sit around and talk."

Kevin and I never got to have that beer. We never got to talk about our strange, parallel experiences. I never got to tell him about his father, Chester Fronczak, and about how proud Chester would have been that Kevin followed him and became a machinist. I never got to tell him how deeply his parents missed him, and how desperately they wanted to get him back, and how his absence in their lives was a wound that never healed. I didn't get to share my family photos with him, and to see his in return, and to talk about our kids now, and to talk about how we were both doing as fathers, and to ask him what I had to look forward to in raising a really energetic daughter.

I never got to give Kevin a good hug.

One other line from my letter stood out: "I wanted to reach out to you today because April 26 is your real birthday, and I want to wish you a Happy Birthday, Kevin." I realized I'd sent that first letter to Kevin two years before he passed away. Back then, I truly believed that in that time, at least some of the pain of the past might be soothed by the blending of our families, the bringing together of a mother and son, the righting of some wrongs.

It turned out two years was not enough time to make all those wishes come true. Perhaps there wasn't enough time in the world to make them happen.

I folded the letter and put it away, and I thought about what I would say to Kevin now, if I was given some miraculous chance to finally talk to him. It wouldn't be any of the things I wanted to tell him—all of that seemed superfluous now. No, it would be a very simple message.

Your mother and father loved you always, Kevin, and I love you too. Rest in peace, my friend.

CHAPTER 26

I was still trying to understand why the Atlantic City Police Department failed to open a missing persons case for Jill, after leading me to believe, for a full year, that they had. Why had Det. Jenkins personally handed me a case file number if he never intended to open an actual case? I was confused and I was angry, really angry, but my friend, the investigator Nino Perrotta—who spent hours working his contacts with the ACPD to get Det. Jenkins to finally respond to us—talked me down.

"Listen, I'm angry too," Nino told me. "I'm so angry, you don't even want to know. But maybe we can use this to our advantage. This is our chance to pull the case away from him."

I took Nino's advice and didn't try to find out why I'd been lied to by the ACPD. A whole year had been wasted in the search for Jill, but, okay, I had to get over that and move forward. Nino said he would try to open a brand-new missing persons case with the New Jersey State Police—a much more efficient and accountable department than the local ACPD. If we could do that, we'd be back in business, and I might finally be able to get some answers about Jill.

Meanwhile, I posted the age progression images of Jill on my website, and sent them to some newspapers. What I really needed was for NCMEC—the big national organization devoted to finding missing kids—to circulate the images through their vast network of contacts, but they couldn't do that without an open missing persons case, and, well, you know. So, for now, it was up to me to spread the images of Jill as widely as I could.

Around that time, I got a message on my website from a woman named Angela Thompson Smith. She was a PhD who ran a research company called Mindwise Consulting, and she taught classes in the practice of remote viewing. "I usually give my students current or local cases to work on their third day of training," she wrote. "Last week we tackled the question, 'Where is the twin sister of Paul Fronczak, and what happened to her?' Through remote viewing, my students got a lot of information. RV is not always 100% accurate but there may be something in their data that helps."

I did a little research to learn more about remote viewing. It's described as something like a supernatural power—the ability to access accurate information about a distant place, person, or event through means other than our five known senses. But unlike psychic phenomena, remote viewing was a skill that anyone could be trained to learn. The ability to do it, apparently, resides in us all, and I guess it's a bit like intuition. Angela mostly taught the skill to individuals, but occasionally she worked on criminal investigations. In one case, she told police a missing girl could be found in a box in a shed behind the murderer's house. Sheriffs soon confirmed that she was right.

I called Angela, and she took me through how her three students tried to find Jill. "The term remote viewing was developed by an artist and writer named Ingo Swann, and he described it as sending his mind to a location and bringing back information," she explained. "Even the military has developed a protocol which they call Controlled Remote Viewing. Anyone can be trained to do it."

Angela's three students—one in Canada, one in Scotland, and one not far from me in Reno—were each given a set of randomized letters and numbers, or alpha-numeric coordinates, that they used to identify their "target," which in this case was Jill. On their own, the numbers meant nothing; they were a tool used to help the students focus their minds intensely on their target. What the students were not given was any information about Jill or I—no names, no details about us being twins, nothing to identify us in any way. "It is totally blind," Angela explained. "They have no specific information about the case."

Angela, who knew all about Jill and I, took the students through three sessions of remote viewing. In the first, "I did not direct them where to look," she said. "I let them loose in their own locations for an hour." In the second session, they all compared notes, and Angela gave them a little bit of direction to focus them on the target. In the third session, her direction and guidance were even more specific; the students had narrowed their searches down to a number of places and people, and Angela told them to focus solely on "the missing biological."

In the first session, the three students came up with different but similar information. One perceived "swampy, weedy water like a lake, and she also perceived there was movement or relocation of the biological." Another had "a wet feeling he described as rain." The third "felt a sharp pain on the left-side temple of her head, and she felt warm, and she also felt frustration that brought her to tears."

Ominously, all three "felt astonishment, frustration to the point of crying, and a sharp feeling of pain. There was also a sense of a one-sided argument and the feeling of 'How unfair.'"

In the second session, one viewer perceived "movement across water and land, possibly air travel over many miles, perhaps crossing borders, territory or a country." That was followed "by a sense of freedom." The location shifted from water "to a rocky area, a mesa, and to a large structure. The land was flat and large." The second student felt "a location that was humid and a tight space. It was breezy, and there was a hollow. He also perceived a suspended or structural beam and a long road." The third saw "a cave or a hole in the ground. The environment was flat, plains, and red dirt, with a vista of red-sandstone pillars. She perceived a white camper van with a sliding door and a long, straight, flat road, like Route 66."

Incredibly, the third student—who still didn't know any details about the case—also "perceived information that matched the target:

a second-related biological, a baby infant. She questions if it was buried. Hidden underground in a cave. She also perceived a male was hurt and stressed, but showing no emotion. During her session she was blinking her eyes and feeling nauseous."

For the third session, Angela gave the students some feedback: she told them the missing biological was a female infant, and she asked them to describe her and her location.

The first viewer described a female infant with brown eyes (Jill's birth certificate did not include an eye color). It was possible that the infant "was bleeding from something sharp, and bruised. And there was a sense that there should be four people but there are only three. And—there is a male child involved somehow. Someone is hiding, and there is the perception of lending a man some help. There is a man, and weaponry is perceived. The man has a record."

As for the location, the viewer now moved to "a location near a lake and a pier. People swim there. Then, a multiple-floor apartment building, inexpensive, a cheap rental. There is a car park behind and a motorway alongside where the speed limit is 70 mph. A second-hand car, a four-door, with a scratch or a dent on the driver's side door. Vegetation like a cactus. A red rock mesa with a rock formation that resembled a man holding a hat."

Her final perception was that the case involved "a boy and a girl—twins."

The second viewer "perceived an infant with blond hair, either two months or two years old [which fit me at the time I was abandoned] and a father who is tall and tan with brown hair [which fit Gilbert Rosenthal]." The third viewer "once again sensed blinking, as if coming out from the dark into the light. Perceived an underground cave that was stuffy and in the mountains. There was a humming sound, droning, like a generator. An overhead map view showed yellow, parallel lines and a pylon. The cave was on the other side of the mountain."

When Angela and the three students got together to summarize the findings, they felt the crucial ingredients were a cave, the long flat road leading to it, the town it was in (possibly at a high altitude), and a possible nearby airstrip or airport. They also felt the head injury to the infant's left temple was significant, and, sadly, they all perceived the distinct possibility that "the infant may not be found."

All this information, Angela explained, would only be helpful to me if it lined up with anything I'd already discovered in my research. On its own, the information was probably too vague to help—though all the stuff about mountains and cacti and caves and trailers and red rock formations and Route 66 sure sounded to me like Arizona, which was one state over from me. At one point in the sessions, a viewer came up with some kind of registration number—CAXY63262—which I dug around for but had no luck in finding.

Neither had I come across any evidence that Jill might be out west somewhere, or specifically in Arizona or Colorado or any state like that. What seemed clear from all their viewings was that Jill was somewhere she had no business being: traveling across state lines, in the mountains, in a cave, across the country from where she'd been born. All of which pointed to foul play.

I thanked Angela for taking the time to speak with me and explain the results of the RV session. I found it all fascinating, and I had to admit it was pretty incredible that a viewer somehow discerned that the case involved twins. But I didn't see any practical way to use the information. All I could do was file it away for future reference. Angela told me two of her students wanted to target Jill in future sessions, and she agreed to let me know if they came up with anything new.

Around that time, I also signed up for a hypnotherapy session with a licensed therapist in Nevada.

Hypnotherapists use relaxation and concentration techniques to lift you to a heightened state of awareness, from which you might be able to access information from your subconscious. People warned me against it. They said that if I succeeded in freeing up a torrent of memories from my past, I wouldn't be able to handle it emotionally and psychologically. I would be overwhelmed with whatever trauma or tragedy I discovered lurking in my subconscious. Start with regular therapy, they said, and build your way up to it.

It was probably great advice, but I didn't take it. I was too impatient. I was hoping hypnotherapy would allow me to remember what I had seen when Jill and I were still together, in the days before the mysterious event that drove us apart.

I sat down with the therapist and gave her the highlights of my story. She seemed genuinely surprised by the twists and turns. I asked her if she'd ever met anyone she couldn't hypnotize.

"No," she said. "Everyone can be hypnotized."

Our subconscious, she explained, is far more powerful than our conscious mind. But the conscious can only process a small fraction of what is stored in our subconscious. If it all came out at once, the therapist said, basically our heads would explode. Instead, you had to tiptoe into the subconscious, where memories are randomly stored all over the place, like a warehouse with a million drawers and boxes and file cabinets. What we were trying to do, she explained, was find and access one of those drawers.

She had me sit in a chair that reclined nearly all the way until I was essentially lying down. There was a trippy Hindu mural on the ceiling, and she asked me to pick a spot in the mural and focus intently on it. Then she counted backwards from fifty, inserting little whispered words between the numbers. I tried to fully relax and allow myself to be transported to some other state of being, but the deepest I got was a sensation of my arms seeming to float in the air. When she was done counting, the therapist guided me through scenarios from my past.

When she asked me to imagine myself in a crib alongside Jill, back when we were together, I felt myself start to cry.

"What would you say to Jill?" the therapist asked softly.

I felt the tears on my face, and I imagined myself sitting across from tiny little Jill, and the words just came to me.

"Jill, I am trying to find you," I said aloud. "I am trying so hard to find you."

"And what would Jill say to you?" the therapist asked.

Now the tears poured out of me as I listened for Jill's words.

"I am so glad you found me," I heard her say to me. "I thought I would never be found."

And as she said this, and as the tears ran down my face, I focused every ounce of my concentration on Jill's face, trying to see her, trying to see what she looked like, trying to *know* her, but I just couldn't get there, her face was just a blur, and after that the spell was broken, and I stopped crying and wiped away the tears.

I had been so close—*so close*—but not close enough.

After the session, the therapist apologized.

"I don't know what happened, but I just cannot get into your subconscious," she said. "The walls are really up around what happened in your first two years."

"Well, can you tear them down?" I asked. "Can you find a way to tear the walls down?"

"It doesn't quite work that way," is all she said.

I was disappointed. I was the first person she couldn't properly hypnotize. I did feel somewhat transported, and I felt the raw emotions of my powerful time with Jill in the crib. And I felt extremely sad that I hadn't been able to see her face. But I never felt like it wasn't me sitting in a chair in an office in Nevada.

Still, I can't say the experience was a bust. I wondered if another therapist might be able to succeed in somehow scaling or blasting right through those walls. And the release of all that emotion felt good.

As for my moment with Jill in the crib, and what she said to me, it only strengthened my resolve to find Jill in real life. She was afraid she might never be found; she was vulnerable and frightened. That was all the motivation I needed to keep going.

In the fall of 2020, a woman named Alda was watching TV and flipping through channels, until she landed on a repeat airing of the news show *20/20.* The episode was devoted to a single true crime case—the Baby Fronczak case.

After watching the show, Alda Googled my name and landed on my website. There, on the first page, were the age progression photos of Jill. When she saw it, Alda had an immediate thought: "Wow, that looks just like my friend."

Her friend's name, it turned out, was also Jill.

"I've known her for five years, and we've never talked about her past," Alda told me. "So when I saw the picture on your website, I immediately called her and asked, 'Hey, do you know who your birth parents are?' And she said, 'No.' Then I sent her the picture of Jill, and she freaked out."

Alda asked a few more questions. She found out that Jill—who actually changed her name to Jillian, but still sometimes gets called Jill—had a birth certificate with no name for either parent. The couple who raised her told her they'd adopted her when she was nearly two years old. Back then, they wanted to give her a different name—Holly—but they went with the name Jill instead.

Jillian had been told she was born in 1963, the year Jill and I were born.

At first, Jillian was hesitant about looking into her past, but Alda convinced her she should talk to me, and so I called her. Enough pieces fit to make the conversation worthwhile—unknown parents, an apparently fake birth certificate, and a mysterious adoption at age two, which is when Jill disappeared. And there was her resemblance to the age progression image of Jill, specifically when it came to the prominent Rosenthal chin.

I asked Jillian if she'd ever wondered who she was and where she came from during her childhood and teen years. "My parents told me I was adopted, which, when I was two, I didn't even know what adoption meant," she said. "They also told me my biological mother was a college student who couldn't keep me, and that I spent two years in the adoption center, probably because I had a birthmark on my face, and no one wanted me. Anyway, that's what I was told, and I never questioned it."

I asked her if she still had that birthmark on her face. She said she didn't and couldn't recall having it.

When Jillian enlisted in the U.S. Navy, she answered any medical questions by going with whatever her parents had told her. When her adoptive father died, he left her a safety deposit box that held a copy of her birth certificate. "It was a weird looking thing, with no parents' names, and it definitely could have been a forgery," Jillian says. "But I never looked into it."

Like me, Jillian never saw a single baby picture of herself. Her parents told her every photo of her got washed away in a flood. In fact, she never found a single official record about herself before the age of two. She was a clean slate.

I asked her if the possibility that she could be my twin made her any more interested in finding out the truth about her biological parents. "I had a really, really good life with the parents who raised me," she replied. "People would ask me, 'Don't you want to find your real parents?' and I would say, 'No, why should I? They didn't want me, and my parents now want me, so why would I go backwards?'"

I didn't yet dare ask her if she would submit to a DNA test, so instead I kept asking her about herself. The more we talked, the more she seemed to me like she might be Jill. She said she was very undersized as a kid, which fit not only with being a twin but also with being malnourished. When I was found, I was so small the police thought I was around sixteen months old, instead of my actual age, twenty-one months. Like me, she went into the military in her early twenties and, like me, she worked in the communications division. We discovered we both have astigmatism, we love tomato sandwiches, we curse way too often, and we like drinking beer (though not the same brand). Our conversation was easy and unforced, and before long we were both cracking jokes and laughing. We seemed to like each other.

I had a funny feeling that was entirely unfamiliar to me: I felt like Jillian could actually be my twin.

At the end of our call, we talked about her taking a DNA test, so we could find out if we were indeed related. By then, we'd become so friendly that Jillian agreed to take the test. I sent her a DNA kit, and while it was being processed, we spoke a couple of times a week. Jillian said she was having a really hard time waiting for the results. Normally, it might take about a month for the test to be completed, but because of Covid, I checked to see if there were any delays in processing.

I learned that, due to the virus, and the fact that Jillian sent in her test right after the holidays, the absolute busiest time in the ancestry business (DNA kits are a popular Christmas gift), the wait time was now more like two or three months, and maybe even longer. That was another bad break, but nothing in my journey, I knew by then, was ever going to be easy.

After I got the email from Ray Harp at NCMEC letting me know there was no missing persons case on file with the Atlantic City Police, I wrote him back and asked him to confirm that we hadn't gotten the case number wrong, or made any other mistake—that there really *wasn't* any open case. Ray Harp emailed back and said it was time for us to talk.

On the phone, Ray spoke with a slow, serious tempo, and to me he sounded a little like the actor Billy Bob Thornton. His title at NCMEC was Program Manager, and his background was in law enforcement; he was a retired cop from Arlington, Virginia. His specialty on the police force had been finding bodies—in backyards, in storage sheds, wherever they wound up.

Ray confirmed the ACPD had never opened a missing persons case. He told me he'd checked with several different people at the department, none of whom could find it. I asked why in the world the ACPD would tell me they'd opened a file, and then not open it. He said he was as baffled as I was.

Ray then told me he wanted to help me with my case. He was the father of two adopted children, and he felt personally invested in my story. He also felt bad that I'd gotten the runaround from police and hadn't yet received any help from NCMEC. "You're being victimized again," is how he put it. And he explained there was only one way to approach a missing persons case that was as cold as this one was.

"You have to work the neighborhoods," he said.

In other words, talk to people, get the stories, find out who knows what. *The truth is out there.*

Speaking with Ray Harp was one of the most positive moments I'd had in my entire journey. He was smart and experienced and aggressive, and he seemed to live and breathe the business of finding missing people. I couldn't have dreamed up a better person to help me learn the truth about Jill. Suddenly, it didn't matter why the ACPD had lied to me and buried my case; what mattered was that the delay had led me to Ray Harp.

"You came into this for a reason," I told him.

We spoke for about forty minutes, but it seemed to me like Ray didn't want to stop talking. He obviously felt some deep connection to the case. He told me he would use his contacts to get someone from the New Jersey State Police to open a brand-new missing persons case, and then actually work on it.

The very next day, Ray called me with the name of a New Jersey state trooper who would immediately start working on finding Jill. "He's one of the best at this," Ray told me.

Honestly, I wanted to scream with relief and joy, but I didn't want Ray Harp to think I was crazy, so I just said, "Thank you."

CHAPTER 27

Late in 2020, when the Covid restrictions eased up just enough to allow for some plane travel, I went up to northern Wisconsin to see the old man.

We sat on folding chairs in his backyard and talked over a couple of beers. He told me he'd been a much heartier drinker when he was younger, but had slowed way down with age.

"Don't get me wrong, I've been on a few tooters since then," he assured me. "But a two-day drunk costs me a week with the hangover, and it ain't worth it. Anyway, the good Lord takes care of old drunks and fools. I'm not sure which I am, maybe some of both."

The old man told me a story about the days when he took no guff from anyone, and occasionally wrapped a pool cue around someone's neck. It involved a neighbor who shot a deer on his own property, then watched the deer stagger over into the old man's property and die there. He asked the old man if it was okay for him and a friend to go claim the deer.

"He was very polite, and I said, 'Sure go ahead,' and I asked him what he got."

"An eight-point," the neighbor responded.

"Okay, then," the old man said. "Can I get a look at him when you get him out of there?"

The neighbor and his friend agreed, and they drove a four-wheeler out to where the old man had his own deer blind. About ninety minutes later, the men drove back with the eight-point tied across the front of his four-wheeler. When he saw it, the old man's face turned red.

"They'd already gutted him out back!" he told me. "Gutted him and left all the entrails on my property! Right where I do my hunting! I said, 'Excuse me, what the hell is this?'"

The neighbor, who'd known the old man's father, was defiant and told him he had a bad attitude. The old man did not back down one bit.

"If you'd done this to my dad, he'd have shot your ass," he told the neighbor. "So get going and don't come back or I will shoot you myself.'"

By the next day, the entrails were waiting for the neighbor on his front lawn.

"I've mellowed out since then," the old man said.

In one of our earlier talks, the old man had mentioned that Lorraine had a good friend back in Chicago, and that this woman had sometimes helped her with Kevin. Someone else who knew Kevin told me he talked about an "aunt" who helped raise him. I figured out this was the same woman, and I asked the old man about her. He told me her name was Aura Baty.

He didn't tell me much about her, but he did admit that Lorraine borrowed her friend's last name and used it for Kevin. That was the answer to one of the many perplexing mysteries surrounding Kevin—where did his last name come from? Lorraine had been married at least four times, but none of her husbands were named Baty. The lie Lorraine told Kevin was that his father was a Detroit Lions football player named Baty. But when I checked every Detroit Lions player roster from 1960 to 1970, I didn't find anyone named Baty who ever played for them.

This, however, made sense. Lorraine got the name from her friend, Aura Baty.

But now, sitting across from me in his backyard, the old man told a different story.

"I lied to you," he said. "I'm not a liar, and it's bothered me since I did it. The truth is, there is no Aura Baty. I made her up. I made her up to throw a wrench in your investigations."

In fact, I'd spent several hours trying to track down anyone named Aura or Aurora or Orra Baty, with no success.

"So where did the last name come from?" I asked.

The old man shrugged and said, "I have no idea. Maybe she pulled it out of the blue."

I didn't know if I should believe him. I didn't know if I should have believed him then when he told me about Aura Baty, and I didn't know if I should believe him now that he was saying he made her up. I felt a knot in my gut, and I got the feeling I'd traveled up to see the old man for no good reason. I couldn't be sure anything he told me was even remotely close to being true.

Most likely everything he told me was a lie.

Still, I stuck around and listened to more of his stories. Soon enough, he told me the most astonishing story of all.

I thought long and hard about even sharing the story in this book. A big part of me didn't want to. I didn't believe it when he told it, and I certainly don't believe it now. But I've tried to be totally honest in this book, and the old man's story was his final conclusion about what happened in 1964. It is part of the journey, so I'm sharing it now.

When our conversation shifted to the kidnapping of Baby Fronczak, we went back and forth like we usually did, me pushing, him pushing back. I was stuck on the idea that Aura Baty not only existed, but was the mysterious woman in the nurse's outfit—the actual kidnapper. I pushed the old man on this point, defying him to give me a name if the name I was looking for wasn't, in fact, Aura Baty.

"Son, back up and listen," he said. "You've done a lot of listening, but you haven't done as much listening as you should. It is all there. I would like the story to come out, but it would have to be absolutely truthful. That's what you're not getting."

I asked him what exactly I wasn't getting.

"There's a whole lot of hidden bodies," he said. "If we're gonna do this, let's do it, let's go down to the basement, let's go to the attic. There's a whole lot of other involvement, if you want to go through that door."

I told him I wanted to do it—I wanted the name of the person who kidnapped the baby.

"Look, the FBI backed out of this. Why? The mob controls the FBI. The FBI has to work with the mob."

"Forget the FBI," I told him. "Just tell me the name."

"What good's a name gonna do you? To name the names of the boys from the big stores? They're all gone. And to try to drag the new ones into this? You don't want to do that either."

"I don't care about mobsters," I said. "Who was the one who took the baby?"

"The lady who took the baby is gone. She's dead and gone. Now Kevin is gone, and his mother's gone too. There ain't nowhere else to look, and besides, what good would it do? It's all still gonna be old history."

"Just tell me," I said. "Just give me the name. Who took him from his mother? *Who kidnapped that boy?*"

That's when the old man looked at me like I was dumb.

"Kidnapped?" he said. "Son, haven't you figured it out already? There *was* no kidnapping. *The boy wasn't kidnapped.*"

Then the old man told me his story.

It was all about money, he said. Money talks and people make mistakes. What she did was a mistake, he said, but when push comes to shove, you either survive or someone else does.

"Who made the mistake?" I asked. "Who is she?"

"The mother," the old man said. "The mother and the father. It wasn't a kidnapping. They were in on it."

He was talking about Dora and Chester Fronczak.

I got really angry at that point, and I wanted to get up and leave. But I stayed in my lawn chair, and I stayed quiet. I thought I might as well hear the whole story. Still, my blood was on fire.

The old man said they were in a situation, and they couldn't get out of it. Call it a gambling debt, he said. And the mob offered them a deal, and they both said no, but the mob said, *Listen, you need to do this,* and the mother said, *Okay, I'll take the deal,* and the father said, *Okay, we'll do what we have to do.*

Okay, so then the fake nurse, I said, and the old man said, No, the nurse wasn't fake. She was a real nurse. "And the nurse was someone who worked for whoever and whatever, you know? So the mother hands the baby to the nurse, and the baby was handed from that nurse to beyond. So, the deal is done.

"But it wasn't supposed to get big like it did. And everyone gets caught in the crap, and how are we gonna clean this up now? It was never a regular family who was gonna get the baby, it was someone in the mob. But then it turns into a bad deal, and the nurse has to disappear, and her life is ruined forever, and the mother changes her mind afterwards and wants the baby back, but by then the deal is done.

"So now the baby is out of the picture, and then you turn up on a street, and they go, here's a good place where we can appease the family, and they can raise him and be happy, that's what happens. Everybody is happy then. The whole pot is nice.

"And it all blows up over a stupid DNA test."

"Paul," the old man concluded, "you stirred up so much shit we ain't got boots high enough for it all."

After hearing the story, all I had was a hollowed-out feeling in my gut. I didn't believe a word of it, not for a second. Dora Fronczak might not have been my biological mother, but she *was* my mother, and I knew her—I knew who she was as a person. She was a kind, decent, caring, and loving person, through and through. She believed in God and went to mass every Sunday, and she raised her sons to be straight arrows, honest and true in all their deeds. My father Chester was the same way. They did not have any evil side to them, or any dark and sinister impulses. There was no conceivable reality in which my parents would have agreed to hand over their firstborn son. None.

It was a lie, told by the old man to deflect attention from Lorraine and absolve her of any guilt.

The old man sensed I didn't believe him, and said, "There is good and bad in all. Good cops and bad cops. Good people and bad people. People pay people off. People do things. Then they move forward, and life goes on, and you're just gonna have to accept that, Paul. Some things, you can't go back and change."

I got up to leave. The meeting was over for me. I could live with many of the old man's lies and half-truths, but not this one. I shook his hand and thanked him for the beers and for his hospitality, and for agreeing to talk to me at all.

The old man's handshake was still firm. He looked right at me and shared his final thought.

"Paul, on my deathbed, I will write a letter to you and put it in the mail. So, one day, you will get a letter that answers all your questions. Until then, we all gotta live with our consciences. Then we get to St. Peter's Gate, and we won't have to answer to no one but God."

CHAPTER 28

One night I had a dream about my twin sister, Jill. The dream echoed a moment in my hypnotherapy session, when the therapist asked me to talk to young Jill in her crib. In my dream, I was in a crib with Jill, and we were looking at each other, and I could clearly see her face. But her face was blank. There was nothing there. I woke up angry and frustrated, mostly with myself.

Why couldn't I remember Jill's face? I'd spent two years looking at it when we were together: shouldn't I remember something about her? Shouldn't I recall something of the event that led to us being pulled apart? A flash of memory? The slightest sense of her presence? But no—nothing. I felt sure that some piece of Jill remained in my brain, just beyond my reach.

To believe that Jill existed in my conscious or subconscious, and yet to not be able to summon any trace of her at all, was truly maddening. It was like, after having so many people refuse to tell me what they knew about Jill, I was doing the same thing to myself. Like I was hiding the truth from myself.

After I was done speaking with the old man, I focused harder on the Rosenthal mystery. I was finally able to talk with a woman named Katherine Chapman Pope, a specialist with the National Missing & Unidentified Persons Systems, or NamUs. This was an organization that lent far-reaching technical and forensic support to agencies, like the FBI, involved in finding missing persons. I'd always known about them, but I hadn't turned to them for help because it would have meant filing a missing persons report for Jill, something I held off on doing while I did most of the searching myself.

But now that I finally had an open missing persons case, I got on the phone with Katherine to see if NamUs might be able to help. Katherine was kind, reassuring, generous, and direct. "This is a very old case, so it's not considered an acute case, which is what we call more current, ongoing missing children cases," she explained. "But it's also true that this case is acute to *you.* You are still missing a loved one, even sixty years later, so I don't ever want to hear someone say they are too busy to help with this case, or that they're not working on it at all. That's not an answer I will accept."

Katherine explained how missing persons cases are not standardized in the field of law enforcement, which means that protocols and investigations differ from state to state. That can present problems, and NamUs steps in to help solve those problems. She said the factors that can make a big difference in cold cases like mine are having surviving family members who can help create a robust family tree, and, ideally, having the missing person's exact DNA. In Jill's case, we had a great many uncooperative relatives, yet we still managed to put together an extensive Rosenthal family tree. But we didn't have any of Jill's DNA. The best we had was my DNA, fifty percent of which I shared with all my siblings, including my fraternal twin.

What Katherine could do to help was coordinate with the lead investigative officer in the missing persons case, and offer all the support he might need. For me, this was really good news. It meant I had a team in place that included high-quality backup. I felt like I had smart, dedicated, professional people on my side—something I hadn't always felt.

"Time is ticking, and you deserve answers," Katherine said, before adding a caveat I'd heard many times before. "There are extenuating circumstances. The pandemic. The age of this case. A surge of newer, more urgent cases. You need to take that into consideration going forward. There are many families who have done everything they possibly could, the best detectives, the best investigators, and they still didn't get any answers. It is a struggle, and you have to keep your expectations realistic."

"But please," Katherine said finally, "please know that you are not alone. We are on this case with you. So do not give up hope."

I also spoke with the New Jersey state trooper who took over Jill's case after the Atlantic City PD sat on it for a year. He was, in contrast to other officers I'd worked with, an impressive figure. He knew a lot about my case, and he asked me pointed, detailed questions about whatever he didn't know. In just a few minutes of speaking with him, I knew I was in good hands. "This is what I do," the state trooper assured me. "Find people."

I told him what I'd told other investigators before him—that I believe there is someone alive who knows what happened to Jill, or at least knows more than anyone else, and that is my biological sister Linda. The trooper said he would do his best to question her, but I know how difficult she can be to get through to. My hope is that the trooper, with all his resources, will be able to get an honest story out of Linda, something I failed to do.

In the meantime, I answered emails from women who'd seen our age progression images of my twin and wondered if they might be Jill. Some of them simply didn't match up chronologically, or for other reasons, but sometimes there was enough probable cause to make us want to do a DNA test. One woman, whose name is Laura, said she remembered being teased by relatives about the nursery rhyme "Jack and Jill," yet not understanding what it had to do with her. At sixteen she was emancipated from her parents, who threatened her harm should she ever take a DNA test. Later on in her life, one relative confronted her and insisted her name was Jill. Her family history was deeply muddled, full of lore and lies and made-up stories; even the baby photos she had of herself were, she later learned, actually of another child.

"I am looking for answers," Laura told me. "Paul, you may be my last option. I don't know where else to turn."

Unfortunately, a DNA test showed Laura and I were not related.

I was, by then, a veteran of disappointing DNA test results. I can't remember how many times I've been on the receiving end of bad news regarding a promising potential match. Sometimes the pieces seemed to fit so well, and a match seemed so likely, that I allowed myself a kind of reckless optimism. Yet every time, I'd been let down, quickly and coldly.

And not just me, but also the many possible real Pauls and possible Jills I've crossed paths with. They, too, were on journeys of self-discovery, pushing through setbacks, enduring year after year, dealing with dead ends and dashed hopes. I felt bad for every one of them, every time. I think I understood their pain. The finality of a DNA test can be a terrible shock, wiping away as it does every last shred of hope. Most of the time, we live in a murky netherworld of clues and leads and possible outcomes, all of which encourage hope. But then, with the harsh brutality of a slap across the face, reality intrudes in the form of incontrovertible evidence. The faint and brittle hope of not knowing can sustain us for a long while, but a disappointing truth can plunge us into months of darkness and despair.

Yet even knowing how stacked the odds were against me, I still allowed myself to be optimistic about one possible Jill.

This was the woman named Jillian, who I've mentioned earlier. She'd been told she was born in 1963, the year I was born. She was told she was adopted at two, the age when Jill disappeared. Her birth certificate didn't list a name for either parent. Later on, when she went searching for her identity, she couldn't find a single public record about herself before the age of two. And she looked just like our age progression image of Jill, which meant she shared some of my distinctive facial features, most glaringly my chin. Coincidentally, her grandson's middle name was Jack.

But beyond these data points was the feeling I got when we spoke. We had a completely unforced familiarity and comfort level with each other, and our phone conversations were filled with jokes and laughs. I'm not sure if I ever felt that comfortable that quickly with anyone before. We learned we both worked in a communications division in the military, both had astigmatism, and both loved tomato sandwiches. Before long we admitted to each other that we were hoping we were brother and sister. "That would be so great," Jillian remarked in one text. "I am so, so excited to find out."

For most of her life, Jillian told me, "I seriously never even thought of looking for my family, because I just figured whoever had me didn't want me, so why bother?" But now, she said, "I'm kinda thinking I need a new brother."

The day she dropped off her completed DNA kit at the post office, she texted: "I did it…yay! Cross your fingers!!!! We are doing this!!!"

In early April 2021, I opened another text from Jillian.

> *Well, the results are in and it's looking like we are not brother and sister… I am sorry.*

I immediately hopped onto my own Ancestry page, hoping beyond hope that somehow she'd misread the results. But she hadn't. We were not related. Jillian was not Jill. "Wow," I texted back, "I was really hoping you were my sister." She responded quickly.

> *I was too, and I am sad. I really hope you find Jill. For me, it looks like I have one second cousin out there, but I think I will probably just leave it alone. I am okay with not knowing too much. I was just hoping it was you.*

I told her I thought that she was awesome, and that I'd love it if we could meet one day soon and sit down for a beer or two.

It was, as they all have been, a crushing end to a hopeful moment. For me, it was the closest I'd yet come to feeling like I actually *had* a twin sister. The idea of having a twin had always been abstract to me, but for the two or so months that Jillian and I went through the process of getting her DNA tested, it suddenly felt like it was real. Like *this* is what it feels like to be that close with someone, and to be able to pick up the phone and just talk and laugh, and to have this mysterious force that binds us in ways we can't understand, or ever need to explain.

I know now that the feeling I had in those two months was only an illusion—an artificial manifestation of a desperate wish.

Even so, the truth is that it felt good. It felt *really* good.

And it was bittersweet because it showed me what I'd been missing.

In the years since I discovered my real name was Jack Thomas Rosenthal, I learned a lot about the Rosenthal family, and about what forces brought them to the place where Gilbert and Marie Rosenthal—my parents—could do something as heinous and unthinkable as abandoning their two-year-old son on a street corner in Newark, New Jersey.

Initially, I thought I had a tenuous understanding of what might have happened. My mother Marie was under enormous pressure after having five children in four years, and she succumbed to alcoholism, and—when my father Gilbert walked out on her for six months—was driven to eliminate two of those children in a desperate bid to hold her badly broken family together. Whether my twin Jill was deliberately harmed, or whether she was hurt in a reckless accident, was unknown. But family stories made it seem that Jill's demise was the incident that prompted my mother to abandon me, and wipe out any trace of the twins altogether.

That is a horrifying, nearly incomprehensible scenario on its own, but at least it held together as a plausible theory of what happened.

Then I met Susan Wolhert, the woman who babysat Jill and I just before Jill disappeared, way back in 1965. The story she shared complicated my working theory about Jill. In her telling, my parents had acted cruelly and callously towards the twins long before anything bad happened to Jill. Susan saw us in our barren cribs, our pajamas soiled and filthy, our faces dirty, my eye blackened—two seriously neglected and likely abused young children.

That changed the mystery from "Why did our parents get rid of us?" to "Why did they seem to hate us the way they did?"

After speaking with Susan, I re-interviewed many of my surviving Rosenthal relatives, to see if I could connect our abuse to our disappearance. What was it about either Jill or I, or both of us, that led our parents to shun and neglect us? Did they believe we were developmentally disabled? Were they ashamed of having children they thought were not fit for society? Or were we just a consequence of their badly degrading marriage, and the chaos of their splintering family? There was so much I still did not understand.

But the stories I heard from relatives did not change. There remained an unanswerable question at the center of it all, something no one could explain or comprehend. All they knew was that something terrible happened to the twins. But no one knew what it was, or why it happened.

I spoke with my great-aunt Toby, whose mother was the sister of my grandmother Bertha Rosenthal. Bertha's son Gilbert was Toby's first cousin, and when they were young, Toby and my father spent a lot of time playing together on the beaches and boardwalk of Atlantic City. When my parents got married in a synagogue, Toby was the matron of honor. She remembered the newlyweds hosting her for a dinner in their home in Atlantic City.

"They were so kind to me, and so happy I was there," she recalled. "And then it all fell apart."

I heard this a lot—things fell apart. No one knew quite why they did, just that things changed, and not for the better. A few years after their happy dinner together, Toby ran into Gilbert on the Atlantic City boardwalk.

"He was a policeman then, and we talked for a bit, but it was very, very strained," Toby said. "He was not happy to see me. He wasn't rude, he just wasn't talking or looking at me. He wasn't happy I was there."

Toby also recalled her mother telling her one day that Gilbert and Marie's daughter Jill "was not with the family anymore," Toby says. "I asked what happened, and my mother said, 'I don't know.' She was very, very close-mouthed about it. All she would say about it was that it was a *shonda.*"

Shonda is a Yiddish word that means a person, thing, or act that brings shame or scandal. A *shonda* is a disgrace; something you don't want your neighbors to know; something you never, ever talk about.

Did Toby's mother know what happened and refuse to tell her daughter? That was unanswerable; Toby's mother was gone now, any memories gone with her. Nearly everyone who might have firsthand knowledge of what happened to the twins back in 1965 was gone now, leaving behind only muttered sympathies for some unknown horror. As far as I could tell, only three people in a position to have seen or heard anything of consequence were still alive: the Rosenthals' next-door neighbor in Atlantic City's Pitney Village, Joan Pileggi, and her son, who was about four years old when the twins vanished, and had played in their shared backyard with my two older sisters Karen and Linda before "it all fell apart." And, of course, Linda herself, who claims to have no memories of the twins at all.

Whatever memories any of them have are unknown to me, since they've all resisted my efforts to question them.

Which leaves me, as I continue searching for Jill, with only vague descriptions of some unspoken rupture that led to Jill and I being pulled apart. And unless the New Jersey state trooper working my case can somehow persuade Linda or Joan Pileggi or her son to talk, that may be all I ever have.

Toby told me something else about my grandmother Bertha that I found fascinating. For a while when Toby was young, Bertha earned her living as a fortuneteller in Atlantic City. "She was a great storyteller, and apparently she could see the future," Toby says. "She had a place on Wilson Avenue that was twenty-seven dollars a month to rent, and all these beautiful women in fancy cars would pull up and park outside to have their tarot cards read." One day, Toby asked Bertha if she would tell her about her future.

"And she said, 'Oh, no, no, no, never the family,'" Toby recalls. "She would never read the cards for me or anyone in the family. She just refused to talk to us about our futures, or the future of the family."

Was this just a superstition on Bertha's part? Or did she know, somehow, what sort of bleak future lay ahead for the Rosenthals?

In the spring of 2021, I learned that my second cousin Lenny Rocco had passed away. His daughter Lenai had told me he was ill, first with an inoperable cancer, and then, near the end, with Covid. I tried to prepare myself for when we might lose him, but it didn't help. Hearing Lenny was gone was devastating.

Lenny was one of the first biological relatives I ever found, and certainly the relative who most enthusiastically embraced me and welcomed me into the clan. I told him many times how much his acceptance meant to me, but I'm not sure I was ever able to convey just how meaningful it was. I would endure many rejections, including by my biological sister and brother, and Lenny's open arms were like a lifeboat in a storm. He pulled me out of not belonging anywhere and dropped me right into his life and family. His friendship was more precious to me than words can hope to convey.

Lenny was the one who first warned me about a particular streak that ran through him and others in the Rocco-Rosenthal tree—a mean, self-destructive streak that doomed many in the family to unhappy lives. The streak did not start with him; rather, it was his birth legacy. "Everything you are comes from your genetics, from your family," Lenny's daughter Lenai said in one of our conversations. "Lenny was a very good person who came from a very troubled background. His parents were very rough and abusive and tribal. My father did the best with what he had, and he did some truly amazing things. He was the greatest friend to people, and he literally saved lives. But he could not escape who he was born to be."

Lenny had three great passions in life—singing, boxing, and women. "He was a gorgeous man, very handsome, and he was a charmer," says Lenai. "He had a beautiful voice, and he was extremely proud of his career as a doo-wop singer. But he could have gone much further, and he could have been as big a star as any of the big doo-wop singers, if he hadn't been so stubborn. You could never tell Lenny what to do. That was the Rocco streak."

In the few times we met and spent time together, I knew Lenny to be one of the friendliest, warmest humans I've ever met. And he was that, in every way, says Lenai, except that "he also had a sadness to him all his life. It all came from his family. His parents never said anything nice to him. His dad beat the hell out of him. He lived in a tough neighborhood and got into fights all the time, and he got kicked out of every high school in south Philly. And that made him hard. It made him hard on himself.

"I think that's why he was so misunderstood by people," Lenai went on. "Everyone saw him as this really tough guy, but he was much more vulnerable than that. He had a real emotional intelligence, and he was very self-aware. He knew he needed to change, but he also knew that he could never change no matter how hard he tried. That was why he was sad."

Lenny was devoted to his wife, Barbara, who sang backup for him on his singing gigs. When she passed away two years ago, "Lenny never got over it," Lenai says. Then Lenny began to lose weight, and his skin took on a yellowish tone. He was diagnosed with advanced pancreatic cancer.

"To the end, he never complained, not even once," Lenai says. "He never even took a painkiller. And earlier in the year, he'd still been working out in the gym, still taking gigs and singing on stage. That all had to stop."

I called Lenny just as soon as I heard about his diagnosis, and by then he found it hard to talk. Still, we stayed on the phone for a while, and I told him, more than once, how much I cherished his love and friendship.

"Paul," he replied in a thin, raspy voice, "I am so gad I got to meet you. You are my family. But I've had a great life, and now, I am ready to go."

Lenny was diagnosed in November 2020. The following April, he passed away. Because of Covid I was not allowed to see him at the end, and neither was Lenai.

When you have a minute some day, I urge you to go on YouTube and type in Lenny Rocco. If you do, you'll find videos of him in his later years, still hearty, still singing, still entertaining crowds with his eight-octave range well into his seventies. You'll also find a video that plays his two big doo-wop hits, "Sugar Girl" and "Rochelle," with a picture of Lenny in his heyday on screen. You will see his slick-backed, jet-black pompadour, and his pearly white teeth, and the obvious all-consuming joy he felt while singing. Lenny was a true artist, and a real American character. He was kind and gracious, and he had a huge, loving heart. He gave me something remarkable, and something I'd been desperate to find—the sacred bond of shared blood, the embrace of a blood family.

Lenny was the closest I ever came to the white picket fence.

I love you, Lenny Rocco, and I will forever hold you in my heart.

As I write these words, I still haven't found my twin sister Jill.

When I started writing this book, I believed that by the end of it, I would have the answers I'd been searching for. But then, as Katherine Pope put it, there were extenuating circumstances. The inexplicable yearlong neglect of the Atlantic City Police Department. The desolate months of the pandemic. The passage of time, that destroyer of all that once there was.

The reluctance of some to tell what they know, out of fear or dread or God knows what.

None of that, however, has stopped me. I have a new team in place, and my plan is to keep going, keep searching for answers. I will circulate more age progression images of Jill, hoping to get lucky. I will keep hunting for long-missing records, from hospitals and foster homes, and even from the FBI and the Newark Police Department. I will keep listening to stories and theories, and waiting to hear that one elusive detail that might, just might, unlock everything. I will get hypnotized again, so that a little bit more of that impenetrable wall around my memories might get chipped away.

As of those of who have followed my story from the beginning, or picked it up along the way, I ask one thing: do not stop rooting for me, or give up hope. Your support keeps me going.

Together, I truly believe with all my heart, we will one day find the solution to this mystery—and perhaps even find my twin sister, Jill.

CHAPTER 29

I was thinking about lone wolves again.

I read a little about them, and one of the things I learned is that a lone wolf is more likely to die before his time than a wolf in a pack. That's because wolves hunt in packs, and together they can bring down much larger prey than a wolf hunting on its own. Without the support of a pack, a wolf will find it harder to survive in harsh conditions. A lone wolf can always try to form his own pack, which is much easier than the alternative—joining an already existing pack. For a wolf to be assimilated into a biological pack—father, mother, and offspring—is pretty rare.

Thus, most lone wolves remain just that—unfortunate outcasts in the wild. You can always tell one by his long, lingering howl in the night, a desperate plea to lure other lone wolves.

It all goes back to April 27, 1964. The before-and-after day. The opening scene of an endless tragedy.

The day that changed everything.

I've reconstructed the events of that day more than once. I've focused on Room 418-B in the maternity wing of the Michael Reese Hospital, a stately gothic structure long since torn down. I've pored over every detail I could find, down to how cold and cloudy it was that day. I've replayed those events in my head like a movie: the mysterious nurse first entering the room at 9:30 a.m. to lift the blanket covering Baby Fronczak and get her first look at him; her return at precisely 1:53 p.m. to take the baby from my mother's arms; the mad scramble in the hallway as nurses and orderlies desperately tried to find him.

The surreal moment a few days later, when my mother was finally discharged from the hospital, and all the nurses gathered in the hallway to see her off and wish her well, a sea of women in white uniforms—each a kind of specter of the very person who stole her son.

These events are immutable and play out the exact same way every time. But there is room there for a thousand what-ifs.

What if a security guard had been patrolling the fourth floor at 1:53 p.m., and not some other floor? What if a taxicab hadn't coincidentally been idling outside the hospital, forcing the kidnapper to wait or flee on foot? What if my mother had given birth not at Michael Reese but at the MacNeal Memorial Hospital, a mile or so away, where every new infant was foot-printed? That might not have helped find Baby Paul, since he didn't turn up for more than fifty years. But it would have shown, in 1966, that I was not the real Paul Fronczak, altering my life in ways I can't imagine.

Yet for all the research I'd done into the events of that day, there was one person I hadn't really talked to about it.

My mother Dora.

Even though I learned about the kidnapping when I was ten years old, neither of my parents ever discussed it with me until I was nearly fifty. That was when I asked my mother, "Don't you want to know for sure that I'm your son?" which set up the DNA test that finally revealed the truth. After that, though, my parents didn't speak to me at all for two more years. And even when we reconciled, we only briefly touched on the kidnapping, since I knew it was a subject neither of them really wanted to talk about. I interviewed dozens and dozens of people for my first book, but my mother was not one of them.

Now, I felt the time was right to sit down with her in her home in Chicago and spend a little time talking about that day.

I wasn't interested in specifics. I didn't need to take her through the painful timeline of April 27. All I wanted was for us to have had at least one meaningful discussion about how that day impacted both our lives. My mother was fine with that, and she wound up speaking of that day with ease and clarity.

In fact, she told me something about April 27 that I hadn't known, and it broke my heart.

She told me that after she finally learned her baby was missing, a doctor at the hospital came into her room. "He looked at me and he said, 'You should have known,'" Dora recalled. "He said I should have known that since the nurse wasn't wearing a cap, she wasn't a real nurse. Like it was my responsibility to know who was a nurse and who wasn't. I felt a little bitter about that. You think you're protected in a hospital, but you're not."

I was astonished that a doctor would have scolded my mother like that at the moment of such intense grief and shock.

"That makes me angry, Mom," I told her. "Your child was taken, and they're blaming you?"

"He basically told me I was stupid because I hadn't asked the nurse more questions," she said.

I wondered how much the doctor's words had added to the staggering burden of guilt my mother carried with her for the rest of her life. Surely, they just made everything worse.

The hero in that story, my mother said, was my father Chester. "Not once did he turn on me and say, 'Well that was stupid of you,'" she said. "He could have done that, but he never, ever did. It was the kind of thing that could have led to a divorce, but your father wasn't like that. He was nothing but supportive."

I felt so proud of my father when I heard that.

I asked my mother if, when I was brought into a conference room in New Jersey in 1966 and presented to my parents as possibly their stolen son, she felt sure that I was Paul.

"The truth is, from that very first moment, I never really doubted that you were my son," she said. "Over the years, I noticed the differences between you and Dave, your looks, your personality, but even then, I never questioned it. I just wouldn't put it in my mind to think about. I mean, I loved you and I was always proud of you, so why would I question it? You were the son that we raised, and that was that."

My mother's approach had been the opposite of mine. Knowing the absolute truth was not important to her, because, quite simply, what difference would it make? Digging through the past and turning over every apple cart just wasn't necessary. There was no point to it. I was the son they raised. That was all that mattered, because there was nothing that could change it.

Even so, my mother was not willfully blind to the reality of my physical disparities, and, deep down, she knew I wasn't Paul. She'd told me that before. Early on, "I used to pray and pray and pray that he would be found," she said. "But I kind of gave up on that. As the years passed, I thought, 'Well, no one's going to be looking for him now, so I guess this is something that is not meant to be.' After that, all I ever prayed for was that he was doing well and living a happy life wherever he was."

I asked her how she felt now that the real Paul had been found. Did it make her happy, or something else? My mother took a long pause before answering.

"I am glad that he was found," she finally said. "I'm glad we finally got an answer. But the thing that always used to make me feel better was the hope that whoever had him would be able to give him more than he would have gotten from us. Maybe he was with some wealthy family now, some big executive of a big company. I prayed he'd been that fortunate. But from what I've learned, I don't feel like he's had many opportunities in his life. He married very young. He didn't go to college. He was raised in a small rural area. So, was he better off? Did he lead a happy life? I just don't know.

"But I remember thinking, 'Why would somebody kidnap him if they couldn't give him a really good life?'"

My mother and I talked about the period of time when we didn't speak to each other for more than two years. I told her I knew that reopening the whole affair was against her wishes, and I apologized to her for that. I told her I hoped she knew I never did it to hurt her or my father. My mother surprised me by saying that, during that time, she had actually defended me when others called my actions despicable.

"We were all very upset at first," she said. "We felt you were turning against us, that you weren't happy with us as parents. And that was the way the majority of our relatives looked at it too. But after a while, I stood up for you. I said, 'Don't think he did this to hurt us. That is not why he did it. He did it for his own reasons. And because he did it, a lot of things have worked out for the better.'"

I told her again that all I ever wanted was to reunite her with the son she lost. My mother just shrugged.

"Just because you want something to happen doesn't mean it's going to happen. Sometimes you just have to go along with it and believe that whatever happens was for the best."

My mother truly believed in this philosophy. Or I guess you could call it faith. Be patient, let everything play out, and it will all end up in a better situation. *Things will always turn out for the better.* It would be easy to dismiss such thinking as naïve, but that's not what my mother was saying at all. She was telling me that trying to change the past was the busy work of a fool. Some things could not be changed, no matter how much you wanted it or how hard you worked. In the face of that harsh reality, my mother's answer was faith. Mine had been to dig even deeper.

For the first time in my entire search, I thought hard and tried to envision what my life would have been like had I answered reality the same way my mother had—with faith.

But it was too hard for me to imagine such a scenario, so I gave up trying. And anyway, it was too late. I chose the way I chose. I chose to risk everything to find the truth.

There were so many loose ends to the story of finding the real Paul that I knew my mother and I wouldn't be able to wrap it all up in a tidy bow. The relationships she began to develop with the three women who were her granddaughters sadly stalled and sputtered, and possibly fractured, for reasons that aren't really clear. She got to meet them all, and spend time talking, and it looked like they might become friends. But that didn't happen.

I know the pressures on Kevin's family at that time were enormous. People were asking them about Lorraine, even as Kevin was grievously ill. The world they had known was gone now, replaced by something surreal and unsettling. It would not have been fair to expect them to do everything right, since none of us knew what was right and what was wrong in such a fraught, heightened situation.

Still, it's sad to think of the moments that might have happened, but didn't. No one sat down with my mother and showed her photographs of Kevin throughout his life, something I know she would have enjoyed. No one told her funny stories about him, or about the many ways he was probably just like his father and his brother Dave. No one introduced her to her great-grandchildren, a blessed event for any mother.

Maybe these things will still happen. I hope they do. But my mother has given up on hoping. Instead, she is patient and waits for everything to play out as it should.

"Wouldn't it be nice if we could all just meet as one big family?" she once remarked to one of Kevin's daughters, envisioning a dinner table with her and her granddaughters and her great-grandchildren and Dave and I all gathered around it.

Everyone agreed that it would be nice. But just because you want something to happen doesn't mean it will.

I did more research based on everything the old man told me, but I can't say it led me anywhere. I looked up a bunch of Chicago mobsters from the 1960s—men like Sam "Teetz" Battaglia and "Milwaukee

Phil" Alderisio and Rocco Fischetti, a cousin of Capone's who ran a floating craps scheme and was known as "The Big Game." But there was nothing to connect anyone to a child-kidnapping ring, much less to the events of April 27, 1964. Mobsters tend not to leave too long a trail.

I also kept searching for Aura Baty, who may or may not have been real. I couldn't find anyone that could have been her. But even if I had, how would that change anything? The best I'd ever be able to do, I figured, was to make an educated guess as to the identity of the mysterious woman in white. But short of corroborating evidence—photos, witnesses, confessions—that wouldn't classify as solving the crime.

As I write this, that part of the case is still cold.

All that remained was for me to answer the questions that had been driving me for the last eight years.

Had I done enough?

Did I fail in my mission?

Did it even matter if some things remained a mystery?

It's like that old saying the psychic Bobbi Allison used when I sat for a reading.

"You can't find peace if you can't find all the pieces."

I wondered if that was true.

There was something else Bobbi said that really stuck with me.

She compared me to Dorothy in *The Wizard of Oz*, in terms of the journey I was on. "You're in your house, and the house is spinning, and it lands on the Wicked Witch, and you go down the yellow brick road, and this is what you have chosen, with everything good and bad in it," she said. "But then you're like, 'Where am I, how do I get home, what do I do? How do I know how I'm supposed to live now?'"

Now that I was on the journey, Bobbi said, "You have to let it all happen. Let it all fall and let it all crack open and let all the emotions come out. This is how you heal. It's a very sad thing, but you are strong enough to handle it. Your spirits want you to purge, purge, purge and find out what you need to know and let your emotions swim in all of it, and then get positive about it. No matter what happens, you have to understand that *you lived the life you were supposed to live.*"

In other words, there was a cut-off point. I needed to do what I'd done—throw myself into the journey with abandon—but then figure out when enough was enough and, most importantly, take everything I'd learned and see it in a positive light. No matter what happened along the way, it was always going to be up to me to decide how the story ended. It would be what I decided it was, nothing more, nothing less.

For me, that was a really liberating idea.

There was someone else I wanted to talk to about the whole journey—my ex-wife, Michelle. My worry, however, was that she might not be as forthcoming with me as she might be with someone neutral. So, I asked Michelle if she would be okay with a friend of mine interviewing her. She said it would be fine.

Michelle talked about her feelings during the difficult time of our divorce. "Yeah, it was hard," she said. "My family had fallen apart, and I was sad and guilty. I mean, I understood Paul's need to know. I totally get it. But I was trying to keep our family together, and at one point I knew there was no stopping him. I only had so much control. But I knew I was lucky that I had a relatively normal childhood compared to what Paul went through. I always felt for him. I knew he needed to do it. I don't know if there was anything I could have done differently."

What I hadn't thought about was that, after the divorce, Michelle had to contend with her own identity issues. She had to figure out who she was now, the same as I was trying to do. "It's a huge adjustment," she said. "It's a brand-new identity. Suddenly I'm doing everything alone, working full time and also a single mom. Everything felt like it was up in the air and crazy."

She was like Dorothy, too, caught in a spinning house.

My friend asked Michelle if she thought I was finally coming up on the end of my journey. "I believe he is, because now he has found the real Paul," she said. "But I also know that he will never give up on finding Jill. Will he ever find one hundred percent peace? I don't know. Maybe he'll always be a little broken, always searching, always wanting to know more."

Michelle also said she believed I'd learned a lot about myself over the last eight years. "I think he has a better appreciation of what his mother went through. I think he is more willing to look at things from different angles and really consider other people's opinions and feelings. But the thing is, Paul is a very good person. I know that. We never got to the point where we were at each other's throats. We always got along. I like who he is, and he likes who I am. There was nothing scandalous in our marriage that led to an explosion. I've always loved Paul, and I never stopped."

Michelle was right: we were never pitted against each other, only against this massive intrusion that I wheeled into our marriage. We never harbored any hate for each other, or even stopped loving each other. And we never for a moment stopped being the best parents to Emma that we could be.

That is still true today. In some ways, Michelle and I are closer than we've ever been. We regularly get together for two-mile hikes and then have dinner with Emma, and it's always a fun and happy time. Not long ago, Michelle sent me this text:

> *Things I am thankful for: the Fronchies, Emma and Paul, your kindness and patience, our dinners together.*

I told her I feel the same way. I love Michelle, and I am grateful she is a part of my life. She and Emma are my very best friends in the world.

I thought about something else Bobbi Allison told me in our reading—a way for me to find peace and positivity in my journey. She asked me if I had a family, and I told her about Michelle and Emma. "Okay, here it is," Bobbi said. "Love your family as hard as you can. Let that love be unconditional. Let that love wrap itself around you. The people who love you don't want you to be a victim of circumstance. You are worthy of more than that. So experience the gamut of emotions and let them flow through you, and figure out what you need to figure out, but don't let it all get stuck inside you. *Wrap yourself in the love.*"

The truth is, I will be slowing down in my efforts to learn the entire truth of the Fronczak kidnapping. Not giving up, just slowing down. There aren't that many more people I can talk to, nor are there that many people who still care about knowing the truth. My mother, God bless her, doesn't need to know any more. And the FBI, as far as I can tell, hasn't been knocking on any doors lately. My brother Dave is still determined to somehow find justice for our mom, and to hold someone accountable for the kidnapping. I would like to know who that person was, too, even if nothing comes of knowing. Maybe I just don't like leaving such a glaring loose end. But as I said, I feel like I've exhausted most of the roads I could go down.

It's a little like what the old man told me:

> *"You ain't ever gonna find the real rock bottom truth. Cause there's no such thing anymore. It's all gone now. The sooner you accept that, the better."*

Can I come to any meaningful conclusions about all I learned? I am leaning towards believing that Lorraine, the woman who raised Kevin, was not the actual kidnapper. It's true Lorraine's mother, Blanche, was a nurse's aide, which perhaps gave Lorraine access to a nurse's uniform, which the kidnapper wore. But the witness statements all said the kidnapper was between five foot four and five foot seven, and of unexceptional build. That simply doesn't match up with Lorraine's appearance. Maybe the old man was telling the truth when he said someone else did the kidnapping, before the baby ultimately wound up with Lorraine. Maybe the real kidnapper was this mysterious Aura Baty.

Still, that wouldn't absolve Lorraine of any guilt, as long as it's true that she was part of the mob that arranged the kidnapping, and as deeply involved in its aftermath as the old man said she was. She would still be every bit as guilty as the actual abductor, and certainly she broke the law by harboring an infant she knew had been stolen from his mother. From all that I learned, the woman who raised the real Paul was as responsible for his kidnapping as anyone else.

And the theory that it was the Outfit in Chicago that planned and executed the kidnapping? I couldn't find any hard evidence to support it. But neither did I find anything that suggests it wasn't true. It's definitely plausible, and it could very well explain how anyone could have been so heartless and cold-blooded as to take a day-old infant from his mother's arms. The mafia, after all, is not known for its compassion.

Today, I feel I solved some aspects of the mystery of Baby Paul's disappearance, while others remain unsolved. The most important discovery was finding the real Paul, so that at least he got to speak to his mother before he passed. I probably won't ever know how much worth that had for Kevin, but I'm pretty sure it wasn't as monumental as I'd imagined it would be. After all, how could it be? The emotions going into it were so complex and so distorted by the passage of decades, and untangling that thicket would take a lot more than a few phone calls. For me to have believed that a reunion would somehow help in the healing of deep wounds a half century old was, I guess, naïve.

I thought of something a professional in the field of missing children told me when I used the word "closure" in one of our talks. "I don't like that word," he said. "People don't want closure, they want answers. And when they get those answers, then they have to find a way to live with them."

That sounds like something I will be doing in the coming years—learning how to live with what I have discovered. Again, I'm not giving up on finding the whole truth. I'm just subscribing a bit more to my mother's approach—let it play out, and believe that everything works out for the best.

I will also devote myself even more fully to helping other people in the middle of identity journeys like mine. I get so many letters from people who've been inspired by my story to start their own searches, and I take great heart from knowing they have a resource I didn't have—the two books I've written about my journey.

That is the very reason I wrote them in the first place: to help others in similar spots know they're not alone. There is no good manual for how to do what I did, no moral guideposts, no roadmap showing the peaks and pitfalls. My books aren't manuals, and they certainly aren't definitive. They're just one man's story. But I hope they give readers a sense of what it's like to undertake an identity search, from the awesome blessings it may offer to the terrible destruction it may cause.

So, look for me on a podcast or a TV series devoted to guiding people through the land mines of such searches and hopefully leading them towards the answers they need. I truly believe my experiences will be helpful for others. And all the while, I'll still be trying to find my twin sister, Jill. I'll be right there with all the other searchers, turning up rocks, digging holes, poring through dusty records, and hoping that at the end of it all, I will find what I need to become a whole, authentic, happy human being.

If I haven't found it already.

Just after I thought I'd finished writing this book, my story took yet another strange and remarkable turn, in a way I never could have imagined. I'd like to share that twist with you now.

I always looked at the mystery of my missing twin Jill in the context of the Rosenthal family unit—my biological parents, Gilbert and Marie, my siblings, Linda, Karen, and Fred, and me and my twin, Jill. A family of seven, which suddenly became a family of five. The fact that my mother had five children in the span of four years helped to explain the enormous pressure she was under and shed light on her decision to abandon me.

But what if there was more to my mother's story than I knew?

In July 2021, one of my newfound biological cousins, Rhonda, sent me a document she'd found while digging into our family history. I'd never seen it before, and it shook me to my core. It was a birth certificate for someone named Richard Duncan, who was born in St. Thomas Hospital in Akron, Ohio, in 1958. The certificate left the space for the father blank, but it did name the birth mother.

It said Marie Louise Duncan—my biological mother.

I had to read the name three or four times before the truth sank in. My mother did not just give birth to five children, as I'd thought. She gave birth to *another* child just two years before she married my father Gilbert in Atlantic City.

This meant I had *another* biological brother, or maybe half-brother, I'd never known existed.

But there was more. As I researched the certificate and Richard Duncan, I discovered he only weighed two pounds at birth. I also learned the St. Thomas Hospital in Akron was operated by the Sisters of Charity of St. Augustine and was the first hospital in the country to ever treat alcoholism as a medical condition. In fact, the hospital campus was the scene of the very first Alcoholics Anonymous meeting ever held, a meeting that was run by AA's founder, Bill W.

One of the few things I knew about my mother Marie Rosenthal was that she had a very serious drinking problem; several relatives told me so, including Marie's brother Frank Duncan. Immediately I wondered if her alcoholism pre-dated her relationship with Gilbert Rosenthal, and if it was the reason why she was admitted to St. Thomas Hospital.

Then came the real shock. I looked everywhere for any information I could find about the baby, Richard Duncan, hoping that he was somehow still alive. A baby born weighing two pounds was certainly less likely to survive in 1958 than today, but Richard did survive, at least long enough to have his tiny feet inked and printed for identification on his birth certificate. But did he make it into adulthood?

I found a database of death certificates issued in Ohio, and there was no such certificate for a Richard Duncan born in 1958. But those records only went back to 1963. I was referred to a historical society that kept earlier records, but I couldn't find his death certificate there, either.

Then, crucially, I looked at the 1961 birth certificate for my sister Linda, the first of Gilbert and Marie's five children. That certificate had a space for listing the number of other children born to Marie Rosenthal.

The number she put down was zero.

Which meant that between 1958, when Marie gave birth to Richard, and 1961, when she had Linda, Richard had, for some unknown reason, vanished from the official record.

Just like that, there was another mystery, *this one going back sixty-three years.*

How could this be? How could I have yet another missing sibling? I knew Richard had not been stillborn—he survived long enough to be issued a birth certificate. I wondered if he'd only survived a short time—but if that were true, I should have found a death certificate for him from either 1958 or 1959, and I didn't.

There were other possibilities—my mother and Richard could have quickly moved out of Ohio, and Richard could have died in another state, and without knowing that state, I couldn't search for a death certificate.

Or he may have lived into adulthood, and was either still alive (he'd be sixty-three) or passed away in another state. But if he survived, why didn't my mother list him on Linda's birth certificate in 1961, just three years after he was born? Had she given him away at birth? Had the Sisters of Charity of St. Augustine raised him, or given him up for adoption? Had Marie given him to a relative to raise?

Or, I wondered, had Marie abandoned this child, too, just before leaving Ohio to marry Gilbert in Atlantic City?

This last possibility was horrifying to consider. If it were true, it would change the entire nature of my story, and my understanding of why my mother did what she did to me. Up until then, I'd presumed she made the decision to abandon me because of the enormous stress she was under—a husband who left her, five children who needed her, not much money, and a dangerous drinking habit. But what if that wasn't the case? What if Jill and I weren't the first of Marie's children to disappear?

I cannot help thinking about all these possible scenarios, but I don't want to get ahead of myself—there may be a very simple explanation for what happened to my brother Richard Duncan, and I just have to find it. I've already tackled three fifty-year old mysteries—what's one more six-decade mystery added to the pile?

One of the great themes of my search is that every answer has only led to another question, and every solution has only created another mystery. Even so, I can hardly believe it's happened again. I am only at the very beginning of this new adventure—the quest to find my brother Richard—and of course I will keep all of you posted on my progress. For now, I just wanted to share this strange new twist to the story. What comes next, I can't even imagine. But I hope that Richard is still alive and out there somewhere, and if he's not—or if I never find out what happened to him—I have come to understand that's just the way life goes.

Not every question gets an answer. Just like not every family is destined to stay a family.

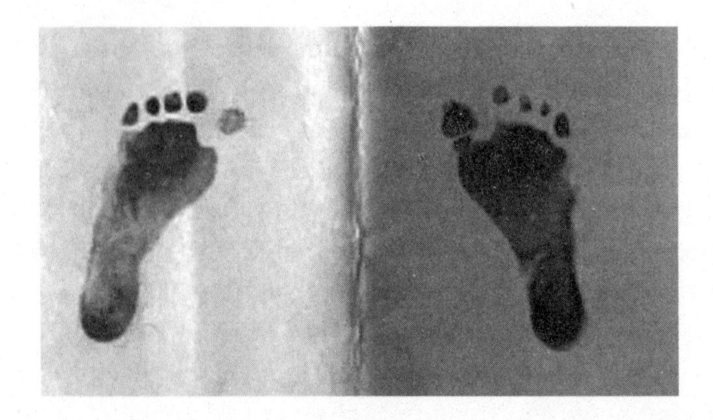

EPILOGUE

In February 2020, I was invited to give a speech at the annual conference of the Institute for Genetic Genealogy, an organization founded by my friend CeCe Moore and devoted to furthering the use of genetics as a tool for genealogical research. The conference was held in a cavernous arena in Las Vegas, and I stood up on a vast stage with a massive AV screen hanging over my head. The topic that day was my life.

I am used to telling my story, so I was able to take the packed audience through all the highs and lows without a script. I've always said that sometimes it feels like I'm talking about someone else's life, and I'm just the detective who's digging through it. I guess it feels a little like that when I give a presentation too. I think I need that bit of distance, or else I might not be able to tell my story at all.

That day, I had a little surprise for the audience.

"Before we end, I want to bring up my daughter real quick," I told the crowd once I was done. "Come on up, Emma."

It was my daughter's idea. She was eleven years old and very interested in the details of my searches. She wanted to be a part of the journey, and she wanted to be up on that stage with me. At home, she really wore out her short presentation, basically committing it to memory, though she still came up with her little script, handwritten on loose leaf paper. She wasn't really nervous—she's very comfortable in the spotlight—but she might have been a bit more anxious than usual.

"Are you ready?" I asked her when she got to the podium.

Emma just looked at me and said, "No."

But that didn't stop her. "Hello, I'm Emma Fronczak, Paul Fronczak's daughter," she began. "Thank you for letting me have a quick moment to talk about a few things."

I stood off to the side, literally beaming with pride.

I thought back to the day Emma was born. I'll never forget the emotions that washed over me when I held her for the first time. Emma was, in one sense, the first blood relative I could ever remember touching. And she filled me with a powerful sense of belonging that I'd never, ever felt before.

I also thought back to when Jill and I were young, though I couldn't actually remember that time. The memories, I told myself, had to be there in my brain, it's just that I couldn't access them. A memory of being in a crib with Jill. A memory of recognizing she was my twin. A memory of having loved her because she was my sister, my family.

These memories *had* to still be in there. They just had to. I didn't want to think that they were gone forever, because they were the few things I had of Jill that I could call mine.

Memories, though, are mysterious, elusive, and not nearly as fixed as we think. Especially a child's memory, and especially when there is trauma involved. "For a small child, violence is an overwhelming, uncontrollable and terrifying experience," the psychoanalyst Stephen Grosz wrote in his book *The Examined Life*. "Its emotional effects can last a lifetime. The drama becomes internalized; it's what takes hold of us in the absence of another's empathy."

Sometimes the drama becomes so internalized that we can't recall it at all. And even if we could, those memories "are not fixed and immutable, not a place way back there that is preserved in stone, but a living thing that changes shape, expands, shrinks and expands again, an amoeba-like creature," the memory researcher Elizabeth Loftus wrote. "Our representation of the past takes on a living, shifting reality."

In other words, the original memory is not reality; the only thing that's real is what the memory looks like once we dredge it to the surface.

So—trying to enact a future that somehow changes the past can never work, because we can't even accurately remember the past. Me searching for my true identity by peeling back layers and layers of history could only ever be so effective, because in truth there is no such thing as a true identity. I was trying to pin down a butterfly that wasn't there.

This is one of the reasons I haven't legally changed my name yet. I am still Paul Joseph Fronczak, though Emma likes to call me Jack. Actually, she likes to call me Jack Cheddar. She thinks that's hilarious. And she's right. I laugh every time she calls me Jack Cheddar. I recently started a new job, and my colleagues there, once they heard about my story, began calling me Jack. I have to say, I liked how it sounded. It felt right. Maybe one day I will change my name, but I'm in no hurry to do so. It's only a name, after all. It doesn't define who I am.

My daughter, Emma, on the other hand, does.

I looked at her as she wrapped up her presentation at the I4GG Conference, and I understood that this very moment—Emma and I together on stage—was more real than anything I could ever discover by digging a hole.

"As you may know, my dad's been through a whole lot in his life," Emma said in finishing. "My dad may not know this, but I think he is really cool."

I gave Emma a double high five and told her she was awesome. And I realized she'd just given me what I'd been searching for all along.

My daughter thinks I'm cool.

What more do I need to know about my identity?

ACKNOWLEDGMENTS

Thank you to my daughter, Emma Faith… The reason behind everything I do. I am so grateful for every second we share together. To Michelle for being the most amazing ex-wife, ever! Our hikes, talks, laughs, and together, raising the absolute coolest daughter, ever! Thank you to my mom, Dora Fronczak, for loving me unconditionally, and finally traveling this road together. To my dad, Chester; we miss you and love you every single day. To David, for just being David. Thank you to Cece Moore for all you have done and continue to do, and for the Key Speaker opportunities. Thank you to Nino Perrota, the real-life Jason Bourne. Thank you to Trooper Jason Maloney and the New Jersey State Police for taking on my missing persons case and the search for my missing twin sister, Jill. Thank you to Frank Weimann, the legend lives on, and Sylvie Rabineau (WME) for your expertise and guidance.

Thank you to the one and only, George Knapp, C2C AM and KLASTV. We started in 2012 and traveled back to 1964! Who needs a DeLorean! What a journey this has been!

Thank you, Lenny Rocco; you are deeply missed and loved by all. I am so thankful I had the opportunity to spend time with you, play bass with your band, shoot a film with you, and just talk. Thank you, Lenai, for your hospitality and love. Thank you, Joy, Sandy, Aimee, Fran, Joe, and the entire family for your love and support. Thank you, Toby, for hanging out with me and sharing stories on the Boardwalk in Atlantic City.

Thank you to Susan Wolhert, for bravely coming forward and sharing her important story with me. A special thank you to Angelo's Fairmount Tavern in Atlantic City; your hospitality, food, and customers are truly outstanding, and you have the coldest Stella in AC!

Thank you to everyone at RAW and CNN Films for believing in my story. I'm so excited to be working with such incredibly talented people.

A big thank you to Paulie Drake (First Cardio) the real Abe Froman; your friendship and support will always mean everything. Jimbo and Jon Bach—we grew up together and have grown together ever since. Best friends. True friends. Brenda—from teenagers to now…reconnecting; never missed a beat! Even after the Lake House incident and the hose-down!

Thank you to Oasis Lodge #41 F & AM, Las Vegas, and all of my Brothers; including Scott, Keith, Logan, Rick, John, Jake, and Hal.

Thank you, Eric and James (Wolfpack), for keeping me humble and hungry.

A special thank you to Alex Tresniowski (*Look at me, Ray!*) for staying the course on this crazy adventure! Bones, I can't wait to hit the road again. Shovels in hand! From "Get Shorty" over Heineken to the adventure of a lifetime! And thanks also to Rainey Stundis, for putting up with Alex's nonsense.

Thank you to Band-X; Rick, Dan, Henry, Justin, and Darren Dice—and to our "One show every few years after 30 years" Tour! We got the band back together!

A big Thanks to Steve (Chuck), Rachel, and the entire F clan! Your friendship, and Axe Cap, mean more than you know! Thank you, Dr. John Nassar, DDS; creating the best smiles, and coffee—Tru Bru!

Thank you to Rickenbacker Basses and Fender guitars for keeping me sane, creative, and always inspired.

Thank you, RUSH; Dirk, Lerxst, and Pratt—for the soundtrack of my life and the reason I started playing bass.

Thank you, Harley-Davidson Motorcycles...the only way to experience Valley of Fire!

Thank you, Greg and Sharon at Sampsel-Preston Photography (LV)...you are truly the best in the business!

Thank you to the crew at Lucky's (Cactus Jacks) Roger and Noel for always quenching my thirst, and the team at Padrinos—Vito, Barrie, and Whitnie—where everyone knows your name! Or all three names!

Thank you to all the great people at Post Hill Press: publisher Anthony Ziccardi, production editor Rachel Hoge, production manager Alana Mills, associate production manager Christina Chun, publicity director Devon Brown, and my wonderful editor Maddie Sturgeon.

And finally, thank you Spooky and Scully: The truth is out there and I do believe!